July

S0-AKX-504

To Bill and Ina Marlieb
With respect and affection
Judy Gold

Monsters and Madonnas

Monsters and Madonnas

The Roots of Christian Anti-Semitism

JUDITH TAYLOR GOLD

NEW AMSTERDAM
New York

Copyright © 1988 Judith Taylor Gold

All rights reserved.

First published in 1988 by
NEW AMSTERDAM BOOKS
171 Madison Avenue
New York, NY 10016

First Printing

Gold, Judith Taylor.
    Monsters and madonnas : the roots of Christian anti-Semitism /
Judith Taylor Gold.
    289 p. 33 × 50½ cm.
    Bibliography: p.279
    Includes index.
    ISBN 0-941533-28-X
    1. Christianity—Controversial literature.   2. Antisemitism.
I. Title.
BL2775.2.G59   1988
201—dc19   88-25331
                                                      CIP

This book is printed on acid-free paper.

Printed in the United States of America.

TO JOSEPH GOLD

With gratitude and love I acknowledge his great labor of love for Monsters and Madonnas. *His valuable comments, his editorial skills and his arduous work have been a driving force in bringing this book to fruition.*

In remembrance of my father, Victor H. Taylor

Contents

Introduction

WE ARE ALL, IN A SENSE, VICTIMS OF THOSE ELEGANT, SO-
phisticated thoughts of Copernicus, Darwin, Einstein and
Freud. Science and technology have pushed us to undreamed
frontiers. The impact of nineteenth- and twentieth-century
physics and biology continues to reshape the social sciences.
Yet, in a world fraught with profound social change, political
upheavals and advanced technology, we are constantly reminded of our past: we must still reckon with the presence of
the archaic; rocks and fossils, fish and ferns tell us their silent
story. And in response to the questions of life we still continue to fashion pictures and scrolls, temples and tombs. In
many ways we have not changed. Only our modes of expression have changed.

Human evolution is a history of our changing expressions,
physical and psychological, under the pressure of time and
events. We have developed in that we have changed. But the
drives which move us have remained essentially the same. We
no longer eat with our fingers, but this is not to say that
utensils are "superior" and eating with the fingers is "in-

ferior." It is merely a change of expression. Hunger remains the same. We have gone from hand to spoon, from bow and arrow to nuclear warheads. Evolution is a process of sophistication.

This process of sophistication is really what we mean when we talk of civilization. On a personal level civilization is an attempt to push back the unharnessed forces within us and rechannel them into sublimated, useful outlets. Externalized, civilization is the process of understanding and controlling nature. To what end is of course another question.

Today, despite our advanced state of sophistication, man is still confused about his nature. The idea that he is half-holy, half-animal has literally condemned him to a constant duel with himself. That he be all-holy has led him to both socially acceptable and socially unacceptable schizophrenia. That he be all animal, free to unleash suppressed desire, has led to his spiritual dissolution.

No system of ethics has ever been reconcilable with man's nature. There has always been a disparity between his idealized and his actual behavior. But then no system of ethics has ever viewed man as a function of ancient expressions, refined—though not fundamentally changed—into an ever-contemporary portrait. Moreover, we can never successfully interpret this portrait relative to any point in time because it is essentially jumbled. It is as though we sit before a mirror, seeing only the face of the present, unaware that this particular mirror presents a long series of reflections from the past and that in reality the face looking out at us is the sum total of a thousand faces that have gone before.

Man's best comprehension of his present may be by insight into his past. He may not remember his past, but Nature will not let him forget. For he is surrounded by vestiges of his primitive existence. Like clues they lie embedded just under the veneer of everyday life. They infect our literature, our speech, our laws, our customs, our holidays, our beliefs, our art and our music. They are analyzed, sifted, scrutinized and reflected upon by a host of disciplines. And they can be observed in our children as primeval and amorphous perceptions.

Man has achieved a measure of understanding of his past, of the state of sophistication in civilizations far removed in time. He has been able to unearth and assimilate the relics of his former existence by means of studied objectivity—at a respectable scientific distance. He is free to approach and examine in finest detail the tools and forgings of his forebears with a spirit of detachment; he concludes that these artifacts no longer bear immediate relevance to his present life.

In the area of antique humanities, rites and rituals, feasts and festivals, drawings and dances—all that body of knowledge which reveals to us how primitive man thought and behaved—our spirit of detached independence begins to break down. We may regard the tools of Neanderthal as curious, but the idea that ape and man may have a common ancestor can be disquieting. Ideas that challenge our personal security and threaten to destroy our elaborate systems of self-defense, inspire boundless resistance. Even in the scientific disciplines, Galileo had trouble reconciling his physics to the prevailing opinions of the day.

Man has become bedazzled by his technology, intoxicated by knowledge that can be demonstrated and predicted, and by forces that can be controlled. He seems unaware that in many of his present day customs and thought patterns, he compulsively obeys commands from the past—commands that no longer make sense and are often contrary to what he knows to be fact. That a multitude of primitive beliefs and superstitions continue to remain essential and acceptable forms of his behavior, he apparently discounts. In his infatuation with the scientific method, he has relinquished interest in the viable part of his past.

In the beginning there was no language. Its development,

while a distinct technical achievement, must also be viewed as a vulgarization or debasement of thought, since a word becomes an imperfect representation of a thing or action, often carrying attenuated emotional connotations. With the development of verbal sophistication, the emotional distance between the original object and the word must have inevitably widened. Today language is to a great extent a system of symbols possessing the power to convey an essence—often far removed from its first and exact definition. While this essence may be universally perceived, it may also be universally obscured to the point of distortion because of the disjunction between the original object and its succeeding derivative symbols. The will to live—and to be safe from death—may not be discernible in some of today's complex word ceremonies and intricate theological doctrines, but were most certainly "essences" upon which man first sought to placate the gods.

The old gods have fallen and have been replaced by the new but the essentials of life have not changed. Life is more complex; and death is no more understandable today than it was for our ancestors. But life has changed in that Nature's secrets have been formulated, predicted and to a large degree, controlled. We are no longer Nature's vassals. Much of the terror has gone out of the night.

But not completely.

For a realm of darkness has remained intact over the ages. It is a land of angels and howling devils which, from the very beginning of history, have vied for the soul of man. Within its domain objects of the supernatural still find root; like persistent and prevalent weeds, they have remained resistant to the trowel of time.

We are going to explore this land of the supernatural, beginning with some of its chief inhabitants, *the monsters*. We shall try to track these apparitions—the vampires and werewolves, the demons and witches—back to their hidden lairs. For the monsters lie in a well-camouflaged pool of primitive thought, superstition and myth—a pool regarded as shallow and meaningless, relegated to the land of childhood and viewed through a lens of laughter. Our journey will take us down well-trod paths and some not so well-trod and we shall be surprised when and where these paths meet and cross, overlap and diverge. And by what we discover along the way. When we finally arrive at our destination, we shall see that the waters of the pool are deep and dark, and from its great tides flow far-reaching currents.

CHAPTER ONE

Monsters and Their Attributes

THE MONSTERS ARE VERY OLD. PERHAPS AS OLD AS MAN himself. Their pictures are found in prehistoric drawings on the walls of caves. They have come to us in the myths of Asia and Asia Minor; in the folktales of Europe; in the stories and legends of the New World. The idea of monsters exists in every culture; their prevalence is universal, their persistence nothing short of phenomenal.

In the Ardennes there is a representation of a horned man—half-human, half stag, dating back over 40,000 years; in the jungles of South America there are legends of a faceless people of the Upper Amazon; in the sands of the Sahara, great stone sphinxes still keep vigil among silent tombs; and through Nubia, Ethiopia and upper Egypt wander the Blemmyes, depicted in aboriginal art, a race of headless people. In contrast are the Great Heads of the Iroquois Indians—giant, bodiless, man-eating craniums. There is Shutu, a guardian

1

demon of ancient Babylonia, and his fellow-countryman, Oannes, half-man, half-fish—prototype of the mermaids and mermen that have come to us through European heraldry. Within the realm of monsters stride the giants: Cyclops, the one-eyed monster of Homer's *Odyssey;* Beryon, with three bodies and three heads; Briareus, with fifty heads and one hundred hands; Wathatotarho, of the American Indians; and the giant, Maushope, of Martha's Vineyard, which can eat a whale in a gulp.

Here in the land of monsters flies the Phoenix, the fabled Egyptian bird, which has its counterparts in many nations: the Arab Salamander; the Persian Simurg; the Hindu Garuda. The Phoenix builds a nest of twigs, cassia and frankincense in which to die. After death a worm emerges from the body of the dead bird, and from this worm a new bird grows. The new bird was said to appear at the ancient Egyptian city of Heliopolis every 500 years, bearing a ball of myrrh that contained the body of its father which it then buried in the Temple of the Sun. The Bible mentions this bird ("I shall die in my nest, and I shall multiply my days as the Phoenix," Job 29:18) which Christianity later adopted as a symbol of the Resurrection.

Another birdlike creature, the griffin of ancient Greek mythology, purportedly had a feather-covered body of a lion, but the head, wings and claws of an eagle. It had an affinity for buried treasure and built its nest of gold in remote and dangerous places. Despite its perilous nesting sites, men were always attempting to seek it out. The griffin was a kind of mascot to the Rimaspians, a one-eyed people of Scythia.

The sky is host to myriad other monster-like creatures: Lemura of the Greeks, Xtabai of the Incas and Mayans, Tengues of the Japanese, Estorie of the Hebrews, Lilith of the Old Testament—all vampire-like creatures. In addition, there is Tornit of Eskimo folklore, a cannibal that secures its food by heaving stones at its victims; the cannibalistic mothers of the Iroquois; the Gaki of Japanese folklore, creatures with swollen bellies and emaciated bodies, having huge mouths extending from ear to ear, and cursed with being always unsated; the Harpies, bird-women with lethal claws; and the Callo Gruis, the crane-necked men of ancient Tartary.

Other monsters include the winged elephant of the Hindus; the monkey-like Ahuizoth of Mexico, with four heads protruding from its body, and a fifth head at the end of its tail, which discriminately feasts upon the teeth, nails and eyes of its victims; the cockatrice, to whom death comes only when it catches its own reflection in a mirror; the dragons, multiheaded, fire-breathing man-eaters. There are the Oni of Japanese folklore which range from giants who devour the whole world to ogres, vampires and mischief-makers. The Oni are usually pictured as hideous creatures that come up from the infernal regions to drag down a sinner. They are portrayed as possessing monstrous mouths, a third eye, three toes and three fingers, from which grow sharp talon-like nails.

In this land of strange beings also roams the unicorn, the odd-looking quadruped distinguished by the soft horn protruding from the middle of its forehead and whose ferocity and wildness could be tamed only by the touch of a virgin. In ancient China it was widely believed that the unicorn ate no living vegetation, never walked on green grass, was always present at the birth of sovereigns (as it was at the birth of Confucius), and that to injure it brought death.

The origin of monsters is lost in antiquity, but it may be conjectured that it would be improbable for man to conceive of anything that does not or did not at one time exist, at least in some sense. Earliest monsterism may well represent the physical embodiment of psychological distortion, particularly distortion relating to the animal kingdom then extant. This is strikingly illustrated in prehistoric art where cave drawings showed human life as inextricably bound up with animal life. Animals represented not only a constant threat, but also a source of food and clothing, which meant that their fertility and reproduction were essential to human survival. Animals were therefore vital to the life of primitive man, and this dependency for the sustenance of life itself, coupled with the tendency to anthropomorphic identification, undoubtedly contributed to animal worship. As animals became objects of worship, their attributes and powers became increasingly subject to human distortion and exaggeration.

Millenia later, the unearthing of immense and conceivably grotesque animal parts, together with their giant fossils, served to perpetuate the concept of animal-derived monsterism. Indeed, in recent history—during the last five thousand years—these mammoths have been extinct, so that man has had to rely on imagination to conceive them, thus fanning through the centuries the flames of fantasy as they relate to these creatures that have been submerged in humanity's unconscious throughout time.

Natural disasters, too, no doubt helped germinate the idea of monsterism in primitive thought. Earthquakes, volcanic eruptions, violent storms, tidal waves, floods and eclipses were originally attributed to unexplained powers. In time these natural disasters became causally related to some concrete object—usually animal or plant—so that the particular object became endowed with the power to either destroy and disrupt, or to promote and ensure, the security of man's environment.

Over the ages the monsters have become more sophisticated and diversified, until today they exist in infinite variations. Moreover, with each generation there seem to be "contemporary monsters" introduced into monster lore.

One of these is the celebrated abominable snowman or yeti, "dweller among the rocks." Sherpa porters of Tibet describe these manlike apes or apelike men as standing eight feet tall at maturity, covered with blond or reddish-brown hair except for the soles of their feet, palms, upper half of the face and head. The face is apelike, the hair on the head is dark, straight and rather short. The creatures reputedly eat both flesh and vegetation, but do not cook their food. They wear no garments, walk upright, and if the big tracks photographed do indeed belong to the *yeti,* they have a comparatively short stride and toe outwards. The natives of the Himalayas, lamas, explorers, merchants, porters and soldiers claim that the snowman's feet can turn backwards at the ankle, and that the creatures possess an offset rear toe that enables them to grip while climbing. This offset toe is comparable to the thumb of man. A monastery in Pangboche, Tibet, is supposedly in possession of the scalp of such a creature and two other monasteries reportedly have mummified versions of the complete snowman.

The North American counterpart of the abominable snowman is the *sasquatch* ("Bigfoot"), whose territory extends from the coastal California range to Toba Inlet, British Columbia. Descriptions of the *sasquatch* are strikingly similar to those of the *yeti.* A mountain dweller, this creature eats vegetation and occasionally shellfish, wears no clothes, but outdoes his Far Eastern cousin by having the power of speech. Generally considered harmless, the *sasquatch* has nevertheless been accused of kidnapping Indian maidens. The Chehalis (American Indians), who have reportedly encountered the beast, are very reluctant to talk about their sightings, apparently because they have been subjected to severe ridicule. Not so scientists and laymen who do not share the reticence of the Indian, and whose sightings of "Bigfoot" have resulted in the creature's widespread popularity.

Another contemporary apparition which has evoked increasing attention is the Loch Ness Monster. Allegedly dwelling in the depths of Loch Ness in Scotland, it has been the object of scientific study in which year-round observation teams scrutinize the lake; residents of the area describe the monster as serpentine in character, and sonic tracings and photographs exist that purport to represent the creature. Similar "prehistoric" denizens reportedly have been sighted in the Chesapeake Bay and Lake Champlain areas of the United States.

Monsters may also assume a futuristic frame of reference. Sightings of UFOs or "flying saucers" have attracted international attention. While these encounters with extraterrestrial phenomena, like the sightings of the *yeti* and the Loch Ness Monster, remain to be proved, UFOs have come to represent a classical monster-form cloaked in modern technological terms.

Although diverse in number and variety, monsters share common characteristics and functions, as is apparent from their definition. The word *monster* is derived from the Latin *monstrum,* meaning evil omen, and is defined as something unnaturally marvelous: ". . . departing greatly in form and structure from the usual type of its species; . . . showing a deviation from the normal in behavior or character; . . . a legendary animal; . . . of great size and ferocity; . . . compounded of elements from several brute forms; . . . a threatening force; . . . an engulfing power; . . . an animal of strange and often terrifying shape; . . . a being of unnatural or excessive ugliness; . . . deformed . . . wicked . . . cruel."

Perhaps the most common attribute of monsters is that of animalism; many are depicted as half-animal, half-human. These extraordinary creatures are not mere amalgams of species. They are mistakes of evolution, products of natural processes which somehow went awry. They are deformed mentally as well as physically and are capable of wreaking horror and bringing about prodigious evil. As such they are conceived as part superanimal, part superhuman, and their psychological projection is fear.

Monsters are also depicted in all-animal form, including birds and winged creatures, quadrupeds, unicorns, cats, and serpentine and insect forms. The animal monsters plot and scheme like humans—not ordinary humans but those that are supercunning and cruel. They are perceived as special creatures, endowed with evil powers and capable of attaining their sinister ends either through their own means or as instruments of others.

Monsters also appear in all-human form, often distinguished by a physical impairment or exaggeration, or by omission of a body part or parts. Included are faceless people, people with huge mouths or ears, giants, elves, trolls, one-eyed beings, a head alone, a pair of hands. Ghosts belong to this category, their defect being a lack of cytoplasm. A variant may include those in whom there are no defects, exaggerations or omissions—the beautiful woman and the stereotypical hag (both witches), children (innocence masking latent evil). Any human form possessing unusual characteristics such as left-handedness, mental retardation, genius or grossly atypical psychological behavior may fall into this category.

The remarkable mergings and manifestations of animal-human forms are dependent on a second basic feature of monsterism: transformation.

Transformation is the ability of an object or being to change or be changed from one form, structure or appearance, to another. Transformations in nature, such as larvae to butterflies or water to ice, are common. But monster transformations are of a different character; they are outside nature. Such unnatural metamorphoses may take place between animals and humans, between animals and animals, between humans and humans, between animate and inanimate objects, or between inanimate objects alone—and result in the production of extraordinary creatures and things. In these transformations, species are crossed and the traditional concept of time is violated.

Unnatural metamorphoses may occur as a result of the

utterance of magic words and incantations, of ritual (the performance of a series of prescribed, specific acts) or the use of elixirs or potions. Or they can be spontaneous, resulting from the snap of a finger or the wave of a wand. In this sense, transformation is also the power of an external force to change something or someone else into another form.

Some of the common transformations described in monster literature are: individuals who become animals, trees, flowers, rocks and stars; beings turned into salt or gold; heroes changed into serpents; and rocks turned into precious stones.

Not all transformations are grossly apparent. There are also implied transformations, in which inconsequential creatures become the manifest agents of some evil force: a black cat that systematically drives its guilty master to the gallows; a tiny lizard that suddenly shows itself capable of devouring a city; a snake that carries out the commands of its master, showing the oneness of master and serpent although no actual physical transformation has taken place between the two. Implied transformations generally involve a person or animal that becomes the slave or representative of its monster master, fulfilling the monster's purpose but not actually undergoing a metamorphosis itself.

Disguise is an attempt at transformation; it is, in effect, an incomplete transformation. Practiced for the most part by humans, it requires the aid of no special supernatural powers, but rather the accoutrements of makeup, mask, costumes and the like. While disguise must therefore always be recognized as a pretense, it still attempts to convey that an impossible or unnatural change has taken place, and can thus—like a real transformation—frighten. A masquerade ball, while fascinating and entertaining, may also contain an element of latent horror.

Transformation is a *modus operandi* of monsterism. It gives the monster unlimited maneuverability and the security of appearing in benign forms. It looses all finite fetters. In general it allows the monster, unable to achieve its ends in one guise, to assume that form which will best serve its ends. Transformation also occurs as a protective device. (Noble characters in literature are turned into "stars" or "flowers" or "trees" so that they may escape harm.) But even these benign-appearing transformations, which are ostensibly for good, can inspire terror; the randomness of transformation, whether for good or bad, is perceived as the result of a capricious force that can produce formidable results. It is a process over which there is no control, contrary to all known laws and in direct violation of nature. The psychological impact of transformation, like that of all monster attributes, is fear.

A third distinct feature of monsters is giantism. Many monsters are perceived in terms of supersized creatures, having tremendous proportions, accompanied by great strength and power. "Gargantua," "King Kong," giant dragons and lizards, huge robot-like beings, fall into this category. Giantism is one of the most general features attributed to the monsters, and dates from earliest times:

> There were giants in the earth in those days; and also after that, when the sons of God came in unto the daughters of men, and they bare children to them; the same became mighty men which were of old, men of renown.
>
> —*Genesis 6:4*

Although giantism was believed to be bound up with the genesis of earth and man (it was common thought among the ancients that the union between the sons of gods and the daughters of men produced a race of giants), man's relationship with giants was far from amiable, their strength, power and size being enough to inspire feelings of intimidation and inadequacy:

And there we saw the giants, the sons of Anak, which come of
the giants: and we were in our own sight as grasshoppers, and so
we were in their sight.

—Numbers 13:33

Giants were reputed to possess awesome appetites, especially for humans. This cannibalistic attribute courses
throughout monster and mythological literature and may
account for the prime fear generated by giantism: namely,
that big monsters have big appetites.

Examples of giantism abound in the biblical literature. The
giant of Gath (2 Samuel 21:20) was described as a "man of
great stature," possessing six fingers on each hand and six
toes on each foot. The bed of Og, King of Bashan, measured
nine cubits (the equivalent of nine times the height of a man)
in length and four cubits in width (Deuteronomy 3:11). Goli-
ath stood six cubits and a span (1 Samuel 17:4). The Amorite
giant was the height "of the cedars . . . strong as the oaks"
(Amos 2:9).

A variation of giantism is its opposite: dwarfism. Monsters
are often portrayed in terms of excessive smallness. The
superhuman strength and brute ferocity of giants are replaced
by the superhuman cunning (physical power replaced by
mental) of "little people." These tiny beings—dwarfs, elves,
leprechauns and their myriad cultural counterparts—are depicted as capable of changing men into beasts, casting evil
spells and fomenting enchantments. They are viewed as arch-
schemers, brewers of magic potions, and practitioners of
sorcery—particularly that which interferes with the affairs of
men. Fairies (feminine) work mischief chiefly in the field of
romantic love; the rest of the fairy people (masculine) are
active in promoting deeds of frank evil.

That something very small is capable of doing great harm
is implicit in the idea of dwarfism. In outright monster tales it
is a frequent theme that inconsequential acts or things can

wreak great havoc: a huge and ominous beanstalk springs from a handful of carelessly tossed seeds; a small salamander evolves into a carnivorous dinosaur; ants devour man and beast. Dwarfism is thus a mirror image of giantism, in which small size belies the enormity of potential threat, and it is this latency, always on the verge of becoming manifest, that is seen as sinister.

Invisibility is another important feature of monsterism, found widely in horror literature. It is a state in which a thing or being becomes objectively or subjectively unseen, but not unperceived. There is corporeal absence, but incorporeal presence. In this regard invisibility is a special type of transformation that provides a monster-form with an ultimate disguise: nothingness comingled with presence. Objective invisibility (with the object actually invisible) results from the use of potions, unguents, incantations, and so forth, by a person or thing seeking invisibility; it is not seen because it is "not there." Subjective invisibility (with the object actually visible) occurs as a result of hypnotic states induced in the viewer, rendering the viewer incapable of "seeing." In both instances the cardinal feature is presence without visual perception.

Perhaps the classic example of objective invisibility, which continues to pervade all cultures, is the concept of ghosts. This category includes spectres, spirits, spooks, phantoms, apparitions, banshees, poltergeists and others. Usually the ghost itself is not seen but its presence is felt. Sometimes the ghost chooses to show itself by materializing into ectoplasm or by making noises, but in most instances ghosts are perceived by their specific and characteristic activities. A further example of objective invisibility is illustrated in H. G. Wells's *The Invisible Man*. In this story a scientist develops a potion that makes him invisible; he finds himself unable to become visible again; the powers stemming from his invisibility turn ultimately to evil, and it is death which finally restores his visibility.

Subjective invisibility is exemplified in a character popularized by radio broadcasts in the United States in the 1930s and early 1940s: "The Shadow." This character had the ability "to cloud men's minds" so that they could not see him even though he was present. The purpose of this most unusual endowment was to enable the invisible "Shadow" to fight criminals and bring them to justice, especially those whose means of destructiveness were of a quasi-metaphysical nature. Yet the psychological effect of this socially appreciated personality was disquietude, for it was perceived that the "Shadow's" ability to achieve subjective invisibility had the potential, like all unnatural transformations, of being turned to evil purposes at any moment.

(In contradistinction to invisibility are the illusions magicians perform, such as causing a rabbit to disappear in a hat. These are not felt as anxiety-provoking or malevolent, since there is a "total disappearance." In this case corporeal absence is complete absence; the animal is unseen but also unperceived. When the rabbit reappears the viewer is aware of trick, not transformation.)

The concept of invisibility is lent credibility by the fact that in nature there are examples of *bona fide* invisibility. Gases, which are matter, are invisible in their usual states but are nonetheless perceived as capable of sustaining or destroying life (fitting the classic description of monster invisibility). Some solids have the ability to sublime through the liquid phase to the gas phase, rendering the liquid phase essentially invisible (iodine, carbon dioxide, etc.). The air is filled with electromagnetic radiations of various frequencies—cosmic rays, x-rays, ultraviolet rays, radio waves—which, although invisible to the eye, again make their presence known; moreover, some of these have the ability to be translated into images and voice. The products of fission and fusion of atoms, themselves invisible, are examples of purely physical phenomena that can be perceived as having potentially destructive components (invisibility turned to evil use). Bacterial and viral agents, invisible to the naked eye, may be harmful or lethal. Higher biological forms—certain fish such as the phantom glass fish, the transparent knife, *Ambassis lala, Chanda ranga*—exhibit total or almost total invisibility (only their eyes and backbone can be seen). The idea of invisibility as it pertains to material things may thus not totally be a figment of the imagination but rather an extension into the metaphysical of the host of examples afforded in the physical world.

Invisibility provides two advantages for the monster. First, it allows the monster to watch the doings of others while remaining unobserved (omniscience coupled with omnipresence); second, it affords the monster the opportunity of engaging actively in plots and schemes, unobserved (omnipotence coupled with omnipresence). These passive and active functions are fundamental to invisibility and pertain equally to all its expressions.

Anonymity is a form of invisibility. It resembles invisibility, in that it is a state in which an individual strives to watch while being unobserved: by immersing himself in a crowd, by hiding himself, by becoming identical with and thus indistinguishable from like "objects." He also tries to perform actions that are not traceable to him: the anonymous donor, the powerful businessman who through circuitous means destroys his competitors, a saboteur, a frustrated suitor. Anonymity can confer on an individual a sense of great power and on his victim a sense of deep fear. Anonymity therefore accomplishes for the human what invisibility accomplishes for the "monster."

Invisibility in all its dimensions is a mimicry of death. It presupposes a dualism of body and spirit—a state of presence mingled with corporeal absence—nonlife which is not quite death. The particular monster-function associated with invisibility (horror) in effect derives from its being perceived as a confrontation with death.

Thus arrayed, as well as with such other additional attributes as hairiness, toothiness, bizarre locomotion, a propensity for victimizing children, a taste for blood, etc., the monsters make their timely appearance as the *dramatis personae* in contemporary tales of horror.

CHAPTER TWO

Construction of the Horror Story: Setting

MONSTER TALES ARE DISTINGUISHED BY SETTINGS IN which time and place are used interchangeably. In these settings a sense of time is achieved by depiction of place; deserts, mountains, swamps, moors, or places such as antique shops, museums, ruins, graveyards, all convey a sense of time. In nonhorror literature place and time can be distinct entities; but in the horror story a setting is always a place that strongly suggests a particular inference about time. In tales of horror place and time are inextricably alloyed.

Tales of horror are characterized principally by natural settings. These commonly depict nature in its wildest and most primeval forms, often including the vivid portrayal of scenery—mountains, valleys, gorges, seascapes, storms, sunsets, fogs—and are readily recognizable by their anomalous, bizarre, transcendental, misanthropic and in general hypernormal content.

For example, although they are beautiful and wondrous they are also awesome and threatening:

> Then the mountains seemed to come nearer to us on each side and to frown down on us. . . . There were dark, rolling clouds overhead, and in the air the heavy oppressive sense of thunder.
>
> —*Dracula*

> . . . the close-pressing green and granite slopes hinted at obscure secrets [which might] be hostile to mankind. . . . There were awesome sweeps of valley . . . gorges where untamed streams leaped, bearing down toward the river the unimagined secrets of a thousand pathless peaks. . . . The only thing which reached my ears was the gurgling, insidious trickle of strange waters from numberless hidden fountains in the shadowy woods. . . . The dense, unvisited [forest] . . . seemed to harbour alien and incredible things.
>
> —*The Whisperer in Darkness*

In these settings hyperbole converts thunder and lightning into a war in the sky. It is a tempest, never a rainshower. A seascape becomes formidable by virtue of a whirlpool. Nature is extended to outer space in the fury of a galactic storm, and is characterized as untamed by man:

> The storm appeared to approach rapidly . . . the thunder burst with a terrific crash . . . flashes of lightning [made] the lake appear like a vast sheet of fire. . . .
>
> —*Frankenstein*

> . . . the whole sea—was lashed into ungovernable fury . . . the vast bed of waters seamed and scarred into a thousand conflicting channels, burst suddenly into phrensied convulsion—heaving, boiling, hissing—gyrating into gigantic and innumerable vortices. . . .
>
> —*A Descent into the Maelstrom*

The storm was still rising . . . the ascending gas streams . . . carrying . . . into the bitterly cold regions ten thousand miles above. . . . The million-miles-an-hour wind . . . [carried] . . . up the great funnel it had torn in the photosphere. . . .

—*Castaway*

Natural settings in tales of horror are additionally characterized by an absence of civilization. Such settings are remote chartless places. ". . . the castle Dracula is located in the wildest and least known portions of Europe." The whirlpool of the *Maelstrom* lies within "a panorama more deplorably desolate [than] human imagination can conceive." Frankenstein pursues the monster he created to a land at the top of the world which has no end. These settings are reminiscent of the Beginning, manifest in a "first-man-like" quality.

. . . as far as the eye could reach rose the leagues of endless crowding Bush, desolate in its lonely sweep and grandeur, untrodden by the foot of man. . . .

—*The Wendigo*

. . . Was this the garden, then, the Eden of the present world? And this man . . . was he Adam?

—*Rappacini's Daughter*

Cut off from, shut in by or otherwise immutable to time, they become isolated psychologically, their temporal and physical remoteness rendered indistinct.

. . . imprisoned amidst the ancient woods, shut in an olden land of mystery and dread . . . as if all was long ago and forgotten by the living outside . . . now and then repeating . . . evil . . . unchanged, unchangeable.

—*The Black Seal*

In the convergence of place and time natural settings in

tales of horror become progressively metaphysical. Although geographic, they are perceived as other-wordly, permeated by the presence of extranatural forces:

> . . . one is on the edge of life, of the unforeseen. . . .
> —*The Creatures*

> It was . . . a place where spiritual agencies were within reach . . . a "beyond region" . . . another evolution not parallel to the human. . . .
> —*The Willows*

> "Lucky's Grove is . . . 'sacred'. . . ."
> —*Lucky's Grove*

Host to unnatural psychical occurrences, they are endowed with legend and mystery:

> Though the day of the Druids is now long past . . . it is said that shapeless invisible horrors haunt the vicinity. . . .
> —*The Spirit of Stonehenge*

> . . . There are peculiar spots on those mountains which are . . . inhabited by the evil influences. . . .
> —*The White Wolf of the Hartz Mountains*

> . . . every known superstition in the world is gathered into the horseshoe of the Carpathians. . . .
> —*Dracula*

Ostensibly giving the appearance of a legitimate history of these scenes, legendary accounts of natural settings constitute a core of shared experience—a "memory net"—evoked by remembrances of past events. In presenting their content in a quasi-factual, quasi-objective manner, the main thrust of these descriptions is not in the development of historical credibility but in the creation of an arena of alien forces. Such legends serve to portray the anomalous character of these settings, giving unsubtle clue as to what must recur within their confines and investing them with a foreboding, menacing, threatening metaphysic.

Tales of horror are likewise characterized by symbolic settings. These include houses, buildings, castles, ruins, museums, antique shops, graveyards—anything capable of connoting a type of age or antiquity refractory to time and civilization. In these settings symbolic material takes the place of frank exposition of nature, extending to a variety of apparently benign objects, such as a portrait, a jewel, an antique or a being (or part of a being) perceived as "bewitched," or anyone or anything represented as "possessed." The function of symbolic settings mirrors that of natural settings: the portrayal of a timeless, primeval, and potentially threatening state.

Perhaps the most ubiquitous and classic of symbolic representations, enunciated by Pliny the Younger already in the first century, is that of the haunted house:

> There was at Athens a mansion, spacious and commodious, but of evil repute. . . . In the dead of night there was a noise as of iron, and . . . a clanking of chains . . . a specter used to appear, an ancient man stinking with emaciation and squalor, with a long beard and bristly hair, wearing shackles on his legs and fetters on his hands, and shaking them. . . . The mansion was accordingly deserted . . . condemned to solitude . . . abandoned to the dreadful ghost . . . .
>
> —*Letter to Sura, Book VII*

Such structures are anything in which spirits, ghosts, memories or happenings—which have the power of materialization or repeating or recreating themselves as if for the first time—repose. Commonly set apart from the mainstream of life, they are buildings that have fallen into a state of ruin, often appearing abandoned, unlived-in (but not necessarily uninhabited). These dwellings are typically large in size, sometimes containing many rooms and chambers, and are frequently distinguished by exterior features such as stonework, elongated windows, arches, parapets, massive doors and heavy ironwork. In effect, however, any structures may be portrayed as haunted; there is no set standard for their appearance. Nevertheless, certain features are common to them all.

Haunted houses are typically *old*. Their antiquity is marked by superannuation and age, specifically an oldness characterized by decay and stagnation:

> Here was the flight of stairs . . . the railing fallen away in a heap. . . . The plaster of the walls . . . broken away in sheets . . . the presence in the house of decay's very soul.
> —*Where Angels Fear to Tread*

> The building was of gray, lichen-blotched stone, with a high central portion, and two curving wings, like the claws of a crab. . . . In one of these wings the windows were broken, and blocked with wooden boards, while the roof was partly caved in. . . .
> —*The Adventure of the Speckled Band*

These dwellings are portrayed as encased, entombed, vaulted in time, many having remained over the years in a state of intact decrepitude—static, fixed, unchanging.

> . . . there was much that reminded me of the specious totality of old wood-work which has rotted for long years in some neglected vault, with no disturbance from the breath of external air.
> —*The Fall of the House of Usher*

. . . the clock downstairs sent up its faint silvery tune of forgotten days. . . . I resumed my reverie, letting . . . impressions of the past . . . permeate me. . . .

—*Oke of Okehurst*

The damp logs spluttered on the hearth, and a wailing wind swept down the valley. . . . [His consciousness] . . . fell into long trains of thought leading far into the dim past.

—*My Brother's Ghost Story*

Their psychological thrust is toward the past, and the nature of this time is implied to be a state which, under the right circumstances, could be reanimated:

. . . unless visitors such as we come to disturb them, they will never wake of their own accord.

—*The House of the Past*

I sat there, thinking of bygone times . . . summoning half-forgotten faces out of the mists . . . listening . . . to voices that long ago grew silent. . . .

—*A Ghost Story*

. . . in this haunted spot, darkened by the towering foliage that rose on every side, dense and high above its noiseless walls . . . my heart sank as I thought my friends were . . . now about to enter and [rekindle] this triste and ominous scene.

—*Carmilla*

Haunted houses also possess a history. Murder, intrigue, suicide, insanity and other sordid, bloody and cruel events are said to have occurred within them. Moreover, memories of these destructive events are thought to linger within the house, and thought capable of recurring under the proper circumstances.

The dust of ages seemed to have settled on [the chamber of the tower], and the darkness and . . . horror of its memories seemed to have become sentient in a way that would have satisfied the Pantheistic souls of Philo or Spinoza.

—*The Squaw*

"There've been mighty strange things a'goin' on about this house . . . and I'm afraid things'll be goin' on again after a bit."

—*The Return of Andrew Bentley*

. . [they] were fated to re-enact their fearful tragedy. . . .

—*The Chronic Argonauts*

Haunted houses are characterized by interaction with their occupants. While various structures may be host to spirits or memories, their special powers are manifested only in the presence of occupants or witnesses. Within this frame of reference the mind of the occupant acts as a psychological projection and extension of the physical structure itself.

. . . by a merging and interplay of identities between himself and his beautiful room, he might be preparing a ghost for the future; it had not occurred to him that there might have been a similar merging and coalescence in the past.

—*The Beckoning Fair One*

Mr. Kincaid's achievement . . . was nothing less than reaching the time of Joseph and the Pharaohs in one's very person. . . the essential element was mathematical and mental involving the reorienting of the mind in hyperspace.

—*Mr. Kincaid's Pasts*

The haunted house serves as a physical surrogate for natural settings. The age and antiquity of these structures, their psychological thrust toward a static and deathly past, their memories and sinister associations—all act to duplicate the threatening, awesome, remote and other-worldly character of these settings, conveying their inherent malignancy and underscoring their overriding motif that chance, randomness and forces outside nature reign supreme.

Settings of horror stories tend to produce a "dream-picture" of time at its beginning: ". . . [he] walked in the garden . . . as if . . . in Eden. . . . [Was he] mistaken in thinking that he had seen a sinuous, dark . . . thing undulating . . . down the stem of that particular apple tree . . .?" *(Couching at the Door).* However, this dream-picture is basically nightmarish. This is a paradise belonging to Cain. For within these settings nature is revealed as capricious, incomprehensible, ungovernable and menacing. The timelessness, immutability and eternal character of these settings, their antiquity and their lore, serve to evoke a sense of time in which the supernatural—events, legends and superstition—can be *perceived,* as distinguished from conventional time, which renders these as abstractions. In rejecting the timetable of man's consciousness, such settings induce a state in which logic and reason are rendered ineffectual and in which the psychological primeval emerges dominant.

In this milieu an earlier time-set prevails. Human thoughts, behavior and emotion revert to more primitive expression. The restraints of civilization fall away. Rationality and reason recede, while the more elemental emotions—fear, terror, anger, hate, the impulse to murder—come to the surface. In this parallel depiction of nature and human nature as stormy, destructive, unsublimated and unpredictable, horror story settings usher in their characteristic state of incipient violence, a violence perceived as both physical and metaphysical, over which man has no control and to which he must ultimately fall victim.

Horror stories likewise evoke a morbid sense of destiny. This recurrent theme, mandating that what has occurred in the past must inevitably occur again, indelibly marks all tales of horror and is present in virtually every aspect, animate and inanimate, of their settings. Legends, stories and accounts all invoke a premonition of things to come. Metaphysical histories indicate what must inescapably be repeated and relived: "A tingling long-lost sense of pleasure came back to me. . . ." *(Frankenstein)*. The antiquity of the settings implies a time past, a time that can characteristically be reawakened to (and remains differentiated from) the present: ". . . the borough of Vondervotteimittiss has existed, from its origin in precisely the same condition which it at present preserves . . . ." *(The Devil in the Belfry)*. Descendants of the original inhabitants of haunted houses, as present occupants of these structures, are often marked by some physical or psychological anomaly which runs in the family—webbing, birthmarks, extra digits, atypical epilepsy, depressions—indicating the propensity for the malevolence of the past to be rekindled in the present. The implication of fulfillment of past prophecies, predictions, signs and dreams in terms of coming events, in effect obliterates the temporal and physical integrity of these settings. In this manner, destiny acts to efface the distinction between past, present and future, rendering these as psychological equivalents.

Unlike the settings of other kinds of literature, those of horror stories thus function to eradicate a sense of usual or conventional time and substitute for it a sense of pseudo-time inherent in and inseparable from the settings themselves. Whether it is the timelessness generated by a depiction of time at its beginning, a time of incipient violence generated by the unstable physical and psychological surroundings, or a time of the past *becoming again* generated by a fearful destiny, it is this sense of "other time" that distinguishes these settings, that imparts to them and the story as a whole their essential transcendental quality, and that makes credible the supernatural events, happenings and occurrences they present.

CHAPTER THREE

Construction of the Horror Story: Characterization

CHARACTERIZATION THROUGHOUT TALES OF HORROR IS basically similar, although variations in character portrayal exist from story to story. The majority of horror stories contain three main characterizations representing diverse forces in dynamic tension with one another. These forces, a triad configuration of characters, include in their simplest form an older man, usually as antagonist, representing evil; a young man as protagonist; and a young woman, typically passive, caught in the conflict between the young man and the older. The characters are usually cast in the hyperbolic mode—good versus evil—and often lack in-depth human qualities.

The older man is presented, actually or symbolically, as representing the older generation in relation to the younger counterparts in this triad. He is portrayed as powerful, especially in the realm of the magical and metaphysical, and brilliant, typically engaged in a scientific venture. These pursuits, quasi-medical in nature, often involve experiments on the body. The older man is frequently distinguished by the title of doctor or professor, or by a title of nobility. He may also be mad in the classic fashion peculiar to horror literature, his so-called scientific explorations going outside natural law and beyond the known. Often pictured as physically ugly, he is sometimes portrayed as repellently attractive, displaying a veneer of gentlemanly charm, elegant language, encyclopedic knowledge and courtly mannerisms. His magnetism and strength of personality, however, are bent toward evil; his outstanding quality is his evil nature. He is the monster figure, the perpetrator of ill—a corrupter, especially of the young, an arch-schemer, always looking for new recruits whom he can enslave to fulfill his evil designs. The immediate object of his designs is the young woman, the apparent prize of the conflict. The exact nature of his intentions is gradually although never completely revealed. He is the master, exerting a powerful hold on those associated with him. Operating in a milieu of the macabre—castles, dungeons, laboratories—and surrounded by the accoutrements of torture, he presents a formidable obstacle to the young man.

The young woman is depicted as beautiful, romantic, eager and the epitome of goodness. She is typically fair with ". . . soft voice . . . sweet glance of celestial eyes . . . the living spirit of love . . . hair . . . the brightest gold . . . blue eyes cloudless . . . lips . . . so expressive of sensibility and sweetness . . . ." *(Frankenstein).* She is innocent in spirit as in body, a virgin, chaste, classically feminine in the Victorian sense. She is devoutly religious, exhibiting a strong sense of moral obligation; she ministers to the less fortunate, to the old and poor, to children and injured animals. She is supremely virtuous. She, too, is the descendant of an illustrious family.

The young woman is solicitous to the point of excess. She is obedient, dutiful and polite, expecially to her elders. She is submissive and does not question the rules, regulations and proprieties of her society. Passivity dominates her relationships. This is especially true of her relationship with the monster figure. She is tied to him, either by blood or in some equally binding way. She often lives in the same dwelling with him, fluctuating between the condition of unwilling guest and outright prisoner. She is frequently "under his spell" and thus an accomplice in his scientific experiments. She assists him in these experiments only when she is not in full posesison of her mental faculties. She is sympathetically portrayed as not being responsible for the evil that occurs during episodes of memory-lapses, sleepwalking, trances, drug reaction and other aberrational states induced in her by the monster. In her lucid, waking moments, when her reason, powers of discrimination, judgment and sense of right and wrong are restored, she is appalled and horrified by the power that the older man exerts over her, but is psychologically unable to break away.

It is only through the young man, as he supplants the older one as the primary male figure, that her liberation becomes possible. Her attraction to the young protagonist assumes the form of hero worship—he is the wish-fulfillment of her secret dreams. While sometimes portrayed as aligning herself with the young man in manifest opposition to the monster figure, more often this alignment is a passive one; she merely waits to be rescued. Her relationships with the two men are in this sense identical: she is wholly passive with respect to both.

The young man frequently serves as the pivotal character in a horror story. The story is mediated through him, and he is often the first person narrator. Presented as a character ostensibly opposite to his older counterpart, he is depicted as possessing a superrational outlook on life, professing faith in science and empiricism and a disdain of the supernatural. He is strong, youthful (or young in spirit), courageous, brave, good-looking; he is religious, respectful of the conventions of society, and is described as having an acute sense of morality, knowing what is good and bad, right and wrong. Those things that offend this morality (i.e., experiments that go "beyond nature") he considers sacrilegious. Logic and religion are his champions and first line of defense in his repudiation of the metaphysical challenge of the monster figure. However, not unlike his older counterpart, the young man, too, is a gentleman, with good manners, a command of language, well-educated, of distinguished family background, a student of science or erudite in equally important fields. In these respects the two characters are congruent.

The story in general progresses as a function of the young man's attraction to the young woman. This attraction is portrayed as girl worship, a basically depersonalized relationship in which the qualities of beauty, virginity and purity of soul are idolized. The young man sympathizes with the young woman's bondage and sees himself as her liberator; it is this circumstance that compels him to engage the monster. But as he pits his acumen against the older man, he is revealed to have a decided bent toward the metaphysical himself and is shown to be as well versed in the "black arts" as his rival; the scientific front he had espoused quickly dissolves. In the end the vanquishing of his foe is accomplished not by any form of rationality, but by a mixture of metaphysics and religion.

The young man, the only figure in the triad configuration who undergoes an apparent change in character as a result of the experience of the story—moving from a supposed nonbeliever to a believer in the metaphysical—thus becomes strikingly similar to the old man. His hold over his associates is as strong and of the same nature as the monster's hold over his subjects. His ability to inspire loyalty, fraternity and unity is every bit as great as the monster's ability to inspire terror and disunity. His reputation as a hero, as godlike and as a crusader for good, is quantitatively the same as the older man's reputation as a demon and conscriptor for evil. And in the end their relationship to the young woman is also similar: she is possessed by the young man through the institution of marriage, never as a person, and by the old man through familial propinquity, never as a person. The principal differences between the two men appear to be in their ages and apparent motivations: one is depicted as representing evil, and the other good.

Characterization in horror stories is frequently modified by recurring sets of circumstances pertinent to the triad figures—such as missing characters, interchangeability of character traits and the presence of particular kinds of auxiliary characters. These circumstances may affect one or more of the triad characters. In the portrayal of the old man, there is a *conspicuous absence of any female counterpart*. He is usually depicted as having no wife, no helpmate, no female contemporary. The event of a *journey* is a circumstance especially pertinent to the young man, who is commonly portrayed as embarking on some kind of quest. These excursions show him to be in a state of maturation; he is cast as a youth coming of age, about to leave home, to sever old ties and set out on an adventure. These journeys also involve the discharging of an obligation on the part of the young man (fulfilling a last request, falling heir to a will, and so forth), further promoting conditions under which the young man must meet the opportunity and challenge of becoming a man. Still another recurring circumstance surrounds both the young man and young woman. They are portrayed as *sexual novices* (especially the young woman), for whom the ideas of chastity and virginity have great significance. However, both young people are commonly portrayed as being on the threshold of sexual experience. They are usually single, about to fall in love, in love, about to be engaged, engaged, about to be married or just married. Also applicable to either or both young people is the circumstance of a *missing parent or parent figure*. The absentee may be a parent *per se*, a grandparent, aunt, uncle, relative or any member of the older generation perceived as a parent substitute toward whom the young person bears a filial affection or relationship. Whether these absences are explained or remain unexplained, the missing parent figure is always made apparent, either by allusion or symbolic representation. *The creation of a myth surrounding birth, parentage and genealogy* is a circumstance pertinent to all members of the triad. The characters are commonly portrayed as being of noble blood or being otherwise distinguished by their genealogy. Even when the origin of one of the characters is unknown, a romantic birth is invented and a history composed to ensure a special beginning. Also applying to members of the triad and closely associated with the idea of special genealogy is the condition of *genetic destiny:* the passing on of an inherited characteristic of doom. The trait of doom that runs in the family is manifest in the older man in his physical deformity or madness. The young people fear the latency of this trait within themselves and its supposed contagious quality. Eliciting or catching this trait is correlated with contact with the monster or the monster's attack.

In some stories the basic triad configuration is altered by the absence of one of the characters, most typically the young woman; in such instances the principal action seems to be confined between monster and protagonist (as in *The Strange Case of Dr. Jekyll and Mr. Hyde*). A character in the triad may be physically absent but still present. The character may be replaced by an equivalent substitute or may make a symbolic appearance. He or she may be present through dreams and allusions, even through abstractions—a thought or ideal—or through concrete representations, such as a portrait, a jewel or some tangible object. Often the absentee makes an appearance in a seemingly inconspicuous role, similar to a theatrical walk-on—for example, the young maid in *Jekyll and Hyde* who makes a brief appearance as a witness to a murder (and is construed within the framework of the story to represent the missing young woman in the triad).

Sometimes traits commonly attributed to one character are shifted to another. Such interchangeability of character traits may be illustrated by the portrayal of a monster figure in terms of youth or beauty rather than their opposites. Also, there may be an interchangeability of sex roles, in that the two young people are confronted with a female monster figure. Variations within the sexual configuration of the triad change the sexual relationships between characters. The portrayal of a young and beautiful female monster whose primary victim is the young heroine implies a basic alteration in the sexual relationship between monster and victim. In terms of nonhorror literature, deviations from standard characterization are for the purpose of character amplification. But changes in characterization within tales of horror always imply a message. For example, the combination of youth and sinister nature can convey the idea that the evil classically associated with the older man can also be present in the younger. The breaking of the stereotype of young equals good, old equals bad, is not alien to the horror story in view of the fact that both the older and younger men are frequently revealed to share basically similar characterizations, and in some instances (*Jekyll and Hyde*) they are indeed the same person.

Auxiliary characters are frequent participants in tales of horror; they may include helpers or assistants to each of the triad characters, foreigners, children and clergy. Each participates in modifying or expanding the characterizations of the three major figures.

The helper of the older man commonly belongs to the younger generation and is of the same sex as the master he serves. Blind loyalty and obedience are his lot. He is often portrayed as being a semi-idiot, mentally deranged, or physically deformed, exhibiting in more acute form one or another of the aberrations that afflict the older man. He is sometimes depicted as being aware of his enslavement to the monster figure, but under his spell. In effect he carries out the monster's orders and derives pleasure in so doing. However, he, too, is often described as being empathetic to the young woman; he is sometimes depicted as having one redeeming feature left within him, and in the last analysis he betrays his master for the sake of the girl, usually at the expense of his life.

The assistant (frequently more than one) to the young man is portrayed as a contemporary, a best friend, characterized by staunch loyalty. He is spiritual brother to the young man, possessing all of the shining virtues of the hero, in a somewhat lesser degree. These friendships are often depicted as being anchored in childhood and based on the sturdy values of brotherly love, comradeship and shared experiences. The assistant to the young man is also attracted to the young woman—platonically—and like the monster's assistant, he, too, usually loses his life in association with her defense, often dying in place of the young man.

The assistant to the young woman is also of her generation and sex. Her relationship to the young woman may be of long, enduring friendship; she may also be a casual acquaintance or even unknown (but known about) to the young woman. Whatever her status, the "other girl" is characterized as essentially a replica of the young woman (a recurring difference is that the young woman is described as classically fair, while the other is typically dark). This nearly identical counterpart serves as a proxy for the young woman, especially in relation to the monster: events that govern the fate of the other girl forecast the impending fate of the young woman.

Foreigners are frequent personages in tales of horror. Such characters may be portrayed as coming from another place or land, affecting speech, manners, customs or dress alien to the existing culture. They are in general portrayed as sub-civilized, often lacking in birth and background, equated with the wildness of nature, frequently more animal in their perceptions and feelings. They may also be characterized by their *joie de vivre,* their lack of inhibitions, their exuberance and their capacity for pleasurable pursuits. Foreigners may include anyone perceived as "different" within the context of the story—nonconformists, members of ethnic and minority groups, and so forth.

Americans are commonly presented as foreigners. Since many of the horror stories are of European origin, the American is perceived as classically nontraditional, not only coming from another land, but more importantly, symbolizing a basically alien idea in tales of horror: the idea of free will. Often characterized as brash, friendly, outgoing and open to life's adventures, the American is the embodiment of free enterprise of the spirit. He is also perceived as representative of a land that is new and unencumbered by the weight of the past, a place where man has wrested changes from nature. The American epitomizes hope for the future, since he is viewed as a symbol of individual freedom and of a system of law and justice anathema to the ideas of predestination. As the counterpoint to the dominance of a violent, random nature, the American, paradoxically, serves to accentuate the futility of free will in tales of horror.

The gypsy is equally symbolic. A wanderer, without roots, he is always the stranger, in effect the classic foreigner. He is portrayed as wild and free, unfettered by the bonds of society, a figure outside the law, commonly suspect. His uninhibited nature is viewed as basically sensual. Within tales of horror the gypsy often appears as a female—dark and beautiful—frequently characterized as a woman of anti-Victorian qualities. The presence of the gypsy underscores the premise that improper behavior (disregard for law and convention) is destined to meet with retribution.

"Colored" people—blacks, Indians, Orientals—likewise appear in the role of foreigner. Because most Western horror literature is "white," these people are presented as aliens on the basis of color. But their portrayal is more than skin-deep. Within horror stories colored people are presented as a lower order of beings, unbridled, less civilized. Their past is neither illustrious nor noble, but steeped in superstition and supernaturalism. Indians and blacks in particular are characterized as still having "bush-like" leanings despite the wash of civilization; Orientals are often described as "timeless" and as possessing the secrets of nature.

Children or their symbolic representations are also conspicuously present in horror stories. Often portrayed as the symbol of innocence, they are described in accordance with traditional concepts. Pure creatures unspoiled by the knowledge of good and evil, they enjoy the same basic characterization as the young woman. Such children are commonly cast as the victims of monsters—witches, ogres, giants, vampires, werewolves, and the like—having a special affinity for the young in that they mean to do them harm either physically or through psychological corruption. But children also enjoy another characterization. Portrayed as the offspring of a human and supernatural being, they may also be the agents of Satan, familiars to witches, malevolent evildoers and latent "bad seeds" destined to lose their outward, benign appearance. Whether as defiled innocents or as diminutive monsters themselves—in several stories the mortally wounded monster makes a last desperate cry: "Mama!"—children act to reinforce the innate evil of the monster figure.

Within the horror literature there is in addition a recurrent association between monsters on the one hand and clergy and religion on the other. Descriptions of these may include hauntings of holy places—cathedrals, churches and rectories—incidents of violence occurring on sacred sites, evil beings loose in convents and monasteries, the appearance of monsters on high holidays (especially Christmas) or, similarly, the werewolf who requires a churchyard with a northern exposure in order to complete his transformation, the vampire who is turned back by the sight of the crucifix, the witch who steals an unbaptized infant and celebrates a Black Mass. In this milieu the clergyman functions as a symbol of what is right and moral. Although the clergyman is conversant with the metaphysical, it is the *acceptable* metaphysical that is his realm, the supernaturalism of established, orthodox religion. Usually making his appearance as the advisor to the young man, specifically in the area of legitimate metaphysics (he may also be the central character himself), the clergyman serves to polarize the confrontation between religion and monsterism, between accepted and unaccepted supernaturalism. Implying religion to be the antedote of monsterism, asserting righteousness to be superior to evil, the presence of this figure within tales of horror acts to buttress and expand the characterization of all three members of the triad configuration.

Characterization within tales of horror is thus comprised of three major figures—the younger man, the young woman and the older man, who in effect mediate the plot of these stories. Missing characters, interchangeability of character traits, the presence of auxiliary characters all serve to emphasize the structural integrity of this triad configuration and to point up and intensify the basic constellation of these primary characters of the story.

CHAPTER FOUR

Construction of the Horror Story: Plot

THE DISTINGUISHING FEATURE OF THE HORROR STORY AS opposed to other literature is that the major events of plot occur outside of nature; incidents, explanations and resolutions are a function of the supernatural. As a result these stories bear a basic similarity.

Plot lines in horror literature typically center around the basic triad configuration—the older man, the young woman and the younger man—corresponding, respectively, to the monster figure, the willing or unwilling accomplice (prize or victim), and the protagonist who ultimately supplants the monster. Such literature commonly includes ghost stories in which the primary action is between the protagonist and a manifestation of the monster (head, hand, paw), and stories of the supernatural in which action is represented between a protagonist and a transformation attribute of the monster, such as an invisible figure. These plot lines may have infinite variations but fundamentally all are concerned with a confrontation between the earthly and the nonearthly—the supernatural, extra-natural or metaphysical.

Horror stories generally can be divided into fairly definite plot sequences, consisting of a series of unnatural encounters between monster and victim, graphically described in eyewitness terms. These confrontations comprise the hard core of the plot; they hold the story together and maintain the reader's interest by gradually revealing the nature of the monster. All of the preliminary and in-between action and narrative—settings, characterizations and story line—are in effect a means of advancement of these sequences.

The first sequence, the pre-encounter period, represents the time before any clear confrontation between monster and protagonist. In this phase of the story, the main characters are introduced directly, while the monster is introduced only by implication: only the monster's deeds (sometimes even the death of a first victim)—or other clues—are presented. In this pre-encounter sequence the pervasive yet unseen presence of the monster becomes manifest, suspense is created, morbid curiosity is aroused, and an atmosphere of impending doom arises.

Frequently incident to this first period is the subplot of a journey on the part of the young man. Such journeys may be actual or symbolic—psychological flights, dreams, time displacements. They are presented as ostensibly benign excursions, often endowed with a moral purpose, undertaken as a deathbed request of a close relative or friend or in response to a parental wish to fulfill an obligation. Whatever their rationale, these journeys act to transport the protagonist to the setting—the home of the monster.

The second sequence is the period of direct initial encounter between monster and protagonist. This period serves to relieve the suspense and curiosity built up in the pre-encounter period and gives a first glimpse of the monster, its evil intent but not its exact nature. Often this first encounter between monster and choice victim (protagonist) is the result of the protagonist's own action (utterance of a forbidden word, staring at a portrait, trespassing on sacred ground), known to call forth the monster.

The nature of this direct initial attack of the monster on the protagonist (and his allies) is that of a violent physical assault upon the victim, frequently involving the infliction of pain or the shedding of blood. Often the protagonist is shown to be not in full possession of his faculties at these times; he is depicted as being asleep, drugged, in a trance, under a spell, in a hypnotic state, under the influence of alcohol, sleepwalking, dreaming—generally in a state of "nonconsciousness." These states are usually explained as a result of excess fatigue, the inadvertent administration of a sleeping draught for nerves, or as the work of the monster in preconditioning his victim for the attack (often no reason is given). The victim usually recovers from these assaults wondering, in fact, whether they had actually occurred or were bad dreams. But certain telltale signs of the attacks are present: odors (which may herald the coming of the monster and often linger after the actual physical encounter) and secretions (wet, cold, semiviscous discharges left by the monster upon his victim), that presage the culminating events of the story.

The third and last sequence of the plot is the period during which the frequency of direct encounters increases, their descriptions become more graphic and detailed—revealing the victim's anguished state of mind and body—and unpleasant occurrences befall auxiliary characters. In this phase of the story the full confrontation between monster and protagonist arises, calling forth the inevitable counterattack on the monster. The resulting clash of wills frequently takes the form of counter-metaphysics invoked by the protagonist, despite his avowed disbelief in such measures (magic words, herbs, flowers, and so forth), in addition to the signs and symbols of orthodox religion. As the final struggle ensues, the balance of power between monster and protagonist shifts. The hero becomes the hunter, the monster the hunted. The horror story usually culminates climactically in the destruction of the monster, but it may also end with the destruction of the hero.

Plot in the horror story mediates the major themes first expressed in settings and characterizations—themes such as predestination, the ineffectiveness of logic, the supremacy of nature, the reality of metaphysics, the alienation of free will, respect for established order, retribution for lack of restraint. In pitting the untamed forces of nature against the propriety of convention, plot gives expression to the intergenerational conflicts between the primary triad characters, and their ultimate resolution.

CHAPTER FIVE

Madonnas

MADONNA FIGURES OCCUR IN THE PRIMITIVE RELIGIONS of ancient man. The term *madonna* represents the synthesis of two apparently antithetical attributes, virginity and motherhood. Whatever its origins, the concept of virgin-mother seems to rest on a transference of the physical condition of virginity into a spiritual condition, wherein the purity of body becomes a purity of soul.

From earliest times the state of virginity was considered special:

> If a man seduces a virgin who is not betrothed, and lies with her, he shall give the marriage present for her, and make her his wife. If her father utterly refuses to give her to him, he shall pay money equivalent to the marriage present for virgins.
>
> —*Exodus 22:16–17,*

The virgin—"unsullied, undefiled, untouched, untried or unused"—thus signified a state of spiritual perfection, which invested her metaphysically with an aura of holiness. Within

41

this state of holy perfection the virgin could fulfill her primary female function, to be fertile and reproduce. Under such conditions of metaphysical perfection, immune to earthly considerations, motherhood could be conferred on the virgin and the two antithetical poles of motherhood and virginity be fused into a madonna figure. Such a concept, while contradicting human experience, is easily accommodated within a metaphysical context.

Madonna figures play a role in religions that are characterized by an organized system of beliefs and rituals concerned with the promotion and ensurance of fertility of land and animals. These are the fertility religions, rooted in a time when man was wholly dependent on the land and/or animals for his sustenance and survival. They are primitive religions in the sense that they originally arose when man's control over nature was minimal and his technology was not yet developed to any appreciable degree.

Man's role in these religions was to perform certain rites and rituals to propitiate the gods, ensuring the cycle of nature—the order of the seasons, the ebb and flow of rivers and tides, the rising and setting of the heavenly bodies, the cycle of fertility in man and animals—and preserving the laws of nature, deviations from which could mean disaster. Although there were wide cultural variations among fertility religions, they were all premised on a similar theme, the perpetuation of natural law.

The central deities in fertility religions were the great mother goddesses and the young male god, typically identified as a sun god. These deities were many and culturally variable, but their roles had a singular purpose: to engage in an archetypal sexual drama depicting nature in its seasons—a drama which in turn was reenacted by man in his rites.

In these rites the mother goddess mates with the young god, who is commonly portrayed as her son (sexual union between goddess and god symbolized the sowing of seeds and fructification). After consummation, the young god "withers and dies"—he is usually depicted as suffering and dying violently—and goes to the "regions below." (As a solar deity the dying god symbolizes the change of seasons after the summer solstice is passed and the crops have been ripened and been readied for harvest.) The mother goddess conceives. But to bring forth she must resurrect the dying god since that deity, who represents the revitalizing force, will become her delivered son. The goddess embarks on a perilous labor, a journey to the land of the dead, in order to deliver her son. Her absence from the earth is marked by the absence of fertility, i.e., the autumn or winter seasons. When her time is due, in the season of rejuvenation (spring), she returns to the earth with the resurrected god. In achieving his resurrection the goddess assures in his rebirth the perpetuity of nature.

The principal mother goddess Ishtar, of the ancient Babylonian religion, typifies the role of madonna figures in the early fertility rites. According to the legend Ishtar mates with a sun god, variously portrayed as her son, brother and bridegroom. After conception (according to one version of the myth) Ishtar destroys Tammuz. The dying god goes to the underworld, "to the breast of the earth . . . the land of the dead" from which no one returns. Ishtar, regretting her act and full of lamentations, goes to the land of the dead in order to resurrect her son. There she engages in a struggle with the goddess of the underworld, while the earth above ceases to produce. Ultimately Ishtar emerges victorious; the god is resurrected and nature's cycle is assured[1].

The Ras Shamra documents unearthed at the ancient city of Ugarit (northern Syria) in 1928 reveal a like drama, central to the religion of the ancient Canaanites.[2] These documents, composed of cuneiform tablets, describe the myths and rites of the young god Baal and his consort, the virgin Anat, goddess of love, fecundity and war.[3] Even in the ancient

Egyptian religion, which was male dominated, it was only through the initiative and efforts of the mother goddess Isis that procreation was assured. Her mate Osiris was slain but Isis "erected the tiredness of the powerless one and conceived." Isis brings forth Horus, a principal Egyptian deity incarnated in the pharaohs, in this remarkable posthumous conception[4].

Madonna figures important in similar psychosexual dramas mimicking the processes of nature include the mother goddess Cybele and her son Attis (Phygrian religion), Aphrodite and Adonis (Greek religion) and the deities of the Indians of both North and South America (the Quetzalcoatl legend).

It was a natural consequence that the virgin should come to be the earthly representative of these exalted mother goddess forms, that man's desire for fertility and productivity should be dramatized through the virgin, and that she should become invested with the rite and ritual of his early religion.

Virgins have long been associated with religious purposes and roles, and have enjoyed special relationships with supernatural beings. One of the first of these roles was as a human sacrifice. Virgin sacrifice in order to incur favor with or appease a god or monster is found in both primitive religion and mythology. In primitive religion these sacrifices were a feature of rites to promote and ensure fertility of land and beast.[5] In Greek myth the same situation prevailed: the virgin Andromeda was to be sacrificed to the Gorgon monster in order to assuage the wrath of the goddess Minerva and thereby avert natural disaster, i.e., the loss of fertility. The apparent idea behind this type of sacrifice was that the potential—yet unused—fertility of a virgin could constitute a perfect gift to a vegetation god; or that such potential fertility could be transmitted directly into the land, river or site that received her remains. Whatever the reasons, the practice of fertility religions demanded that to the gods go the "first fruits."

Examples of virgin sacrifice in primitive religions abound. The Egyptians reputedly threw a virgin into the Nile to ensure a good inundation; the Chinese drowned a virgin in the Yellow River for the same reason; in Africa a virgin was sacrificed at the time of the sprouting millet in order to ensure a good crop; in Scandinavia Lapps offered a virgin to the sun god to assure the fecundity of animals; evidences of virgin sacrifice among the Mayan, Incan and Aztec Indians of South America continue to be uncovered. And in North America the "Morning Star" sacrifice of the Pawnee Indians involved the capture of a virgin who was subsequently torn limb from limb, her remains scattered and buried in fields to ensure the magical fructification of the grain. A similar rite was enacted among the Khands of India.

Children—particularly the firstborn—were sometimes victims of these sacrifices. Primitive reasoning held that by conception the firstborn takes away virginity; and by a principal of transference, the power of virginity (fertility) is incorporated into the firstborn. Hence, the firstborn would carry the same or part of the same potential power of fertility as the virgin, and would be a fitting object for sacrifice to a fertility god.[6]

Virgin sacrifice also took the form of symbolic marriages between virgins and natural entities—rivers, rocks, mountains, wind and even animals—things thought to represent or embody a god. Such unions commonly resulted in the death of the "bride." In Peru, girls of fourteen were married to stones, then sacrificed. In parts of the South Pacific, a virgin was wed to the prince of the crocodiles by being thrown into a river infested with these animals; if she did not return, it was inferred that the god was pleased and had taken her.

Virgins have served a religious function also by devotion

and service to the gods. The Vestal Virgins of ancient Rome were young women chosen between the ages of six and ten and trained to be devotees of Vesta, goddess of field and beast. These girls were the daughters or slaves of the king; they belonged to the king and were members of the royal household. They worshipped the fire god and among their duties was the keeping of the sacred fire which burned in the temple at all times. (The keeping of a sacred fire, symbol of divinity, fell to holy virgins in the service of their gods within many cultures.) The main duties of the Vestals were to engage in operations intended to promote fertility. For example, once a year unborn calves were torn live from their mothers' wombs, and their ashes were scattered by the Vestals over the land—a rite not dissimilar to the virgin sacrifice of the Morning Star.

While the Vestal Virgins—and those of other cultures—took a vow of chastity, prescriptive sexual union was a different manner: for virgins also fulfilled their holy function by marriage to the gods. Actual marriage ceremonies between virgins and "gods" took place at certain times of the year on special religious festivals connected with the promotion of agriculture. The purpose of these sacred marriages was to reenact in human terms what man wanted the gods to do, to be fertile and productive (thus assuring the fertility of nature). In ancient Rome the Vestals were married to the fire god; in South America, Incan virgins married the sun god; in Africa virgins were wed to the python god; in Babylonia virgins married Bel, a solar deity; in Egypt virgins wed the sun god Ammon Ra.

In these religions of old the king or high priest (often he was the same person) stood in a special relationship to the deity and was the god's representative on earth or, as in Egypt, he was the god incarnate. It fell to the king or high priest to portray the god and have intercourse with the holy virgins at a sacred marriage ceremony. When the king or high priest masqueraded as the god to act out the fertility rite, he *became* the god. (In mythology a god in disguise often mates with a virgin.).

The union of virgin and god completed the madonna concept with the creation of a virgin mother.

These unions, in turn, produced exceptional personages. According to legend, the offspring of the Vestal Virgins and the fire god were the early kings of ancient Rome. Romulus and Remus, cofounders of the Eternal City, were reputedly born of a Vestal Virgin, daughter of the King of Alba and the fire god. King Servius Tillius was supposedly born of Ocrisia, a Vestal Virgin, who conceived by a "phallus of flame." Summerian kings were supposedly the offspring of a virgin and the god Tammuz, and called themselves "little gods." Egyptian pharaohs, who were regarded as gods incarnate, were reputedly the sons of a virgin and the sun god Ammon Ra. The remarkable nature and parentage of these offspring are exemplified in an ancient inscription found on the Temple of Luxor describing the divine conception of Amon-hoptep III by a virgin and the sun god:

> He [the god] has incarnated himself in the royal person . . . he stood beside her as a god . . . he caused her to behold him in his divine form . . . his lovableness penetrated her flesh . . . .Amon-hoptep is the name of the son which is in thy womb. . . . He shall exercise sovereignty and righteousness in this land unto its very end. My soul is in him: he shall wear the two-fold crown of royalty, ruling the two lands like the sun for ever.[7]

An extension of holy intercourse between virgin and god prevailed in the practice of sacred prostitution, also in the service of the gods. Primarily concerned with the mechanics of procreation, this ancient fertility rite was devoted to the ritualistic repetition of the "act of life"—the acting out of what was desired of the gods, sexual virility.

In parts of Africa, India and Western Asia, girls chosen from infancy or at puberty were trained to learn chants peculiar to their gods. They engaged in sexual intercourse with the high priest and inmates of male seminaries as part of their training. At the end of their novitiate they went forth as holy prostitutes acting under divine inspiration.

Several allusions to religious prostitutes[8] and prostitution are found in Babylonian cuneiform texts. Alluding to this practice, the Greek historian Herodotus describes the sacred shrine situated on the top of an opulent Babylonian temple:

> In the last tower is a large chapel, in which is placed a couch magnificently adorned, and near it a table of solid gold; . . . the apartment is occupied by a female, who, as the Chaldean priests affirm, is selected by their deity from the whole nation as the object of his pleasures. They themselves have a tradition . . . that their deity enters this temple, and reposes by night on this couch.[9]

A similar practice is described among the Egyptians of Thebes, and also at the Temple of Patarae in Lycia (Asia Minor).

Herodotus also describes another aspect of religious prostitution among the Babylonians which also occurred in Heliopolis (ancient Egypt), in Aphace (Greece) and on the island of Cyprus.

> Every native woman is bound to sit in the temple of Aphrodite (Ishtar), and, once in her life, have carnal intercourse with a foreigner. . . . In Aphrodite's precinct sit, with a fillet of cord around their heads, many women (for some are coming, others going); while rope-drawn passages keep every direction of ways through the women, by which foreigners pass through and make their choice. And when a woman seats herself there, she

does not go home before one of the foreigners has thrown money into her lap and dealt with her outside the temple. But when he throws it, he has to say this much: "I invoke over thee the goddess Mylitta (Ishtar)!". . . . The money may be ever so little in amount, for she may not refuse it, for it is not lawful for her to do so; for this money becomes sacred: but she follows the first that throws, rejecting no man. But after the intercourse, she makes expiatory offerings to the goddess, and goes home. . . .[10]

Similar practices are alluded to in the Old Testament (Genesis 38:14, Proverbs 7:8, 12) and also in the noncanonical Epistle of Jeremy (Verse 43).

Thus in the societies of ancient man there existed concurrently the concepts of virginity and prescribed holy sexual intercourse of virgins with earthly god-surrogates, both in the service of the gods. The reason for such unions was the propitiation of the life force. These unions were viewed as a sacred religious rite; they were not the sex acts of mortal man, nor were the offspring of these unions ordinary mortals. Within the context of prescriptive holy intercourse between virgin and god, the virgin could retain her virginity despite impregnation and motherhood—with the consequent establishment of the virgin mother or madonna figure.

The concept of virgin mother has extended into contemporary times in the form of the Madonna of Christianity, the Virgin Mary. Ever popular as the virgin mothers of old, Mary is celebrated in doctrine, dogma and devotion—Mariology—which has developed and flourished primarily as a function of orthodox Christian theology.

Cathedrals, churches, institutions of social service, colleges and hospitals bear her name; congresses are convened in her honor; religious orders are dedicated to her service; and to her shrines millions make pilgrimage. Her feast days and her close association with major religious holidays in the church calendar are commemorated the world over in a commingling of pageantry and religious devotions. She is the subject of litany, liturgy and literature, the object of petition and prayer. Her appellations embody man's high ideals and most human emotions: She is *Our Lady of Peace, Our Lady of Solace.* She is patron saint of every land and of every human endeavor. Among her champions, historically, have been some of the principal theologians of the Catholic church: Justin, Irenaeus, Origen and Tertullian (Patristic literature, second and third centuries, A.D.); Jerome, Ambrose, Augustine and Peter Chrysologus (fourth and fifth centuries); John of Damascus (eighth century); Anselm, Bernard, Anthony, Bonaventure, Albert and John Duns Scotus (eleventh through fourteenth centuries); and numerous popes (Benedict IV, Leo XIII, Popes Pius IX, X and XII) under whose pontificates Mariology was significantly expanded.

The virgin motherhood of Mary is cast initially in two principal events in the New Testament gospels of Matthew and Luke, both of which describe her virginal conception via an emissary of God and her subsequent bringing forth of a special child. In the first, the Annunciation, Luke relates the spiritual conception of Jesus: an angel announces the coming of the child, his name, his divine purpose and mission in life.

> In the sixth month the angel Gabriel was sent from God . . . to a virgin . . . [whose] name was Mary. And he came to her and said, "Hail, O favored one, the Lord is with you! . . . for you have found favor with God. And behold, you will conceive in your womb and bear a son, and you shall call his name Jesus.
>
> "He will be great . . . and . . . will reign over the house of Jacob for ever; and of his kingdom there will be no end."
> —*Luke 1:26–33*

Matthew gives a similar account.

". . .for that which is conceived in [Mary] is of the Holy Spirit; she will bear a son, and you shall call his name Jesus, for he will save his people from their sins.

"Behold, a virgin shall conceive and bear a son, and his name shall be called Emmanuel [God with us]."

—*Matthew 1:20–23*[11]

A second New Testament event, the Christmas story, recounts the birth of the Son in the context of the virgin motherhood of Mary.

And while they were there [in Bethlehem], the time came for [Mary] to be delivered. And she gave birth to their first-born son [Jesus] and wrapped him in swaddling cloths, and laid him in a manger. . . . And in that region there were shepherds . . . keeping watch over their flock by night. And an angel of the Lord appeared to them. . . . And the angel said . . . "behold, I bring you good news of a great joy which will come to all the people; for to you is born this day . . . a Savior, who is Christ the Lord."

—*Luke 2:6–11*

. . . wise men from the East came to Jerusalem, saying, "Where is he who has been born king of the Jews? For we have seen his star in the East. . . ." . . .and going into the house they saw the child with Mary his mother, and they fell down and worshipped him.

—*Matthew 2:1–2, 11*

The virgin motherhood of Mary is further shaped in the New Testament Apocrypha, Christian writings outside the authorized scriptures of the church, composed mainly between the second and seventh centuries A.D. While these unauthorized writings, which purposed to supply added information on the events and personages of the New Testament, were not included in the Bible, they nevertheless enjoyed widespread popularity. New Testament Apocryphal books chiefly concerned with the virgin motherhood of Mary include *The Protoevangelium* or *Gospel of James* (second century), *Pseudo-Matthew* (a sixth-century version of the Protoevangelium), the *Transitus Mariae* literature[12] (sixth century onwards) and the *Infancy Gospels* (sixteenth century). These writings were laced with miraculous events concerning the special character of Mary's life, such as her exceptional birth, her childhood dedication as a virgin in the temple of Jerusalem (a practice unknown in Judaism—Mary was Jewish), her miraculous conception and delivery, her perpetual virginity, her role as Mother of God and her assumption into heaven. Although never accorded canonical status, the New Testament Apocrypha has served as a prolific source for the support of the evolving doctrine of Mary as the Virgin Mother of God.[13]

The concept of Mary as the Virgin Mother of God was also developed and emphasized in answer to the early gnostic heresies—Docetism, Arianism and numerous others. These heresies began in the second century and revolved particularly around the nature of Jesus Christ—whether he was Spirit, Flesh or both, and in what fashion—and therefore brought into question the nature of Mary. In the ultimate resolution of the nature of Jesus' humanity and spirituality (as set forth in the Doctrine of the Incarnation) Mary was characterized as both a real flesh-and-blood mother and as a Divine Mother.

But it is not only the tenets of religion that have supported the image of Mary as the Virgin Mother. The arts, too, have given her principal support in that role. She is celebrated in paintings, sculpture, music and literature, and is the subject of many of the world's artistic masterpieces. After Jesus, Mary is the most widely portrayed of New Testament personalities. Her image is found in catacombs, cathedrals, churches, museums and households. Whether in the faintly smiling "Virgin of the Grape" by Pierre Mignard, the "Mater Dolorosa" of Gabriel von Max, the porcelain-like beauty of Fra Angelico and Botticelli or the dramatic representations of Faldi, Titian, Correggio, Murillo, Raphael, Da Vinci and Velasquez—brush, pen and chisel have figured strongly in mediating through the generations the consciousness and presence of Mary as the Virgin Mother.

As the Madonna of modern times, Mary has emerged as a figure of universal scope and influence. While it was not until the early Middle Ages that the term Madonna (*mea domina,* "My Lady," the ideal woman of the troubadors of Provence) was ascribed to her, as early as the fourth century she was the subject of direct worship (Epiphanius), and in the fifth century Ambrose extolled her as the model after whom young women should pattern themselves. With the passage of time the ascetic values embodied in Mary—virginity, chastity, motherhood, obedience and innocence—became consonant with feminine virtue and propriety. These qualities of the Madonna have become medium and message in the promulgation of feminine mores. Perhaps no other force has so deeply affected the concept of the ideal woman, and so profoundly influenced the relationships of men and women in contemporary society.

These human qualities have also materially contributed to her image as a metaphysical being. For it is her human attributes that serve, by counterpoint, to emphasize her all-powerful metaphysical nature, and at the same time provide a pathway of accessibility to that nature.

For example, from Immaculate Conception to Assumption, Mary is portrayed as the faithful, devout servant of God. In humility, innocence and obedience to His Will, she does what God asks and surrenders herself to the Holy Spirit. She is submissive. She is virginal, chaste and ascetic. She is honest and truthful, as well as brave—she clings to her account of her atypical conception in the face of ridicule and ostracism (Pseudo-Matthew). She is also the ideal wife and helpmate of her husband, Joseph; her marriage is characterized by filial loyalty rather than by conjugality.

She is a devoted mother, willing and receptive, who wants and welcomes her child, despite the fact that at the time of conception she was not a married woman (*Magnificat,* Luke 1:46). She is nurse and protectress, and gives loving care to her Son under difficult circumstances (Matthew 2:13, Luke 2:22–35, 40–52). She is beneficent, merciful, compassionate, forgiving and doggedly loyal from beginning to end. She is present at all the significant events in the life of her Son, Jesus. She is at Cana where he performs the first miracle; at Calvary where he dies; and after the Resurrection, with the Apostles at Pentecost (Acts 1:12–14). Mary is thus portrayed as possessing in the extreme the ideal qualities associated with motherhood.

The qualities of anger, punitiveness, dominance and rejection are absent from her human characterization, as they are from her human personality in general. Mary has no guile, no jealousy, no personal ambition, no temptations, none of the passions that are part of the human condition. Likewise, she exhibits none of the vicissitudes of physical decline; Mary does not grow old. She is always shown as a young and beautiful woman. Jesus matures: he is depicted as a babe, a boy, a man. But Mary remains ageless. (She is calculated to be nearly fifty years old at the time of Jesus' death.) In Michelangelo's famous *Pietà,* Mary holds her dying Son, looking like his younger contemporary. St. Ephrem, a third-century poet, observes the relative ages of Jesus and Mary:

> . . .My Son, to whom I have given birth, older than me Thou art. My Lord, though I carried thee. . . .[14]

The absence of these psychological and physical defects enhances Mary's ascetic qualities, making her human residue that of an all-submissive, easily approachable figure.

Contrasting sharply with these human ascetic values, and intensified by them, are her coexistent metaphysical attributes. These attributes, derived from religious dogma, doctrine, teachings and tradition, endow Mary with those qualities which make possible her virgin motherhood.

Foremost among these metaphysical endowments is her characterization as *Theotokos,* the God Bearer. "Theotokos" signifies that Mary as a human bore a God (not that she bore a man who became God). This attribute, strongly implied in early church creeds, was formally declared to be revealed truth (dogma) at the Council of Ephesus in 431[15]: ". . .We confess that the holy Virgin is the Mother of God. . . ."[16]

Mary is also the spouse of God. She is the handmaid of the Lord (Luke 1:38), ". . .in heart wedded to God."[17] "She is the spouse of God, the abode of the Trinity and the most special resting place of the Son."[18] Summing up her role as mother and wife, St. John of Damascus further characterizes the Holy Virgin as the wife of God who begot God.

> O most sacred daughter of Joachim and Ann [Mary] . . . who didst dwell in the bridal chamber of the Holy Spirit . . . in order to become bride of God and God's Mother. . . .[19]

Divine Mother and Wife, Mary is also accorded the attribute of perpetual virginity. Perpetual virginity signifies that Mary was virgin before and during conception, after delivery and for the rest of her life.

> As a star gives forth its light
> So the Virgin bears her Son
> Like in kind.
> As the light breaks not the star
> So the Virgin by her Son

is not broken.[20]

Mary's perpetual virginity was proclaimed in 449 by Pope Leo I in the *Doctrine of the Incarnation*.[21] Two years later, in 451, the Council of Chalcedon accepted this doctrine. And in 649, at the First Lateran Council under Pope St. Martin, the perpetual virginity of Mary became dogma: ". . .the ever virgin and immaculate Mary . . . without seed . . . and without loss of integrity brought [Jesus] forth, and after His birth preserved her virginity inviolate. . . ."[22]

Mary is also "sinless," declared "immune from all stain of original sin,"[23] by Pope Pius IX in 1854 in the *Doctrine of the Immaculate Conception*[24]. Exempt from the mortal affliction of original sin—"Like Eve before the fall" (St. Ephrem)—Mary thus becomes a *perfect human being*. Mary's human perfection is the most important meaning of the Doctrine of the Immaculate Conception. Because of her exemption from original sin and correlatively from all other sin, she is perfect in every respect and in every attribute, without flaw or fault. In her state of perfection whatever comes from her, whatever is attributed to her, is correspondingly without flaw or fault.

Mary's perfection is complete in her corporeal assumption to heaven. Immune to the vicissitudes of natural law during her lifetime, defying maternity with virginity, sin with Immaculate Conception, so too is she exempt from the corruption of death, ascending to heaven as a complete person, body and soul. The result of her prerogative as the Mother of God and of her holy virginity, Mary's bodily assumption—long celebrated in liturgy, papal teachings, noncanonical writings,[25] feasts and festivals and in popular sentiment—was declared dogma in 1950 by Pope Pius XII in his *Munificentissimus Deus:*

. . .the Immaculate Mother of God, the ever Virgin Mary, having completed the course of her earthly life, was assumed body and soul into heavenly glory.[26]

Having transcended natural law, not only in life but in death, Mary is the Authoress of Miracles. She has the capacity for reappearances and animation[27] after death (corporeal accessibility—an extension of her bodily assumption). She has the power to respond to prayer; she makes possible the impossible, she heals the hopeless, she reverses the irreversible.

Mary is also the intercessor between man and Christ. She carries the prayers of men to the Son. "It is the will of God that we should have nothing which has not passed through the hands of Mary" (St. Bernard). As the petitioner for individual and collective salvation, she emerges as "the most powerful Mediatrix and Conciliatrix of the whole world" (Pope Pius X), an attribute underscored by the many prayers, especially the Rosary, in which both the Son and the Virgin are entreated.

Finally, Mary is the Co-Redemptress of Mankind.[28] She is depicted side by side with her Son, in the heavenly redemption of mankind.

. . .she will be seated in the heavenly city of God by the side of her Son, crowned for all eternity. . . ."

—*Pope Leo XIII*[29]

. . .[Mary is] . . . the Dispenser of all gifts that Jesus acquired for us by His Death and Blood . . . who . . . distributes the treasures of His merits.

—*Pope Pius X*[30]

[Mary] may justly be said to have redeemed together with Christ the human race.

—*Pope Benedict XV*[31]

This royal image of Mary is stressed in her various appellations as Queen of Heaven: Divine Empress (Pope St. Martin); Domina (Pope Adrian I); Perfect Queen, Royal Virgin (Pope Boniface I); Queen of Martyrs (Pope Pius X); Queen of Peace (Pope Benedict XV); Queen of Apostles (Pope Pius XI); Queen of Mercy (Pope Pius XII); Queen of Heaven and Earth[32] (Pope Pius IX). Portrayed as Co-Redemptress of Mankind—essentially as Co-Ruler of Heaven—Mary becomes a Divine Being.

Thus Mary as the Virgin Mother is the embodiment of a dualism of nature, metaphysical and human, expressing itself in a dichotomy of portentous opposites and reciprocals. From the human aspect she is all-submissive, but metaphysically she is all-powerful. As a human figure she is the obedient servant of God, passively receptive to His Will; as a metaphysical figure she is a powerful ruler, Queen of Heaven. As a human figure Mary is a poor, innocent girl who bears a child which is not her husband's; as a metaphysical figure she is the Bride of the Father and Mother of God. As a human figure she is entirely dependent on her Son for identity—she does not exist other than through him; as a metaphysical figure, Mary is an independent object of devotion, petition and prayer. As a human figure she stands accused by the unbelieving of sinful conduct; as a metaphysical figure she is Mary Immaculate—without sin or fault. As a human figure she is Mary of the Sorrows; as a metaphysical figure she transcends human nature and death. As a human she is the anguished mother at Calvary; metaphysically she attains fulfillment in her Son's Crucifixion.[33]

The duality of her nature notwithstanding, this lowly maid-servant and Divine Mistress, obedient subject and Queen of Heaven, Lady of Peace and Prize of the Palios—cast in the image of Virgin Mother of God, Bride of God, Intercessor between man and God, Co-Redemptress of Mankind, Co-Ruler of heaven and earth together with her Son—shares with her forebear mother goddesses formidable and almost identical attributes. Mary the Virgin Mother of the New Testament, incorporating the metaphysics of the old into the theology of the new, traverses but a short distance in becoming the Madonna of modern times.

CHAPTER SIX

Background of the Christ Story: Historical

THE CHRIST STORY IS A STORY OF SACRIFICE, A STORY OF *the human relationships of love and hate, compassion and cruelty, strength and weakness, loyalty and betrayal. A story of one man's faith in his destiny. And of many men's faith in him. It is the story of a new religion that was to spread throughout the world and dominate Western civilization. But most of all it is a story of the events and circumstances, the metaphysical endowment and supernatural dimension, of the birth, death and resurrection of Jesus Christ.*

The Christ story is the subject of the first four books of the New Testament, the gospels of Matthew, Mark, Luke and John. (The remaining twenty-three documents of the New Testament, including The Acts of the Apostles [Luke], Epistles [early Christian correspondence principally attributed to Paul] and final Book of Revelation, a view of the Second Coming [John], deal with the growth and manifestations of Christianity.) Antedated by the Epistles of Paul (the first actual Christian documents), the gospels were written long after the death of Jesus. The Gospel of Mark, considered the first of these and dated from as early as A.D. 50 to as late as A.D. 75, was the work of a Jewish Christian (a Jew who accepted Jesus as the Messiah), who wrote in the Koine, the Greek in common use during the life of Jesus, for a predominantly Gentile (Roman) audience. Matthew, the second gospel and incorporating Mark, is dated variously from A.D. 70 to A.D. 90, written by a converted Jew for a predominantly Jewish audience residing outside Palestine. Luke, likewise dated from A.D. 70 to A.D. 90, incorporates parts of both Mark and Matthew and was written by a Greek physician primarily for a Greek audience. John, traditionally considered to be the last gospel, dates from A.D. 90. While Mark, Matthew and Luke were in general agreement as to the sequence of the main events in the Christ story ("synoptic gospels"), the Gospel of John was different both in setting and character, its treatment of Jesus distinctively cast in terms of Greek metaphysics.

Although the Christ story is set in real historical time (Roman rule of Palestine from A.D. 1 to A.D. 33)—and generally was composed in the historical period following the destruction of Jerusalem by the Romans in A.D. 70, at a time of both repressive Roman rule (A.D. 70–100) and intense vying between Judaism and the new religion—the gospel writers were primarily evangelizers not historians. Already persuaded by Paul that "the crucified Jesus was the Risen Lord," they were men who viewed Jesus as a spiritual figure, men whose deliberations concerned his metaphysical nature. The gospels are thus not principally historical but inspired writings, whose main thrust—the dissemination of the story of Jesus Christ— reflects metaphysical rather than historical concerns. Yet history, ever-present in the events of man, often becomes the servant of metaphysics.

A boiling matrix of innovative, disparate ideas created under the pressure of momentous events, the Holy Land just prior to the first century A.D. was a reflection of the plural influences at work in the Jewish world. A place of cultural, religious, philosophical and political turbulence, this milieu was largely the result of precedent factors, the most important of which were historical in nature.

For at least six hundred years before the Christian era the Holy Land had been ruled by outside powers. Palestine, with its strategic geographical location, often found itself in the path of the invader. These foreign conquerors brought to the Holy Land the deepest expressions of their cultures. Each, in some way, left an indelible imprint on the Jewish world, which was to prove of immediate consequence to the Christ story.

Beginning in 605 B.C., the Holy Land was to feel the stamp of Babylonian conquest. As a result of defeating Egypt, Babylonia became ruler of Judah, the southern kingdom of the Jews. In 587 B.C. the Babylonian King Nebuchadnezzer entered Jerusalem, the capital of Judah, destroyed its temple and devastated the city:

> . . . he burnt the house of the Lord, and the king's house, and all the houses of Jerusalem, and every great man's house burnt he with fire. And all the army of the Chaldees . . . brake down the walls of Jerusalem. . . .
>
> —*2 Kings 25:9, 10*

Coupled with the deportation to Babylonia of major segments of the Jewish population—members of the upper and middle classes, the wealthy, the educated, the skilled, the community leaders—these events were to have profound ramifications on Jewish life for centuries to come. The most immediate and important of these was the establishment of the *Diaspora,* the dispersion of Jews outside Judah (Judea). This major effect of the Babylonian Captivity—lasting until the fall of Babylonia in 539 B.C.—would have two far-reaching consequences for the Jewish world relative to the

Christ story. Those Jews who remained in the Dispersion would be liberated from strict philosophical and religious constraints—and would create the synagogue, an assembly for instruction and public worship which would substitute for the Temple at Jerusalem and which would eventually constitute an important forum for the elaboration of new principles. Those Jews who returned to Palestine (the Jews of the Return or Restoration) would establish a more conservative, strict and codified Judaism which would also encourage the development of new, divergent ideas.

In 539 B.C. the armies of Cyrus the Great conquered Babylonia, and Judah became part of the Persian Empire. This was followed one year later by the edict of Cyrus, King of Persia, which allowed the Jewish people to return to Jerusalem. While some chose not to return—in the fifty years of the Dispersion many had built successful lives not only in Babylonia but throughout the Middle East—those who returned inaugurated a period of stringent religious practice (especially under the Persian-appointed Jewish governor Nehemiah), a period in Jewish history known as the "Return" or "Restoration." For two centuries the Jews of the Return enjoyed a large measure of self-rule under the Persians: the city of Jerusalem was rebuilt, the Second Temple erected (516 B.C.) and the concept of the synagogue introduced into the Holy Land. In reaction to the loosening of religious and cultural precepts under the Babylonians, the Restoration was to see the creation of the Hasidic party, made up of the very pious—and forerunner of the Pharisees, whose influence in matters religious was to become integral to the Christ story.

With the Greek conquest of Western Asia in 333–323 B.C. Alexander the Great added Palestine to his far-flung empire, the immediate result of which was the introduction of Hellenism into the Holy Land. Spread at first by force of arms but later sustained by force of attraction, the philosophy, religion, arts and science of the Greeks became especially attractive to the Jewish populations of the Western Diaspora (the large urban centers bordering the Mediterranean, in contrast to the Eastern Diaspora centered in Babylonia). Newly created cities such as Alexandria swiftly became centers of Hellenic culture, from which significant Jewish-Hellenic literature and thought emerged. Demetrius, the Egyptian Jew, in 225 B.C. wrote a history of his people in Greek. Greek and Jewish values and imagery merged in such works as *The Wisdom of Solomon* (30 B.C.), in writings of the Alexandrian Jewish philosopher, Philo (c. 20 B.C.–A.D. 40). Of perhaps most immediate significance to the background of the Christ story, the second century B.C. was to see the translation of the Hebrew Bible into Greek, the *Septuagint,* which became the Bible of Western Judaism—whose use in the Holy Land was to extend well beyond the first century A.D.

Following Alexander's death in 323 B.C., his empire was divided among several of his generals, two of whom, Ptolemy and Seleucus, assumed control of Egypt and Palestine, and Syria and Mesopotamia, respectively. For 125 years their successors, the Ptolemies and Seleucids, ruled these territories until in 198 B.C. the Seleucids conquered the Ptolemies and Palestine became part of the Seleucid Empire (198–166 B.C.).

The beginning of Seleucid rule of Palestine was to see the continued dispersion of Jews into cities founded by the new rulers, with a corresponding expansion of Hellenic influence in Judaic culture. However, with the advent to power of the Judaphobic Antiochus IV (Antiochus Epiphanes) in 168 B.C., the Seleucid policy of Jewish cultural self-determination abruptly changed, yielding to the initiation of brutally enforced Hellenism in regard to Jewish religious practices: the desecration of the Temple at Jerusalem by erection of a shrine to Zeus and the sacrifice of swine on its altar (Daniel 12:11, 1 Maccabees 1:54), the burning of scripture, the murdering of those who sought to circumcize, the profaning of the synagogues. Under pressure of these events Jewish factionalism became increasingly polarized into two groups, composed on the one extreme of the Hasidim, the pious, devout Jews whose primary concern was their devotion to Judaic beliefs developed since the time of the Restoration, and on the other, of Jewish-Hellenic sympathizers and outright apostates. Their respective viewpoints were to concretize into several religious parties extant at the time of the Christ story, among which were the major holders of religious and political power, the Pharisees and Sadducees.

In 166 B.C. the policies of enforced Hellenization of Antiochus Epiphanes resulted in a rebellion by the Jews of Palestine against their Seleucid oppressors, known as the Maccabean Revolt. Begun by a priest from Jerusalem, Mattathias, and carried forth by his five sons—the most outstanding of whom was Judah Maccabee[1]—the struggle lasted for thirty years, ending successfully for the Jews in 134 B.C. with the ascension to power of John Hyrcanus I, Mattathias' grandson. A period of about seventy years of political and religious independence ensued during which Palestine was ruled by a succession of Jewish priest-kings, descendants of the Maccabee family who were known as the Hasmonean dynasty. These rulers were at once kings and high priests, while before the period the kingship and the priesthood had been separate institutions.

Espousing to reestablish a pure and autonomous religion and a free religious and political state, the Hasmoneans paradoxically extended the process of Hellenization. Jewish names, including those of the priest-kings, were Hellenized; new territories were acquired by military expansion; new converts were gained by forced conversion and religious propaganda. But perhaps most significant for the Jewish world at the time of the Christ story was the inauguration with Rome in 162 B.C. of a reciprocal treaty of friendship and military assistance, the League of Amity, which provided for mutual aid between the two in the event of threats to the existing order (under Hasmonean rule Palestine was one of the most important military kingdoms of the Middle East.)[2]

Reflecting the increasingly corrupt and ineffectual rule of the Maccabean descendants (in time the absolute power vested in the priest-kingship took its toll of those ill-suited to rule), John Hyrcanus II in 63 B.C. invoked the League of Amity, inviting the Romans to help him regain the priest-kingship from his brother, Aristobulus II. The Romans came—but not as mediators. When the legions led by Pompey marched into Jerusalem in 63 B.C., Palestine became a province of Rome.

That Palestine became a province of Rome in 63 B.C. is but a minor occurrence in the overall epoch of the Roman Empire. Yet to the Jewish world of the first century B.C. it was an event of momentous consequence. While the Romans allowed each conquered territory a degree of autonomy in its traditional scheme of government, cultural identity and religious beliefs, they nevertheless instituted far-reaching political, social and civil measures that would drastically alter the religious and philosophical climate of the Holy Land.

In particular the Romans were prolific road builders, establishing a vast network of communications linking one end of the empire to another. Throughout the East people moved on Roman roads, along Roman trade routes, through Roman seaports, accelerating the influx of foreign ideas into Palestine and greatly enhancing the spread and influence of Hellenism.

The system of Roman procurators—provincial governors, replacing in this instance the previously installed "puppet kings" of the House of Herod because of their dissolute rule—exerted a similar influence on Jewish society. Responsible for the appointment of officials to posts of importance, the procurator confirmed all political functionaries. He appointed the publicans or tax collectors, Jewish officials who went among the populace and raised revenue for the Roman tribute, and approved the money changers, members of the Sadducees party who acted as a "state bank" exchanging foreign coinage (which bore graven images forbidden by Jewish law) into local currency. The procurator also garrisoned a large standing army, oversaw the Roman court of his jurisdiction to hear the cases of Roman citizens, was himself the overseer of Jewish courts which heard the cases of Jewish citizens (often within the synagogue) in order to ensure the enforcement of local laws, and presided in general over cases of capital punishment. In effect, through the rule of the procurator, the influence and ethos of Rome—paganism, philosophical dualism, rationalism and gnosticism—penetrated into all aspects of Jewish life.

In another respect the rule of the procurator was to figure prominently in the background of the Christ story. For the procurator appointed the High Priest who presided over the Sanhedrin, the High Court of Jerusalem, the most important judicial body in Palestine. Reflecting the increasingly heavy hand of Rome, it was this court that, in complicity with the Romans, was to play a crucial role in dealing with the scourge of the day, messianic figures.

From the very beginning Palestine was a troublesome territory to Rome. Strategically located on the Eastern front of the Roman Empire, Judea, whose capital city was Jerusalem, was a hotbed of sedition, rebellion and brigandage. In the province of Galilee, too, Jewish rebels carried on a running conflict with Roman authorities, creating political chaos, refusing to pay the tribute, fomenting insurrection and civil unrest. Gaining momentum and direction, these anti-Roman acts coalesced in the emergence of the Zealot party, whose religious precepts dictated that the Jews owed allegiance to no one but God, that the Day of Judgment was fast approaching, that the Messiah was imminent who would deliver the Jewish people from the yoke of pagan rule.

To the Jews the Messiah was a very real person, a historical figure who had both priestly and royal attributes. Anointed to carry out the will of God, he was a descendant of the House of David[3] (the King David of the Old Testament who reigned at the zenith of Israel's power), and an outstanding military leader who would restore the Jewish people to their former glory.

To the Romans the Messiah was anathema. He was the agent of violent overthrow of established rule, the enemy of the status quo, the harbinger of a New Order heralding the destruction of Roman power in Palestine. Accordingly, Jewish messianism, expressed tangibly, was viewed as treason—in contrast to the purely religious messianic expression of other territories which was treated with levity—and elicited the full force of Roman retaliation. In the hills of Galilee messianic aspiration was countered with mass crucifixion. In Judea messianic rebels, teachers, preachers, those who asserted divine inspiration—self-styled magicians, prophets, political dissidents, and often ordinary criminals—met similar fates. The result of heightening political anxiety over the appearance of a Jewish Savior, it was this effect of Roman rule[4]—the aversion to messianic figures and in particular to the ideal of a Jewish Messiah—which was to prove perhaps of greatest consequence to the immediate background of the Christ story.

The forces at work at the time of the Christ story were thus born of a more removed era, the product of antecedent factors set in motion well over 600 years before. These included a series of conquests of the Holy Land beginning in 605 B.C. with the Babylonians and ending in 63 B.C. with the Romans, which resulted in major changes in Judaic customs and beliefs and the confrontation of mainstream Judaism with new concepts and developments that were to become most important to the Jewish world of the first century. Principal among these were the division of Judaism into two branches as a result of the Babylonian and Persian conquests; the introduction of Hellenism into the Holy Land and the concomitant penetration of Jewish thought and expression by foreign ideas and practices; the advent of the concept of Jewish priest-kings; the formation of various religious political parties representing different constituencies; and, finally, the savage antipathy of Rome to the emergence of Jewish messianic figures.

CHAPTER SEVEN

Background of the Christ Story: Political

THE ACCOMMODATION TO ROMAN RULE WAS REFLECTED in the temper and beliefs of the Jewish religious-political parties of the time: the Pharisees, Sadducees, Essenes and Zealots. Each of these parties was to have an impact on the immediate background of the Christ story.

The Pharisees, an outgrowth of the Hasidic party, were composed of teachers or rabbis who functioned in one or both of two ways: as interpreters who made commentaries on religious law, and as scribes who made copies of Hebrew Scripture and other religious works. Usually of humble origin, these men dedicated their lives to the study and interpretation of the Jewish Bible, the Torah—literally "the teaching," commonly called the Written Law—consisting of the first five books of Moses (the Pentateuch) in addition to the

books of the prophets. At the time of the Christ story the
Pharisees represented mainstream Judaism, their orientation
directed towards religious idealism and purity. Cleaving to
the synagogue as their forum, they preached in the synagogues of Palestine, establishing a broad base of support and
respect among the people.

The Pharisees accepted not only the Torah, or Written Law,
but also the Oral Law—the interpretations of the Written Law
which had been handed down from generation to generation.
Comprising the Pharisaic code of behavior known as
Halachah, these interpretations extended mainly to rules gov-
erning ritual cleanliness, dietary injunctions and Sabbath observance. By the end of the first century B.C., Pharisaism
had evolved into a thorough discipline and code of conduct:
the requirements of Halachah had become very exacting, and
meticulous observance of both Halachah and the Written Law
affected every phase of Jewish life.

The Pharisees also accepted the divine revelations of the
prophets which included certain eschatological ideas (concerning the end of the world)—principally the coming of
God's Kingdom on earth to be presided over by the Messiah,
a Day of Judgment and the resurrection of the righteous.
However, their eschatology was strongly tempered by religious pragmatism. Their emphasis lay on the existing
world—on the creation of a living Judaism which bore the
stamp of their scriptural interpretations rather than on the
imminency of a Messiah or appearance of a divine revolutionary. In this respect they were regarded as politically benign by the Romans.

Although containing liberal and moderate elements, the
teachings of the Pharisees had a basically conservative thrust,
functioning to reinforce the ideological gulf between Judaism
and Roman paganism and to counterpoint the emergence of
doctrinally divergent Judaism. Rationalistic, legalistic, pragmatic and politically adept at achieving a peaceful coexistence

with Rome, the Pharisees were the only major religious-
political party to survive the Jewish Revolt of 66–70 A.D., in
which the Romans destroyed Jerusalem.[1]

The Sadducees, dating back to the second century B.C.,
were the party of the ecclesiastic aristocracy. Representing the
Jewish power structure during the latter half of the first
century, they were characterized by their wealth, their influence and their political collusion with Rome.

Religiously, the Sadducees accepted only the Written Law,
the Torah, expressing a more worldly and Romanized attitude, rejecting Pharisaic Halachah, together with various
eschatological ideas concerning the Messiah and the resurrection of the righteous.

Disproportionate to their numbers, the power of the Sadducees in terms of their effect upon the Christ story was
twofold. From the Saducean party came the High Priest and
members of the Jerusalem priesthood, who occupied a highly
respected position in Jewish life and in whom was vested the
institution of organized religion. From their number were
drawn the officials of the Sanhedrin, the High Court of
Jerusalem, which passed on virtually every important religio-
judicial, and thereby political, question affecting the Jewish
people. As custodians of the Temple, the symbol of world
Jewry, the Sadducees also controlled the Temple treasury—in
effect a state bank—collecting the half-shekel tax required of
all Jews, the tithes on produce, the charity contribution of the
wealthy, the fees for approving sacrificial foods and animals,
and the commissions on the exchange of monies from persons bringing foreign currency to the Temple—a concession
granted them by the Romans.

In their capacity as proprietors of state religion and eco-
nomics, the Sadducees' relationship with Rome was one of
functional mutuality. The Sadducees kept order for the Romans by the exercise of religious authority, and the Romans
kept the Sadducees in power. By rejecting Halachah and

eschatological ideas—especially the idea of a Messiah[2]—the Sadducees were likewise regarded by Rome as politically unhazardous.

The Essenes, a widespread esoteric Jewish sect, were a group of religious visionaries whose main doctrines and mystically oriented beliefs and practices were premised on an elaborate eschatology and on their own distinctive interpretation of the Law. Also known as the Jewish Sect of the Covenant, they were scattered throughout the major cities of Judea and concentrated on the northwestern shore of the Dead Sea (Qumran).

Living communally, these men governed their lives by strict religious rules. Their ranks were composed of volunteers who fulfilled certain stages of social and religious requirements before final admittance into the Party of the Community (the Brotherhood). Their doctrines, beliefs and practices were embodied in the Dead Sea Scrolls, a library of religious literature composed in the first century B.C., whose discovery in caves near the Dead Sea dates from 1947.

The Essenes believed in an imminent eschatology, with emphasis on the coming Messiah. Their writings reveal several messianic figures, including their own venerated leader, the Teacher of Righteousness (70 B.C.). Rejecting the Halachah of the Pharisees and denying the validity of the Jerusalem priesthood, they followed their own injunctions on dietary matters, ritual cleanliness and observance of the Sabbath and festivals (their feast days sometimes fell differently from those of mainstream Judaism because of their observance of a solar calendar).

Essentially pre-Christian in nature—"they reject pleasures as an evil, but esteem continence, and the conquest over our passions to be virtue"[3]—the Essenes were religious ascetics (some reportedly celibate), holding to such values as humility, meekness, poverty, and pacifism—qualities of psychological and physical temperance and restraint. Among their practices were baptism,[4] a communal meal presided over by a priest,[5] herbal medicine,[6] prayers of supplication to the sunrise,[7] engaging in prophecy[8] and composing scripture.

"Despisers of riches" who renounced earthly wealth and rejected the practice of slavery upon which the entire economic system of the Graeco-Roman world was founded, the Essenes practiced communal ownership and the sharing of material and spiritual values. They emphasized virtues of love, respect, hospitality and loyalty toward one another and the stranger among them and a tolerance of each man's capabilities and limitations. Espousing a deep devotion to truth and honesty and a corresponding hatred of lying and deceitful practices, they stressed diligence and fidelity to work, study and prayer.

Exponents of philosophical dualism, the Essenes based many of their precepts and doctrines on the inherent opposition of spirit and matter, believing in the essential corruptibility of the flesh and the independent immortality of the soul. Their literature, which mentions angels, demons and a personified devil, echoed their intense preoccupation with doctrines of sin, the flesh, guilt and salvation, anticipating the similar Pauline religious psychology and philosophy by more than a hundred years.

As a group of "men, who weary of life, have been driven by the vicissitudes of malfortune to adopt their manner of living,"[9] the Essenes were unlikely to actively foment political insurrection. Rather they chose to express their animosity toward Rome and the Jerusalem priesthood indirectly. Their writings, depicting eschatological battles of a fantastic nature, show a detailed knowledge of Roman arms,[10] and have been construed as bitter indictments against the existing order.

With their intense messianism, the Essenes could not fail to arouse the attention of Rome. It was only their obvious religious devotion to humility, meekness and poverty—their apparent pacifism, asceticism and devotion to the Law—that mollified the Romans into tolerating them as non-*provocateurs*.[11]

The Zealots were a religious-political group of Jewish revolutionaries characterized by their violent and relentless opposition to Roman domination of Palestine.

A party of fanatic patriots whose strength at the time of the Christ story was centered in the provinces of Judea and Galilee, the Zealots were fiercely devoted to religion and country, and carried on an increasingly effective campaign of organized murder and rebellion against the Romans. Also known as *Sicarii* or Daggermen (because of their practice of secretly carrying daggers), the Zealots also directed their attacks against those fellow Jews whom they considered unfaithful or guilty of sacrilegious acts.

Drawing strength from a wide segment of the population, the Zealots based their actions on the principle of pure theocracy. They believed in the inherent sinfulness of all mortal government and acknowledged "no leader or master but God." They believed the Jews owed allegiance to God alone and completely rejected Roman authority. They believed it was better to die than to live under Roman slavery—a choice that was more than once put to the test.

In religious matters the Zealots held to the Pharisaic doctrine, accepting both the Written and Oral Law, including Pharisaic Halachah, and were particularly attentive to the strict code forbidding relations between Jew and idolator and idol worship. The representation of images (idols) on Roman standards, resulting in the "image riots" of Jerusalem under Pontius Pilate—mirrored Zealot concerns. Like the Essenes, the Zealots embraced eschatological ideas, believing that the messianic kingdom was imminent. However, instead of merely awaiting its coming, these activists felt that they could create a messianic kingdom by revolution.

Both fired by the same religious, high-pitched messianism

and hatred of the foreign oppressor, the Essenes and the Zealots represented different aspects of the same nationalistic and religious concerns. Although their responses to worldly disenfranchisement differed—nonviolent hostility as opposed to armed hostility—intrinsically these two groups had a basic affinity.

It was in the Zealots, however, that Rome's worst fears regarding Jewish disloyalty were realized. Their relationship with the Romans being one of accelerating violence and sedition countered by suppression and torture, the Zealots drew unwarranted attention to Palestine—for which the Jewish nation paid heavily. In Galilee the Zealot stronghold of Sepphoris was completely destroyed by the Romans. Its hills, visible from neighboring Nazareth, were dotted with the crosses of two thousand crucified rebels.

Although denounced by the Pharisees and Sadducees alike for their vigilante spirit that often resulted in indiscriminate death and destruction, the Zealots nevertheless enjoyed a clandestine admiration from segments of all political parties, as well as from individuals without party affiliation. Ultimately blamed by some early historians for precipitating the final fatal clashes between Palestine and Rome, the Zealots were destroyed as an effective party[12] in a dramatic encounter with Roman legionaries at Masada on the Dead Sea in 74 A.D.

The various religious-political parties of the Holy Land, vying for the minds and allegiance of disparate elements within the Jewish world, thus gave rich expression to the immediate background of the Christ story, each contributing heavily to this story's panoply of religiophilosophical content. In the doctrine of mainstream Judaism the Pharisees[13] established a religious code based on the Written and Oral Law, outlining strict observance of the Sabbath and prohibitions regarding ritual procedures and practices which would eventually become integral to the Christ story itself. In contrast, the Sadducees, the ruling priestly oligarchy in whom was vested the reins of organized religion, would put forth a doctrine of muted Judaism, devoid of messianic hope or aspiration, diluted in eschatological expression, bereft of the value of the resurrection of the righteous—and on a collision course with the championing of the poor, the sick, the downtrodden, sinners, publicans, unfortunates, which was also to become a major theme in the Christ story.[14] Into this swirling milieu was to be added still another motif—the thoughts and beliefs of the Essenes—representing the ascendancy of humility, meekness, pacifism, asceticism, poverty, confession, baptism, temperance and celibacy as positive spiritual values. Cut off from the mainstream of Judaism, opposed by both Pharisees and Sadducees, suspect to Rome, brought forth by those who possessed no earthly wealth and carried no political power, regarded as religiously anomalous, the ideas of the Essenes would eventually shape a new religion.[15] Yet a final figure in this arena, Jewish militancy,[16] would be represented by the Zealots. Counterpointing Pharisaic conservatism, Sadducean secularism, and Essene pacifism—giving expression both to the ever-present smoldering discontent with Rome as well as to ever-present Roman dominance[17]—it was this theme of militancy and its inherent challenge to Roman authority that would constitute perhaps the most conspicuous Jewish element in the immediate background of the Christ story.

CHAPTER EIGHT

Background of the Christ Story: Philosophical

.

OF ALL THE INFLUENCES WHICH WERE TO BESET MAIN-
stream Judaism, Hellenism was the most critical. Brought to
Palestine by Alexander the Great, further promoted by the
Romans, the arts, science, religion and philosphy of the
Greeks would constitute by far the most serious, enduring,
and attractive challenge to the Jews. Thoroughly mixed with
many ideas of non-Greek origin (Babylonian, Persian, Egyptian), the concepts that came with Alexander engendered
from the outset conflict and response from traditional Judaic
culture. Characterized by deep ambivalence, the Jewish
struggle with Hellenic ideas ranged from philosophical resistance to philosophical reconciliation, from outright military
opposition (the Maccabean revolt) to outright Jewish apos-
tasy. The end result of all these factors was a deepening of

Hellenic influence, not only within the Judaism of the Diaspora but within Palestinian Judaism itself.

Although thought by some historians to have no significant effect on Judaism in the long run, Hellenism nonetheless was to appear at a crucial time. For it was precisely in the centuries surrounding the Christ story that this culture's effect on the Jewish world was maximal.

Two major aspects of Hellenism were presented to the Jewish world of the end of the first century B.C.: Hellenic rationalism, the development and enshrining of reason and logic as a method of apprehending knowledge of the world and of the self; and Hellenic supernaturalism, the recourse to intuition, faith and emotion as fundamental criteria in apprehending knowledge of the self and of the physical and metaphysical world.

Principally derived from philosophers of the sixth to the fourth century B.C., such as Pythagoras, Socrates, Plato, Aristotle and others, Hellenic rationalism sought to promote man's capacity for systematized thought processes such as inductive and deductive reasoning—to employ logic—as tools to unlock the secrets of the physical world, to explore the psychological world, and to allow man to reflect on his basic nature. Finding expression in the development of early science and medicine, and in abstract values such as truth, wisdom, good and beauty, Hellenic rationalism took as its premise the nearly unlimited possibility for individual achievement. Of universal scope and application, exerting its effects across a wide spectrum of disciplines, rationalism promulgated the ideal man as a heroic and enlightened being, whether in mythology, in drama, in sculpture, in architecture, in physical culture, or in the creation of democratic institutions and forms of government. Resulting in broad social and intellectual gains, in this regard the culture of the Greeks intermeshed well with Judaic ideas and ideals.

By the third century B.C., however, the great burst of

philosophical, scientific and artistic achievement waned. Instead, there developed throughout the Near East a preoccupation with metaphysics, to which the tool of logic began to be applied, resulting in new "theological" formulations. It was with this aspect of Greek thought, Hellenic supernaturalism, that the Jewish world would grapple. This development confronted the Jewish people with formidable religious and philosophical syncretisms (alien beliefs and influences) and presented them ultimately with major cultural and social changes.

Central to the expression of Hellenic supernaturalism was the doctrine of philosophical dualism, which set forth the existence of spirit and matter as distinct entities. Arising during the second century B.C., this philosophy professed the antithetical nature of man and his world—and provided a framework and rationale for other supernaturalistic thought systems current at the time of the Christ story. Rooted in Babylonian and Persian cultures, this Greek view contrasted markedly with traditional Jewish thought that held that man was an integrated being, not a creature of warring opposites; that he was a living soul, higher than the animals, capable of making choices; that man's world was of God's creation, that its products were not separate entities but a result of man's actions and decisions, that the God of the Jewish world was a living God not held in abstraction—an ethical force everpresent in the daily lives of his people. [1]

Philosophical dualism deemed that man was an amalgam of two opposing natures: spirit and flesh (matter), the former described as inherently good, the latter, evil. In the inevitable struggle for dominance of these two natures, the weaker—the evil (the flesh)—gained ascendancy. Man became prisoner of his material side, doomed by his very nature to evil.

Philosophical dualism also held that man's world was the creation of an anti-God, the Demiurge (eventually to be identified with the devil), that the world was a corrupt and iniquitous place, peopled by sinners, irredeemable in nature. Nor did the world beyond escape the same kinds of representation, being itself divided into heaven and hell. The former was a place of rewards and eternal life; the latter a region of eternal punishment and damnation in the nether-reaches of the earth.

As man became a victim of his corporeal nature, trapped in a material world, his power of free will, freedom of choice and reason diminished. Individual initiative, mired in an intellectual climate permeated by psychological and philosophical determinism, focused on the spiritual world. Astrology became the science of the time. God retracted from man and his world; He became removed, transcendental, harder to reach, hidden deep within His spiritual realm. Concomitantly the devil began to evolve as an opposing power.

Incorporating the concept of flesh as a determinant of man's nature, and of God as a removed, transcendental being, philosophical dualism moved in the direction of a further supernatural formulation, fording the very gulf it had created—that of the intermediary. A spiritual entity made material, this agent bridged the gap between man and God, between the material and the apprehension of the spiritual. Although transcendentally out of reach, God sent to the world in the form of quasi-personifications, his attributes: His Wisdom, His Truth, His Way, mirrored in the Christ story as the Doctrine of the Logos.[2] Angels and demons, messengers of God and the devil, respectively (heralding the disciplines of angelology and demonology), represented the materialization of the spiritual. Messiahs, divine beings in human form, embodied similar representations, foreshadowing the principle of spirit made flesh.

In the wake of philosophical dualism the problem of how man was to extricate himself from the flesh and material world, to save his soul and achieve immortality yielded to a second major manifestation of Hellenic supernaturalism, gnosticism. Specifically meaning divinely revealed knowledge, as opposed to knowledge acquired by reason, gnosticism represented ultimate knowledge, the supreme metaphysical revelation of Truth. Premised on a strict dualism of nature, providing answers to all universal questions, *gnosis*[3] revealed the mysteries of life, death and destiny to those properly prepared for receiving such knowledge, and was attainable only through a religious experience that put man in direct union with the deity.

Because matter was the ultimate victor over man, the thrust of gnosticism was toward the spiritual realm, toward faith in the deity, toward preparation for mystical encounter with the deity who, characterized as Revealer or Savior, moved toward man as a result of this faith and state of religious readiness.

A magical happening, the union of God and man with its promise of eternal life and heavenly rewards, could be effected by either of two means: vigorous observance of prescribed ritualistic behavior (not necessarily connected with any system of ethics), or abating the appetites of the flesh which had become, by dualistic deduction, the seat of all sin. The latter could be accomplished both by indulging the flesh through hedonism, in which fleshly appetites were curbed by supersaturation, or by denying the flesh through asceticism. Such measures ranged from self-discipline and self-control as preached by the Stoics to abstinence and eventual "mortification of the flesh" by fasts, self-inflicted injuries, and other forms of self-denial.

Further resolving the dilemma of personal salvation and immortality, a third major expression of Hellenic supernaturalism comprised the development of an elaborate and violent eschatology. Since the world was inherently worthless and unsalvageable, its salvation lay in its total destruction through divine intervention, and the subsequent establishment of a spiritual kingdom on earth. Contrasting markedly with the traditional Jewish view, the resulting eschatological scheme incorporated such supernaturalistic beliefs as a final judgment, the salvation of the righteous, the destruction of sinners, the immortality of the soul, the resurrection of the righteous, the establishment of a spiritual kingdom on earth presided over by the Messiah.

Of all the expressions of Hellenic supernaturalism confronting the Jewish world of the first century B.C., perhaps the most challenging was that of the mystery religions, based on fertility cult ideology. These religions flourished among the people, attracting a large membership who could belong to more than one at a time. They were called mystery religions because initiates underwent secret ceremonies of indoctrination, typically including a baptism of blood, eating and drinking special foods, and engaging in prescribed sexual acts, whereby the answer to ultimate questions was revealed. Among such religions were the cults of the vine (Dionysus or Bacchus and Basilinna), the Eleusinian mystery cults,[4] the cults of Isis and Osiris, Ishtar and Tammuz, Cybele and Attis and—especially prevalent at the time of the Christ story—the cult of Ashtarte and Mithra (the latter, Mithraism, eventually became the state religion of Rome).

Religions based on fertility cult ideology contained many primitive beliefs and practices. At the center of these religions was the great mother goddess, who controlled the fecundity of earth, the beasts and man. Through her, the embodiment of the reproductive energies of nature, the Life Force emanated, her role being to bring forth new life each year. Virgin, mother, wife and lover, she was consort to the male god who symbolized the yearly decay and revival of life; his role was to fecundate the goddess, die, and rise again from the dead to begin the life cycle anew.

Although numerous male fertility deities frequented the world, each with his cultural attributes, some of whom were powerful in their own right, all played basically similar roles within an essentially similar drama: to ensure, together with the goddesses, the eternal cycle of man and nature.

Typical of such dramas was the widely celebrated spring festival of Cybele and Attis, commemorating the union of Father Sky and Mother Earth, taking place in Rome about 200 B.C.:

On March 22 a pine tree[5] was cut, brought into a sanctuary and placed on an altar. An effigy of a young man was tied to the trunk.[6] The following day, March 23, the priests and celebrants, accompanied by blaring trumpets, slashed themselves and the effigy with sharp instruments, bespattering tree, effigy and altar with blood. On this day, the Day of Blood, young men dedicated themselves to the service of the god by castrating themselves in a frenzy of clashing cymbals and horns, throwing on the altar their testicles, which were later buried in a subterranean chamber sacred to the goddess. Requiring the sacrifice of first fruits, these vernal rites supposedly recalled the god to life, ensuring his resurrection.

The next day, March 24, the effigy was taken from the tree and laid in a tomb. The celebrants then embarked on a period of fasting. The eating of bread was forbidden because it was considered a profanation of the bruised and broken body of the god; since the divine life of the vegetation deities was manifest in the fruits of the earth, eating was tantamount to cannibalism of the god.

On March 25, the day of the vernal equinox according to the Julian calendar, the tomb was opened and the god was shown to be gone. The priests whispered into the ears of the celebrants that the god had risen and that they, too, as participants would achieve salvation, issuing triumphant from the corruption of the grave. The resurrection of the god was celebrated with a festival of joy, in which all restraints, taboos, and rules of discipline and morality were suspended. On the final day of the festival, March 27, a procession was led by priests to a nearby stream (the Almo), in which the sacred objects of the ritual were washed and made clean for the next year.[7]

Fertility religions, characterized by an absence of ethics,[8] were generated by and geared to magic. Through certain rites, rituals, ceremonies and symbolic acts the supernatural was courted. Employing stimulants, alcohol, aphrodesiacs and other pharmacological agents, as well as pageantry, music, dancing and sports, these rites reflected the primacy of the mother goddess, who by virtue of her female superiority (while the male god was limited by detumescence, the goddess enjoyed unlimited capacity) accomplished the resurrection and rebirth of the dying god. Expressed also in maiming and mutilation, often self-directed, these enactments fulfilled the mandates of fertility cult ideology,[9] the goal of which was the resurrection, the rebirth and the eternal life of nature, upon which man in ancient times was entirely dependent.

However, by the time of the Christ story a growing shift within the structure of the fertility religions developed, a shift away from the dominance of the goddess to that of the god. Becoming apparent in the goddess' growing ties to a multiplicity of gods, this shift was coincident with the rise of an artisan class, trade unions and guilds (about 200 B.C.), and with the realization that man need not be directly bound to the earth for sustenance. This reorientation toward male dominance was not only an outgrowth of the ability to survive in occupations removed from the land but also a result of the concurrently emergent concept of philosophical dualism. Evil—flesh—began to be specifically associated with woman, namely the first woman and her temptation of Adam.[10] It was deduced that since it was the first woman who was responsible for the fall of man, this propensity was passed on to all her daughters. The equating of woman with flesh and sin had the effect of ranking women as secondary and unequal by reason of "inherent fault." Thus, man's independence from the land, the corresponding rise of technology, and the ensuing metaphysical equation of woman and flesh, conspired to dethrone the great mother goddess from the center of the fertility drama and to set the stage for the dominance of the male.

At the same time a corresponding change took place in the significance of the fertility drama. From ancient times its rituals had purposed the preservation of earthly values. But by 200 B.C., concomitant with the shift in emphasis from mother goddess to god, the goals of these rituals had themselves undergone a shift in emphasis—from the rejuvenation of land and beast and the potency of man to rejuvenation of the spirit and the ultimate immortality of man.

Affecting the world of the Holy Land of the third to first century B.C. and after, the syncretisms wrought by Hellenic supernaturalism resulted in the accrual of new and divergent thought. In particular, philosophical dualism—which separated the individual into two component parts, spirit and flesh—was a concept alien to early Old Testament thought, unknown to traditional and pre-Exilic Jewish practices. The influence of this concept on the Jewish world was to result in a marked departure from the Jewish view of the indivisibility of nature.

For example, the concept of resurrection was unknown to pre-Exilic Judaism; traditional Old Testament Jewish thought ruled out the idea of an independent entity, the soul, surviving bodily death:[11]

> . . . the dead know not any thing, neither have they any more a reward; for the memory of them is forgotten.
> —*Ecclesiastes 9:5*

Although the possibility of bodily immortality was mentioned in the Old Testament (Isaiah 26:19), it was not until 165 B.C. that the concept of resurrection as a function of rewards and punishment appeared in the Book of Daniel: "And many of them that sleep in the dust of the earth shall awake. . ." (12:2). Gaining major expression during the time of the Maccabees, the bodily resurrection of the dead was taught by Rabbi Hillel in the first century B.C., and championed during the intertestamental period and especially during the period of the Christ story. Josephus relates:

> They [the Pharisees] believe that souls are endowed with immortal power and that somewhere under the earth rewards and punishments will be meted out to them, according to whether they have loved vice or virtue. The former will be condemned to perpetual imprisonment, but the others will be allowed to return to life.[12]

Angelology and demonology, similarly, represented foreign expression to Old Testament Judaism. In the Old Testament Book of Job, Satan is sent by God to test Job's faith. Satan is not characterized as a separate entity from God but rather as God's instrument. (Traditionally there is little emphasis in the Old Testament on angels and demons; both were portrayed as emissaries of God rather than as representative of any system of good or evil.) However, with the advent of the Babylonian Exile the concepts of angelology and demonology assumed dualistic dimension: angels were perceived as emissaries of God, while demons, devils and "unclean spirits" were pronounced agents of Satan. Demons sent by the devil purposed to tempt, harass and plague man; angels sent by God were sent for man's well-being.

Exorcism, the art of casting out devils that inhabited various persons, was also an interloper in prescribed Jewish thought. The result of a growing preoccupation with demonology, this exercise was directed chiefly to those afflicted with physical disease, or psychological disturbances, or to those who appeared different or possessed. Addressing the demon by name in order to control it, an exorcist, having the power to speak in behalf of God, recited charms and incantations, threatening the demon with punishment if it did not depart.

According to Josephus, exorcism, although contrary to Jewish law, was widely practiced among Jews at the time of the Christ story.

Astrology, handmaiden of both determinism and gnosticism during the first century B.C., represented an equal intrusion upon pre-Exilic Judaism, contravening such traditional concepts as free will and man's relationship with God. The Book of Isaiah mentions Babylonian "astrologers, the stargazers, the monthly prognosticators" (47:13); The Book of Daniel refers to an extensive lore, "the learning of the Chaldeans" (1:4), concerning the study of the heavenly bodies, divination by means of dreams, omens and enchantments. Common among all Jewish classes and sects at the time of the Christ story, the study of the stars and planets as they related to human events gained importance in fixing the dates of significant occasions, in fortune telling, in interpreting dreams, in foretelling the secrets of the future, in the practice of magic and sorcery, as the forerunner of theology and theological systems, and as the predecessor of the science of astromony.

Equally foreign to Old Testament Judaism were the formulations of eschatology, detailing the violent destruction of the world in association with supernatural events. Pointedly converse to Judaic precedents—in which impending disaster could be reversed by reaffirming the Law—the newer eschatological formulations imprinted themselves on a consciousness preoccupied with the ills that plagued the Jewish nation, with the absence of a theologically satisfactory explanation for the inroads of both Roman militarism and philosophical determinism, with the concern that the Law in traditional terms was not working, and that the whole relationship between God, the world and man was breaking down. In a climate pervasive of spiritual bankruptcy, Greek eschatology cast its shadow over the fabric of Jewish society, countering free will with such values as humility, poverty, and pacifism; countering the traditional perception of the Law with a final radical solution—the Divine destruction of man and his world, and through destruction a subsequent rebirth and resurrection.

Of all the influences foreign to Old Testament Judaism, none would be more formidable than the ideology and ritual of the pagan mystery religions. Contrasting sharply with traditional Jewish practices and prohibitions, this aspect of Hellenic supernaturalism—polytheism, idolatry, sun and moon worship, homosexuality, child sacrifice—was perhaps most inimical to basic Judaistic beliefs:

> And the King [Josiah] commanded . . . to bring forth out of the temple of the Lord all the vessels that were made for Baal . . . and he burned them. . . . And he put down the idolatrous priests . . . them also that burned incense unto Baal, to the sun, and to the moon, and to the planets. . . . And he brake down the houses of the sodomites. . . . And he defiled Topheth, which is in the valley of the children of Hinnom [New Testament, *Gehenna:* hell], that no man might make his son or his daughter to pass through the fire to Molech. . . . And he brake in pieces the images, and cut down the groves. . . . And he slew all the priests of the high places. . . . Moreover the workers with familiar spirits, and the wizards, and the images, and the idols, and all the abominations that were spied in the land of Judah and in Jerusalem, did Josiah put away, that he might perform the words of the law. . . .
>
> —*2 Kings 23:4–24*

Proceeding from the earliest times with but few significant interruptions, Judaistic belief moved uncompromisingly toward absolute monotheism, culminating in the concept of the unity and uniqueness of the Diety:

> . . . I am the first, and I am the last; and beside me there is no God.

—Isaiah 44:6

Creator of the universe and sponsor of all life, the God of the Hebrews (Yahweh) did not father a child by a goddess consort nor by an earthly representative of a goddess, nor did He play out the drama of nature by dying and being reborn again. He was instead a God of the desert, of men's affairs, of their everyday struggles, an all-powerful Deity who made strong individual and collective demands on his subjects, establishing a special Covenant with them:

> . . . Obey my voice, and I will be your God, and ye shall be my people. . . .
>
> *—Jeremiah 7:23*

Symbolized by circumcision and the observance of the Sabbath, the special relationship between God and Israel was antithetical to the ideas and practices of fertility cult ideology—to polytheism, to intermarriage with other nations, [13] to virtually any sexual practice relating to a fertility deity:

> Will ye . . . swear falsely, and burn incense unto Baal, and walk after other gods . . . ?
>
> *—Jeremiah 7:9*

Equating the worshiping of false gods with unfaithfulness to the One God, the breaking of God's Law with all unethical behavior, the religion of the Hebrews maintained constant vigil against "backsliding" ("For Israel slideth back as a . . . heifer"), and manifested unending resistance to the allure of pagan worship:

> . . . for the spirit of whoredoms is in the midst of them . . .
>
> *—Hosea 5:4*

In effect the entire structure of fertility cult ideology struck

Jewish society as an amalgam of abominations, the ultimate departure from God's Law, inimical to and incompatible with the preservation of the integrity of the Jewish people.

Thus, by the first century B.C., the religiophilosophical milieu of the Jewish world was comprised of a number of competing ideologies, wrought chiefly by the superimposition of expressions of Hellenic supernaturalism on the values of pre-Exilic Judaism. Constituting the immediate philosophical background of the Christ story, this competition was manifest in such concepts as dualism, angels and demons as intermediaries, the spirit made flesh, the equation of woman with inherent fault, the immortality of the soul, divinely revealed knowledge, resurrection, and religious worship by means of sexual rites—as opposed to the view of man and his world as integrated entities, free will, the unity of God, and the preeminence of the Law.

CHAPTER NINE

The Intertestamental Writings

THE INTERTESTAMENTAL WRITINGS ARE JEWISH RELIGIOUS scripture, composed from about 300 B.C. to about A.D. 100, encompassing much of the spiritual revelation of Hellenism. Many of these writings were included in the Greek translation of the Hebrew Bible, the Septuagint, composed before the advent of the Christian era. Others, composed afterward, were popularly regarded as scripture and enjoyed wide readership.

These writings are important because they provide a glimpse of the intervening years between the Old and New Testaments, a period commonly called "the silent years," but which, in the light of these writings, is revealed as a time of intense and turbulent religious activity.

About 200 B.C. the Hebrew canon—the authoritative, inspired Old Testament scripture—was declared closed; Jewish law forbade the writing of scripture or engaging in prophecy under penalty of death (Zechariah 13:2–4). This prohibition, handed down by the scholars, supported the intent of the Restoration: the codification of existing Jewish teachings by commentary and talmudic writings and the encouragement of a developing priesthood. However, the writing of inspired scripture and the call to prophecy were not easily damped in a people inculcated with these traditions. As a result scripture writing and prophecy found expression in the intertestamental writings—often signed pseudonymously with the names of famous Old Testament personages so that their authors might escape persecution.

Although composed by Jews, these scriptures were distinguished by their many philosophical and religious syncretisms, ideas foreign to the Judaism of the Old Testament and absorbed by Judaism during the Babylonian Exile and resulting Dispersion. It is these foreign ideas and beliefs that constitute the outstanding significance of these writings.

The intertestamental writings are composed of three main works: the Apocrypha of the Old Testament, the Pseudepigrapha and the Dead Sea Scrolls—each of which contains other books, commentaries and writings. These three works elaborate and amplify the events, personages and ideas contained in the Old Testament.

The Apocrypha[1] contains fourteen books, most of which were written before the time of the Christ story and many of which were included in the Septuagint. Some apocryphal books—Tobit, Judith, Susanna—are now included in both the Hebrew and Catholic Bibles (early editions of the King James Version contained the entire Apocrypha); however, since 1816 all apocryphal books have been omitted from Protestant texts.

The Apocrypha contains histories of the Maccabean period and Hasmonean rule[2], a history of the Return[3], proverbs and philosophical discourses on a multitude of subjects including laws and morals[4], additions to the canonical books of Daniel and Esther, refutations of the practices and precepts of paganism[5], prophecy[6], all reflecting in general the pressure on Old Testament Judaism exerted by the Babylonian fertility religions, the Dispersion and Hellenism. Major apocryphal books include 1 and 2 Esdras, The Wisdom of Solomon, Ecclesiasticus (also known as Sirach or Ben Sira), Tobit, Judith, 1 Baruch, 1 and 2 Maccabees, the Prayer of Manasses, the Song of the Three Children, Susanna, Bel and the Dragon, and Additions to the Book of Esther.

The Pseudepigrapha is a collection of pseudoscriptural writings composed between 180 B.C. and A.D. 100 and signed pseudonymously with the names of Old Testament personages. Not part of the Septuagint, these books are characterized by their apocalyptic nature.

Apocalyptic refers to religious literature in which Divine Revelation is made known through a dream, vision or trance, and in which the ultimate mysteries of creation are disclosed. Written in a style of bold and vivid imagery, apocalypses employ dramatic, hyperbolic descriptions of the "final days": supernatural events and beings, the destruction of sinners, the salvation of the righteous, the advent of a spiritual kingdom under the leadership of Messiah. Examples of such literature in the Old and New Testaments are the Book of Daniel (165 B.C.) and Revelation (A.D. 100), respectively.

Among the outstanding apocalypses of the Pseudepigrapha are: the Book of Enoch, a poetic and dramatic presentation of new religious formulations; the Testaments of the Twelve Patriarchs, emphasizing concepts such as repentance, love, hate, envy, deceit, jealousy—in particular, the Testament of Levi portraying Messianic deliverance[7]; all involve a major reorientation between God, man and nature. Pseudepigraphical apocalypses (and "Wisdom Literature") likewise include a retelling of Genesis and the religious history of the Jewish people[8], a compilation of predictions patterned after the ancient Greek sibylla or oracles[9], a collection of verse describing the corrupt religious conditions prior to the fall of Jerusalem to the Romans in 63 B.C.[10], a compendium of rabbinic proverbs[11], a sermon on the supremacy of reason[12], a rapproachement of Jewish and Greek ideas[13]. Further pseudepigraphical works include: 2 and 3 Baruch, 4 Ezra, 2 Enoch, The Story of Ahikar, The Assumption of Moses, The Martyrdom of Isaiah and others.

Although pseudepigraphical writings, most notably Enoch (100 B.C.), were in wide circulation at the time of the Christ story and were regarded in some quarters as inspired scripture, the bulk of these writings ceased to have religious relevance three centuries later, rejected by Jew and Christian alike. Were it not for the discovery of the Dead Sea Scrolls, which contain copies of many pseudepigraphical works, the Pseudepigrapha would today remain a largely unknown religious entity. At present no part of the Pseudepigrapha is included in any contemporary bible.

The Dead Sea Scrolls are an extensive library of ancient religious literature, written in Hebrew, Aramaic and Greek, and composed mainly in the first century B.C. Discovered only in 1947, this library consists of intact and partially intact leather scrolls, as well as two copper scrolls and thousands of parchment fragments, found preserved in earthen jars in caves near Qumran along the northwestern shore of the Dead Sea, about six and one-half miles south of Jericho. It seems most likely that the scrolls are the original writings of a Jewish religious order that inhabited an ancient settlement near the caves known as Khirbet Qumran. The scrolls—also containing copies of all Old Testament books, with the exception of Esther, and many apocryphal and pseudepigraphical books—were presumably hidden in the caves to save them from destruction by the Romans in A.D. 70. Archeologists have discovered within the ruins of the main building of Khirbet Qumran a scriptorium, and an earthen jar identical to the ones found in the caves.

Repairing to the desert and establishing their community toward the end of the second century B.C., the Jews of Khirbet Qumran—whose priests referred to themselves as "Sons of Zadok," after the ancient, venerated pre-Maccabean priest who had anointed Solomon—did not regard the Hasmonean priesthood in Jerusalem (134 B.C.–63 B.C.) or their Halachah (Oral Law) as valid. Instead they considered themselves God's Elect, a remainder destined to survive the catastrophic events to come and to make a New Covenant with God:

> . . . for Thou hast granted a remnant unto Thy people and a revival unto Thine inheritance. Thou hast raised up among them men of truth and sons of light . . .[14]

Known as the Brotherhood, the Sons of Light, the Elect, the Party of the Community, the Sect of the Covenant, the authors of the scrolls have been identified with the Essenes, the Jewish religious party that flourished during the last two centuries B.C. and faded with the Jewish-Roman war of A.D. 70.

Basically apocalyptic, the Dead Sea Scrolls emphasize a gnostic interpretation of the Torah, in which the Law itself is perceived as a mystical object, the deeper apprehension of which leads to Divine Revelation, and a coming Messiah. Most significant among these scrolls are the Manual of Discipline, a comprehensive statement on the organization of the Qumran community; the Damascus Document,[15] a discourse on the life, beliefs and structure of the various camps of the Sect; the Thanksgiving Psalms, a collection of verse recounting the suffering and enduring faith of a devout figure of righteousness; Commentaries on Habakkuk, Isaiah, Nahum, Micah and Psalm 37, in which Old Testament passages are interpreted as a fullfillment of contemporary events or a prediction of future ones; the Lamech Scroll, a retelling of some of the events of Genesis (the portrayal of Sarah as an extremely beautiful woman of sixty-five, the conception of Noah by means of an angel, the healing of Pharaoh by the laying on of hands); the War Scroll, a description of a final battle between Good and Evil; and the Copper Scrolls, directions to treasure presumably hidden by members of the community at the time of the Roman advance

The Dead Sea Scrolls are of historical importance in that they establish the Jewish origin of certain pseudepigraphical works, previously attributed to Christian authors; pseudepigraphical books found among the Scrolls include Jubilees, Enoch, the Testaments of the Twelve Patriarchs and the Assumption of Moses. They are of further importance in their relation to the Masoretic text of the Hebrew Bible (the Jewish Bible of today)—considered the authentic, authoritative, unalterable Jewish Bible—dating from between the sixth and seventh centuries A.D. and thought by the orthodox to be divinely revealed scripture. With the discovery of the Scrolls came copies of Old Testament books that antedate the Masoretic text by several centuries, especially Isaiah.[16] Some of these older Old Testament books found among the Scrolls vary considerably from the Masoretic text, thus challenging the concept of its unalterability.

In their function as a repository of syncretistic ideas, the intertestamental writings serve as a bridge to the New Testament, and convey the expession of new beliefs and principles that were to find their way to the New Religion and become of fundamental importance.

Among these syncretisms were the concepts of angelology, demonology and exorcism[17]; astrology and the equation of the Cosmic Law of heavenly bodies with the immutability of God's Law[18]; dualism, heaven and hell[19,20]; the preexistence and immortality of the soul [21,22]; sin, repentance and intercession[23,24]; divine revelation, gnosticism ("Through Thy holy spirit, through Thy mystic insight, Thou hast caused a spring of knowledge to well up within me. . . . Thou hast put an end to my darkness, and the splendor of Thy glory has become unto me as a light everlasting[25]; salvation and resurrection:

> And I know that in His hand is the judgment of every living thing,
> And all His deeds are truth.
> And when trouble shall come, I will praise Him,
> And when He saves me, I will likewise utter cries of joy.[26]

Equally embraced were eschatological ideas on Kingdom Come[27,28], concepts representing the compatibility and synthesis of Jewish and Hellenic thought[29,30], the quasi-personification of religious abstraction[31,32], doctrines and practices such as communal meals, grace, religious asceticism, the inherent sinfulness of the flesh, and others:

> And it is by the Holy Spirit of the Community . . .
> That [man] shall be cleansed of all his iniquities.
> And by the spirit of uprightness and humility
> His sins shall be atoned,
> And by the submission of his soul towards all God's ordinances
> When he sprinkles himself with lustral water,
> And he shall sanctify himself with running water.[33]

The syncretisms of the intertestamental writings were not limited to ecclesiastical concepts. Women, likewise, were to undergo a marked change in their characterization. Portrayed over the centuries by the Old Testament as human beings capable of a wide range of human qualities (loyalty, courage, intelligence, leadership as exemplified by Ruth, Deborah, Sarah, Hannah), women came to be defined as formidable sexual creatures, cast in terms of alluring abstractions, such as Truth, Beauty and Wisdom, or as actual instruments of flesh, such as seductresses and possessors of the weapon of sexuality, before whom all men are powerless.

> Her [Wisdom] I loved and sought out from my youth,
> And I sought to take her for my bride.
> And I became enamored of her beauty.[34]

> Come unto me [Wisdom] ye that desire me,
> And be filled with my produce . . .[35]

> . . . she [Truth] is the strength, and the kingdom, and the power, and and the majesty, of all ages.[36]

Because of her attractiveness for Asmodemus (the demon of lust), Sarah, in the book of Tobit, is responsible for the deaths of her seven husbands, who die on their wedding night before sexual consummation. Only Tobias, her predestined husband, with the help of the archangel Raphael, can perform the necessary exorcisms to enable Sarah and himself to marry. The beautiful widow, Judith, in order to save her people, attracts the pagan general, Holofernes, goes to his tent and gets him drunk, whereupon Holofernes, in a moment that promises love, literally "loses his head." Similarly, Esther (an apocryphal-like book of late entry into the canon), building upon her allure, becomes queen, a position from which she saves her people by arranging, through her sexual attractiveness, the death of Haman. Unjustly accused of adultery because of her beauty, the virtuous Susanna likewise triumphs—which results in the promulgation of basic societal rules of jurisprudence.

Still possessing qualities of goodness, women in the Apocrypha can turn their seductiveness to useful ends. The Pseudepigrapha, more influenced by philosophical dualism and its equation of sex, flesh, women, evil, sin and guilt, deletes any allusion to the power of good in women.

". . . womankind are by nature headstrong and energetic in the pursuit of their own desires, and subject to sudden changes of opinion through fallacious reasoning, and their nature is essentially weak."[37]

Echoing the admonition of Sirach in the Apocrypha—"From a woman did sin originate, And because of her we all must die"[38]—Enoch, Jubilees, Fragments of a Zadokite Work, and others, reinforce the sexuality of women as a force for chaos and ruin.

And Eve said to Adam: "Wilt thou slay me? that I may die and perchance God the Lord will bring thee into paradise, for on my account hast thou been driven thence."[39]

Foreshadowing the harsh Pauline antisexualism and antifeminism, however, it is the Dead Sea Scrolls (also part of the Pseudepigrapha) which ultimately characterize women by virtue of their beauty as agents of sin, death and destruction.

For evil are women, my children; and since they have no power or strength over man, they use wiles by outward attractions, that they may draw him to themselves. And whom they cannot bewitch by outward attractions, him they overcome by craft. . . . the angel of the Lord . . . taught me, that women are overcome by the spirit of fornication more than men; and in their hearts they plot against men; and by means of their adornment they deceive first their minds, and by the glance of the eye instill the poison, and then through the accomplished act they take them captive. For a woman cannot force a man openly, but by a harlot's bearing she beguiles him. Flee, therefore, fornication, my children, and command your wives and your daughters, that they adorn not their heads and faces to deceive the mind: because every woman who useth these wiles hath been reserved for eternal punishment. . . . Beware, therefore, of fornication; and if you wish to be pure in mind, guard your senses from every women.[40]

Reflecting a most turbulent period in Jewish history, the intertestamental writings were to give rise to yet another major aspect of religious syncretism, the Messiah.

CHAPTER TEN

The Messiah

MESSIAH, DERIVING FROM THE HEBREW WORD *MASHIAH,* meaning anointed, refers to a person charged with high office, a king, priest, prophet, or leader, whose function was to establish a reign of peace, justice and righteousness. Anointment, the ritualistic application of oil, conferred upon such an individual God's blessing and the power to carry out what he perceived as God's will through his exalted station. Although regarded by many as static, the concept of the Messiah has in fact undergone substantial change, ranging from a figure of quite mortal dimensions to one of considerable metaphysical endowment. Approaching in character the Messiah of the New Testament, the various kinds of Messiah figures that arose in the centuries prior to the Christ story existed within a Jewish religious context. As such, the evolution of the concept of the Messiah represented a major religious syncretism in regard to Old Testament Jewish thought.

The most ancient Semitic concept of the Messiah is that of an idealized monarch. Dating from before the sixth century B.C., this Messiah of the Old Testament was a mortal rather than a supernatural being. Portrayed as a military leader or ruler arising traditionally from the House of David, he was an anointed, a human being manifesting a human nature.

"Behold, the days are coming, says the Lord, when I will raise up for David a righteous Branch, and he shall reign as king and deal wisely, and shall execute justice and righteousness in the land."

—Jeremiah 23:5

The sceptre shall not depart from Judah,
 nor the ruler's staff from between his feet,
until he comes to whom it belongs;
 and to him shall be the obedience of the peoples.

—Genesis 49:10

Lo, your king comes to you;
 triumphant and victorious is he,
humble and riding on an ass. . . .

—Zechariah 9:9

The possessor of vaunted human attributes, the Messiah of the Old Testament was a royal surrogate under whose leadership the Jewish people were to be restored to their former glory. Figures that fulfilled this messianic ideal included Cyrus the Persian,[1] Zerrubabel, governor of Jerusalem at the time of the Return,[2] and Judah Maccabee.[3]

A second type of Messiah occurs in the Book of Isaiah, the so-called "suffering servant" of Chapter 53. Dating from between the sixth and fourth centuries B.C., and coincident with the Babylonian Exile and Dispersion, this figure represents a major shift in the messianic ideal toward the supernatural, embodying as his foremost characteristic expiatory suffering.

But he was wounded for our transgressions,

he was bruised for our iniquities; upon him
was the chastisement that made us whole,
and with his stripes we are healed.

Technically not of Jewish origin—nowhere is it mentioned that the central figure of Isaiah 53 is an anointed, nor is it clear whether the servant is literal or figurative[4]—this Messiah figure suffers vicariously for others, bears their griefs, carries their sorrows, is afflicted for their iniquities.[5] Endowed with attributes skewed definitely toward the metaphysical, he has the power of intercession ("he . . . made intercession for the transgressors"), is destined to suffer a violent and inevitable death—viewed as a regenerative act by which others are redeemed—and is fated for a heavenly reward: "Therefore I will divide him a portion with the great. . . ."

Representing a fundamental departure from Old Testament Judaic belief, the "suffering servant" passage has occasioned much debate as to whether it may represent a later type of Messiah concept, dating from the second or first century B.C. This question may be resolved by a consideration of a possible contemporary source of similar ideas from which the writer of Isaiah 53[6] could have drawn: Was there an immediate prototype of a suffering servant?

In the wake of the Babylonian Exile and Dispersion (the post-Exilic period), heavy pressures of foreign religious beliefs, particularly those of the well-developed Assyro-Babylonian fertility religions, were brought to bear on the Jews. These religions shared the concept of a suffering and dying god, and of the god's inevitable, violent death for the purpose of regenerating nature, as a central theme.

A tamarisk that in the garden has drunk no water,
Whose crown in the field has brought forth no blossom.
A willow that rejoiced not by the watercourse,
A willow whose roots were torn up.

A herb that in the garden had drunk no water.[7]

Tammuz, the lover of youth,
Thou causest to weep every year.[8]

This emotional drama was likewise echoed in the Old Testament literature of the same period (late sixth to fourth centuries B.C.):

> Then he brought me to the entrance of the north gate of the house of the Lord; and behold, there sat women weeping for Tammuz.
>
> —*Ezekiel 8:14*[9]

Whether the suffering servant of Isaiah 53 is a direct reference to a pagan deity or whether it may contain Jewish elements or have been inspired by an actual historical figure, the superstructure of this passage is composed of the same cluster of factors as the superstructure of fertility cult ideology: expiatory suffering, inevitable and violent death, and dying as a regenerative act. Thus a precedent for the messianic figure of Isaiah 53 exists within the cultural milieu of the sixth to the fourth centuries B.C., and may well indicate this figure to be anchored in that time rather than represent a *de novo* concept of later centuries.

In the Book of Enoch human values and supernatural attributes merge in the creation of a third type of Messiah figure, the Messiah of the Parables (the Messiah of Enoch). An anointed of God[10], a future king possessing exalted human qualities[11], he exists in an eschatological context. Dating from between 200 B.C. and 100 B.C., this idealized surrogate presides over the Final Judgment, punishes the sinners, rewards the righteous, and decides who shall be saved in the resurrection.

And he sat on the throne of his glory. . .
And he caused the sinners to pass away
  and be destroyed from off the face of
  the earth. . . .[12]

And [the Elect One] shall choose the
  righteous and holy from among [the resurrected]:
For the day has drawn nigh that they
  should be saved.[13]

A figure far removed from the Messiah of the Old Testament
or suffering servant, he is, by virtue of a consummately
esoteric nature, the Elect One, the Righteous One, a source
of everlasting spiritual strength, the embodiment of hope, a
being of universal appeal, the architect of a new world, and a
peacemaker.

He shall be a staff to the righteous . . .
. . . the light of the Gentiles,
And the hope of those who are troubled of heart.[14]

And his glory is for ever . . .
And his might unto all generations.[15]

"He proclaims unto thee peace in the name of the world to
  come. . . ."[16]

A pre-existent being held in abeyance since the very beginning, he is a Revealer, an intercessor, a figure of formidable
metaphysical endowment, having the power to directly apprehend and communicate with God.

Yea, before the sun and signs were created . . .
His name was . . . before the Lord of Spirits.[17]

. . . in his name [the righteous] are saved. . . .[18]

> And his mouth shall pour forth all the secrets of wisdom and
> counsel:
> For the Lord of Spirits hath given (them) to him. . . .[19]

Termed the Son of Man[20,21], an object of worship[22], a being
of divine destiny, the Messiah of the Parables constitutes a
major departure from all previously held Jewish messianic
attributes, and emerges as an apocalyptic representative of a
new and divergent messianic principle.

In the pseudepigraphical book, The Testaments of the
Twelve Patriarchs, the Messiah ideal undergoes further tran-
sition. Dating from 70 B.C.,[23] this fourth Messiah derives
from the House of Levi[24] and combines both priestly and
royal attributes, emerging preeminently as a priestly Messiah. An anticipated but not yet arrived human being, set
against a background of historical rather than eschatological
disaster (thought to be the Roman conquest of 63 B.C.), he
presents basic Old Testament qualities: he is an anointed, a
judge, a king, a militant. Retaining many of the supernatural
traits of his predecessors, he has the capacity for revelation,
the power of exorcism (transmissible to his followers); he
engages with the devil in his struggle against evil and is the
agent by which the fall of man is refashioned.

> In his priesthood shall sin come to an end,
> . . . the lawless shall cease to do evil.
> . . . he shall open the gates of paradise,
> And shall remove the threatening sword against Adam.[25]

Portrayed as free from sin[26], distinguished by his combined earthly and metaphysical endowment as well as his
combatant role against worldly evil, he reopens paradise,
liberates the saints, binds the devil, refashions Genesis, and

ushers in a Utopian world dominated by a vision of a New Jerusalem.[27]

The evolution of Messiah figures prior to the advent of the Christ story, becomes complete in the Teacher of Righteousness. A historical personality,[28] a venerated leader of the Jewish Sect of the Covenant (the Essenes), characterized by his unalterable opposition to the Jerusalem priesthood (the last of the Hamonean priest-kings), he is indicated as the earthly embodiment of religious purity and idealism. Dating variably from the last third of the second century B.C.,[29] he incorporates many of the spiritual and earthly qualities of preceding Messiah figures, embodying a progressive shift to the supernatural of values ascribed to a human being.[30]

Emanating from the House of Aaron and Israel, he is first and foremost a priest and prophet.

> . . . into [his] heart God put wisdom to explain all the words of his servants the prophets, through whom God declared all the things that are coming upon his people and his congregation.[31]

A man of sorrows, likened to the suffering servant of Isaiah,[32] displaying indomitable belief that he will bring forth the words of God ("Thou hast . . . shed abroad thy Holy Spirit in me"[33]), he is preoccupied with concepts of guilt, sin, flesh and the devil.

> A fabric of dust is he [man] . . . a mass of filth, whose foundation is naked shame . . . an object of abhorrence to all flesh![34]

Steeped in philosophical dualism, an ascetic oriented toward an eschatological resolution of life ("God thunders forth . . . and turns not back until final doom . . ."[35]), he is, like the Messiah of Enoch (Parables) and the Messiah of the House of Levi, a Revealer, an interpreter of the Divine, a mystic, chosen by God to apprehend and disclose the secrets of Life to those who follow him, a messianic deliverer.

> I have reached the inner vision . . . through the spirit Thou has placed within me. . . .[36]

> . . . Thou has set me as a banner in the vanguard of Righteousness . . . one who interprets with knowledge deep, mysterious things . . . a touchstone for them that seek the truth. . . .[37]

> . . . [the] man-child long foretold is about to be brought forth.[38]

A being of divine, preordained purpose, an object of faith, he is a figure of Truth and Revelation, in whom the Law is fulfilled.

> But the just shall live by his faith in the Teacher of Righteousness.[39]

> . . . And the man who reneweth the law in the power of the Most High, ye shall call a deceiver; and ye shall rush (upon him) to slay him, not knowing his dignity, taking innocent blood through wickedness upon your heads. And your holy places shall be laid waste, even to the ground, because of him. And ye shall have no place that is clean; but ye shall be among the Gentiles a curse and a dispersion until He shall again visit you, and in pity shall receive you through faith and water.[40]

As an object of faith, the Teacher of Righteousness achieves unique status; for unlike the Messiah of Enoch who was also an object of faith, the Teacher of Righteousness is not an imaginary figure, a being who reigns over a projected eschatological world.

The Teacher of Righteousness brings to a close a series of increasingly syncretistic Jewish Messiah figures, all of whom existed within a Jewish religious context well before the advent of the Christian era. This figure, moreover, predating the Christ story by more than half a century, illustrates particularly the concept of change in Jewish messianic ideals, as exemplified in the coalescence of two major religious themes, the Law and the Messiah. On the one hand he is the fulfillment of the Law (Habakkuk Commentary); on the other hand he is the priestly Messiah of the House of Aaron and Israel (Damascus Document). Such a merger represents an extraordinary circumstance for Jewish religious philosophy. For when the Law and the Messiah are embodied in one man, then faith in the man obviates the necessity for adherence to the Law—a development heralding the appearance of yet a new Messiah in the Coming Era.

CHAPTER ELEVEN

The Christ Story: Settings, Characterizations and Plot

THE CHRIST STORY IS SET IN PALESTINE ABOUT 2,000 YEARS ago[1] *and moves across the face of the Holy Land. Beginning at Bethlehem and Nazareth, it touches Cana, Capernaum and Bethany, finally ending at Jerusalem and Emmaus. The story takes place in a real physical setting at a real time, and includes historical characters and incidents whose validity can be established by documents outside the New Testament. The acts of these actual historical personalities are signal to the story itself. It was Caesar Augustus (emperor of Rome from 27 B.C. to A.D. 14), whose decree caused Joseph and Mary to go to Bethelehem to be counted in the census, where she delivers her child. A prediction that Herod the Great*

(King of Judea from 37 B.C. to 4 B.C.) would order the "slaughter of the innocents" persuades Joseph and his family to flee to Egypt in order to save the child Jesus. The ascension of the dissolute Archelaus, Herod's son and successor in Judea (4 B.C. to A.D. 6), causes Joseph to take his family to Nazareth in Galilee rather than to Archelaus' province of Judea. Whereupon Pontius Pilate, the Roman procurator of Judea (26 A.D. to A.D. 36), historically recorded as particularly insensitive and excessive in dealing with political insurgents, sends Jesus to appear before Herod Antipas, another son of Herod and procurator of Galilee (4 B.C. to A.D. 39). The latter, referred to in Luke 9:7, Matthew 14:1–12 and Mark 6:14–29 in connection with the murder of John the Baptist, finds Jesus guilty and sends him back to Pilate. Pilate, who represents the final legal authority of the procurator, passes the death sentence on Jesus.[2]

The setting of the Christ story is an actual geographical location whose physical characteristics, awesome and wondrous, are steeped in portentous events. It is the land of Mt. Sinai, of the Valley of Jehoshaphat, of deserts, of the River Jordan, of the Red Sea, of Galilee, Capernaum and Jericho. It is also the land of antiquity, a place of the Beginning, of Creation, of the coalescence of great cultures, the land of the Garden of Eden, of Adam and Eve, of Abraham, Isaac and Jacob, of Moses and Solomon and the prophets, the land of the cradle of civilization in which recorded history began.

The physical setting of the Christ story, however, is modified by certain nonphysical factors. For the Holy Land is a place where Moses is given God's Commandments; where Mohammed receives the Koran; where God speaks directly to Adam and Eve (Genesis 3), to Jacob (Genesis 28:13–16), to Moses "face to face as a man speaks to his friend" (Exodus 33:11), to his spokesmen, the prophets; where angels appear and converse with men.

It is a place of extranatural happenings, where phenomena not quite of this world occur: a bush burns and is not consumed (Exodus 3:2); a rod is transformed into a serpent (Exodus 4:2–3); a sea parts (Exodus 14:21); a leper is cleansed (2 Kings 5:14); a contest of supernatural feats is waged (1 Kings 18:20); a vision of fantastic color and glory appears (Ezekiel 1).

The Holy Land is likewise a setting where the forces of nature can and do go awry. Whether it be the devastations described in Ezekiel 38:19–20 (". . . there shall be a great shaking in the land of Israel. . . . the mountains shall be thrown down . . . every wall shall tumble to the ground"), Isaiah 13:10 ("the stars . . . will not give their light"), Joel 2:30–31 ("blood and fire and columns of smoke [will appear]. The sun shall be turned to darkness, and the moon to blood") or equally in Enoch 1:6 ("high mountains shall be shaken . . . high hills shall be made low . . . the earth shall be wholly rent asunder") or in the Assumption of Moses 10:1 ("the sea shall retire into the abyss . . . the rivers shall dry up")—they are all similar in that they are representative of a land host to psychical occurrences in which the supernatural is directly perceived.

The Holy Land is a place also where real time, although present, is rendered irrelevant. For the Christ story is in effect characterized by apocalyptic settings, depicting the cataclysmic destruction of a "time of the end" in terms of the events of a new beginning. Such references as to Kingdom Come, the advent of a New Order—"Repent, for the kingdom of heaven is at hand" (Matthew 4:17)—convey a background of an incipient merger of time in which past and present, beginning and end, become psychologically indistinguishable.

The time-shift of these surroundings is equally a function of predestination. This ubiquitous theme, intensified by eyewitness accounts, is based on the premise that all events of the Christ story are part of a Divine Plan laid out long ago, ready to be revealed imminently. Whatever will happen is already known; whatever has been predicted will inevitably come to pass. In this scheme the presentation of events in terms of the fulfillment of prophecy nullifies the difference between past, present and future, rendering these as psychological equivalents.

Moreover, the depiction of the salvation of mankind and the world only by Divine Intervention implies that within that context man is not the master of his fate, human endeavor is essentially ineffective, reason and logic are meaningless, and the measure of human existence in terms of fixed events rather than years reflects the loss of a temporal structure in the environment.

Thus the settings of the Christ story, although geographical, are indicated to be of an impermanent nature, dominated by aberrations in natural law and subject to forces over which man has no control. This land of the supernatural is equally characterized by the displacement of conventional time in favor of a psychological milieu in which past, present and future are functionally indistinct.

Characterization in the Christ story, while inclusive of actual historical personalities, is relegated to the triad relationship of its three central canonical figures, in addition to the modifying relationships of numerous auxiliary personages.

Among these central figures is God the Father. Creator and King of the Universe, He is characterized in both the Old and the New Testament as the dominant metaphysical force. "I am the first and I am the last" (Isaiah 44:6). He is the Father of all mankind, all-knowing, all-powerful, omnipresent, possessor of ultimate control over life and death. He has the power to transcend and suspend natural law, the ability to transform Himself and others. He is One, yet Trinity. The Embodiment of Virtue, He is Truth, Light and Love.

He is also the Logos, the Word made Flesh. As Father of Jesus, the "Father" of Mary's Son, His special fatherhood is based on the singular and mystical relationship of His incarnation in Jesus. Jesus states: "Believe me that I am in the Father and the Father in me" (John 14:11). Of Jesus, God affirms: "This is my beloved Son" (Matthew 17:5).

As Father, God is an ethical Being. He is the epitome of goodness, a Being of righteousness, truth and justice. "Mighty King . . . thou hast established equity; thou hast executed justice and righteousness. . . ." (Psalms 99:4). He is the Giver of the Law, His essence inherent in the nature of His Law: "The law of the lord is perfect" (Psalms 19:7). He is the God of mercy, forgiveness and compassion: "The Lord sets the prisoners free . . . opens the eyes of the blind . . . lifts up those who are bowed down . . . forgive[s] the guilt of . . . sin" (Psalms 32:5, 146:7, 8). He is the God of salvation, who guides His people through tumultuous struggles: "I am the Lord your God, who brought you out of the land of Egypt" (Deuteronomy 5:6); who is a personal redeemer, who champions righteousness: ". . . What doth the Lord require of thee, but to do justly, and to love mercy . . ?" (Micah 6:8).

Yet God has another side. To those who deviate from his Law and defy Him, He evinces a different nature. For He is likewise a punitive God, a God of wrath and impatience who wreaks havoc and destruction, manifesting violence. For the primal sin of disobedience in the Garden of Eden, He dictates, respectively—to the serpent, woman, man: "Because you have done this, cursed are you above all cattle, and above all wild animals" (Genesis 3:14); "in pain you shall bring forth children" (Genesis 3:16); "In the sweat of your face you shall eat bread" (Genesis 3:19). He threatens annihilation of all life. "I will blot out man whom I have created from the face of the ground, man and beast and creeping things and birds of the air" (Genesis 6:7). He visits misfortune upon Job (Job 1:13), turns Lot's wife into a pillar of salt (Genesis 19:26), strikes dumb Zechariah (Luke 1:18–22), imposes leprosy upon Moses' sister (Numbers 12:10). His displeasure, moreover, is not limited to individuals. Of nations He proclaims: "I will bring evil from the north, and great destruction" (Jeremiah 4:6), "I . . . will bring a sword upon you . . ." (Ezekiel 6:3). He smites the firstborn males of all Egyptians (Exodus 12:7–12), sends Israel into Babylonian captivity (Isaiah 24:5). Of His capacity for ire and destruction Nahum writes, "The Lord is a jealous God . . . avenging and wrathful. . . . Who can endure the heat of his anger?" (1:2, 6).

God is thus portrayed as a Being with two distinct propensities. He is a God of goodness and mercy, leading those who follow His Way through religious and cultural upheaval. To those who turn from His Way he is a God of wrath and vengeance, unleashing personal and collective disaster.

The second and principal of the triad characters is Jesus. The major canonical figure of the Christ story, he is the Son of God and the Virgin Mary, his most outstanding feature being that he is both human and metaphysical. He is characterized as a babe, a boy and, predominantly, a young man placed in the world to redeem mankind.

As a human figure he espouses rationalism and empathy. He is merciful and forgiving, displays a compassionate understanding for the human condition, is ascetic, submissive, wise. He is astutely aware of the difficulties of life, innovative in his teachings, ethical in his precepts on justice and charity, loyal in his devotion; his distinction between worldly values and spiritual worth make him a visionary, projecting an ideal world based on goodness. Conversely, he is antagonistic to religious hypocrites (Matthew 23) and to the religiously corrupt (John 2:15). He has the charisma to attract large crowds, inspiring loyalty and fraternity among his followers by an attitude of combatant pacifism: "I have not come to bring peace, but a sword" (Matthew 10:34).

As a metaphysical figure, he is the author of extra-natural feats.[3] He walks on water (Matthew 14:25–33), stills a storm at sea (Mark 4:37–41), transforms water into wine (John 2:1–

11), heals the sick—the blind, the deaf, the dumb, the leprous, the epileptic, the palsied—casts out devils, raises the dead (John 11:1–44). He is also the object of extranatural phenomena. He undergoes transfiguration (Matthew 17:1–5), contends in a personal struggle with the devil (Matthew 4:1–11) and is himself raised from the dead.

As both earthly and divine, Jesus is a formidable figure in his own right who, like God, has the ability to rescind natural law, to order the forces of life and death: "All power is given unto me in heaven and in earth" (Matthew 28:18). Yet he is clearly limited by his human aspect. At Gesthemane he prays, "Father, all things are possible to thee; remove this cup from me" (Mark 14:36). And on the cross: "My God, my God, why hast thou forsaken me?" (Mark 15:34). His essential metaphysical nature, nonetheless, is indicated in his subsequent resurrection, his posthumous appearances to his followers (Luke 24:15–51) and his ultimate ascension into heaven.

The third of the major figures of the Christ story is the Virgin Mary. Handmaid of the Lord and the mother of Jesus, she is characterized by a combination of idealized human and metaphysical qualities based on her dual doctrinal role. In the gospels Mary is portrayed as devoted to God and obedient to His Will. She is depicted as observant of religious law (Luke 2:21, 41). "[Joseph and Mary] . . . had performed all things according to the law of the Lord" (Luke 2:39). Mary has eternal youth and beauty, which stand immutable from the corruption of time. She is perpetually virgin, without fault, wholly innocent, chaste, epitomizing goodness, in essence the perfect woman, depicted as conceived without sin (Doctrine of the Immaculate Conception), existing in a state of "static perfection" and raised uncorrupted from the dead (Doctrine of the Assumption). She herself is an object of worship; her grace, her blessing and her forgiveness are specifically addressed by those who invoke her name. To them she displays mercy and compassion, especially to the less fortunate—to the sick, to sinners and to children. She is the Universal Mother, compassionate, loving and merciful, unswervingly devoted and faithful. She is the protective and concerned mother of her own child, Jesus, whose ministry and death she closely follows. She is Mediatrix, carrying messages of the children of God to the Son, sharing in the process of salvation and redemption, and reigning with her Son as Queen of Heaven.

Mary's characterization results principally from her familial relationships. To God she is the passive servant, trusting and dutiful. "The Holy Spirit [Holy Ghost] will come upon you, and the power of the Most High will overshadow you; therefore the child to be born will be called holy, the Son of God" (Luke 1:35). While troubled about the means of conception (she does not ask who the father of her child will be, rather how she can conceive without a man),[4] she submits to the Divine Will, her human nature manifest in her reply to the angel Gabriel's tidings: "Behold, I am the handmaid of the Lord; let it be to me according to your word" (Luke 1:38).

Yet to Jesus she exhibits another orientation. In the several instances of interaction between Mother and Son in the gospels, Mary is shown to be positive, authoritative, dominant. She is pointed as she addresses her twelve-year-old boy (who, unknown to his parents, had stayed behind in Jerusalem), finding him in the temple after a three-day search: "Son, why have you treated us so? Behold, your father and I have been looking for you anxiously?" (Luke 2:48).[5] She is assertive at Cana in Galilee where, seeing that the wedding party had no more wine, she implies to the recalcitrant Jesus that he remedy the situation and orders the servants to follow her Son's instructions (John 2:3–5).[6] While at the Crucifixion her earthly presence stands in contradistinction to his earthly end (John 19:25).

Numerous auxiliary personages—representatives of and

assistants to the major figures as well as clergy, royalty, children, and members of society's outgroups—also appear in the Christ story, modifying and expanding its principal themes and characterizations.

Among the representatives and emissaries of God the Father—who carry out His will, convey His messages and serve as His associate in various religious acts and on various religious occasions—is Joseph. A guardian husband to Mary and earthly father to her child, a descendant of the House of David and carpenter by trade, he stays with Mary throughout her term. He is with her and the babe at the manger (Luke 2:16), becomes the protector of the child Jesus, flees to Egypt to ensure the child's safety and settles in Galilee, fulfilling the child's religious obligations. In so doing, Joseph ensures that the Will of God is accomplished. The angel Gabriel also functions as a spiritual emissary of God, a messenger and spokesman who presents God's Will—to Zechariah, regarding the conception of John the Baptist; to Mary at the Annunciation; to Joseph, instructing him about his role and future actions; to the Magi, warning them of Herod's evil inclinations. The Holy Spirit (Holy Ghost) acts as a further heavenly emissary whose purpose is to carry out God's bidding. It is the Holy Spirit that accomplishes the Divine Conception, that fills Elizabeth when she apprehends that Mary is carrying the Lord, and that suffuses Zechariah at the birth of John the Baptist. Characterized as a manifestation of God Himself, as well as an entity independent of God, the Holy Spirit forgives sins, represents God at various religious occasions and experiences, is present at the revelation of Simeon the priest (Luke 2:26), at the baptism of Jesus (Matthew 3:16), at the mass conversions at Pentecost (Acts 2:41) as well as at the phenomenon of speaking in tongues and prophesying (Acts 19:6). The Holy Spirit functions essentially as an auxiliary arm of God, literally the *pneuma* or ghost by which the metaphysical God makes Himself known.

Representatives and contemporaries of Jesus also function to point up his ascendancy as a Messiah figure, as well as underscore and carry forward the messages and meaning of his ministry. John the Baptist, a cousin of Jesus, acts as a forerunner to Jesus, preaching the same tough line of morality as his celebrated cousin. "He who has two coats, let him share with him who has none," John avers. "Collect no more than is appointed to you. . . . Rob no one by violence or by false accusation, and be content with your wages." He reproves some of the religious leaders as a "generation of vipers" (Matthew 3:7). Of Jesus, he says: "After me comes he who is mightier than I. . . . I have baptized you with water; but he will baptize you with the Holy Spirit" (Mark 1:7–8). A leader in his own right, John nonetheless represents a prototype or proxy figure for his cousin: for what happens to John is destined to befall Jesus.[7] The twelve disciples, the band of faithful followers chosen by Jesus to spread his work, act as Jesus' direct representatives. Jesus authorizes them in his name to go and preach, cast out demons, heal the sick, cleanse lepers and raise the dead. "He who receives you receives me, and he who receives me receives him who sent me" (Matthew 10:40). The disciples in essence become an auxiliary arm of Jesus, assisting Jesus in spreading his ministry. In particular, Peter, the first chosen disciple, functions as Jesus' heir apparent (Matthew 16:18–19), for it is Peter, after Jesus' death, who is commissioned to lead the other disciples in the fulfillment of Jesus' mission; similarly the unnamed beloved disciple becomes Jesus' personal surrogate, for it is to this disciple that Jesus commends his mother at Calvary.

Mary is likewise represented in the Christ story by her cousin Elizabeth. What happens to Elizabeth will happen to Mary. The angel Gabriel announces that Elizabeth, who is barren, will miraculously conceive a son who will "make ready for the Lord a people prepared" (Luke 1:17). Mary is subsequently informed by the angel Gabriel that she, too, will miraculously conceive a son who will "reign over the House of Jacob forever; and of his kingdom there will be no end" (Luke 1:33). In presaging the events that will befall her cousin, Elizabeth acts as a proxy and surrogate to Mary.

Clergy and royalty appear as personages representing the forces of established religion and power, respectively, in the Christ story. Their presence serves to contrast the struggle between established clericism—as vested in the Pharisees and Sadducees, the religio-political parties of power—and those of "the religion of the heart." Simeon, Nicodemus and Joseph of Arimathea all represent priestlike figures whose special orientation to Jesus reinforces this struggle of ideologies. Caesar Augustus, emperor of Rome, is the epitome of earthly power. Pontius Pilate, Herod the Great and Herod Antipas share this power. The Magi, the three kings of the East who come bearing gifts to Jesus, and the "rich young ruler" (Matthew 19:22, Mark 10:21) whom Jesus counsels, represent opposing metaphysical and earthly aspects of this royal power.[8]

Children portray a kind of power in the Christ story different from secular or ecclesiastic power. In healing an epileptic boy (Mark 9:17–27), a twelve-year-old girl (Mark 5:38–42) or in casting out a demon from the Syrophoenician woman's child (Mark 7:25–30). Jesus illustrates metaphorically the power of faith—which, like a child, is innocent, free of corruption, humble and unquestioning: "Truly, I say to you, whoever does not receive the kingdom of God like a child shall not enter it" (Mark 10:15).

Members of society's outgroups—the sick, the insane, the poor, criminals, those who are different—function in the Christ story as a constituency for Jesus (in contrast to the constituency of authority). Zaccheus, chief publican of Jericho, Lazarus, raised from the dead, the Gadarene demoniac, healed of insanity, Barabbas, a condemned murderer, Simon of Niger, a black man, Mary Magdalen,[9] a reformed prostitute all represent the disaffected, the ostracised, the multitudes outside of convention, who are drawn to the equally disenfranchised Jesus, whom they embrace. Their advocacy affords Jesus a growing base of power and support from which to mount his challenge to existing authority.

The principal element of plot in the Christ story concerns the Divine Mission of Jesus, its nature, and its effects. Based on the theological premise that God so loved the world that He sent His only begotten Son to serve as "a ransom for many" (Mark 10:45)—and mediated within a matrix of the supernatural, in which major events, incidents, explanations and resolutions occur largely outside nature—this principal plot element begins with Jesus' conception and birth.

At the Annunciation Mary is informed of the special nature of the child she is to carry: "He shall be great, and shall be called the Son of the Highest . . . and of his kingdom there will be no end" (Luke 1:32–33). At Mary's visitation to Elizabeth, John the Baptist, *in utero,* acknowledges the presence of the Lord: "the babe leaped in her womb . . . for joy" (Luke 1:41–44). At Jerusalem the three wise men from the East, learning of Jesus' birth, declare: "Where is he [whose star] we have seen? . . . [for we have] come to worship him" (Matthew 2:2).

Jesus' special status gains impetus during the second phase of his Divine Mission, his adult ministry. Commencing at about age 30 (Luke 3:23) and preceded by Jesus' baptism in which God confirms "This is my beloved Son, in whom I am well pleased" (Matthew 3:17) as well as his successful confrontation with the devil in which Jesus rejects the temptations of wealth and power (Matthew 4:8–10), Jesus' public ministry is inaugurated with the miracle of Cana, in which he transforms water into wine (John 2:9), and unfolds in an accelerating campaign of healing, preaching, teaching and the performance of wondrous deeds. During this period Jesus emerges as a personage capable of transcending natural law.

Jesus' ministry in essence serves to identify him as the Messiah—"Thou art the Christ, the Son of the living God" (Matthew 16:16)—and to generate conflict with existing authority (the Romans, the Sanhedrin, the Pharisees); this conflict in turn sets in motion the remaining plot mechanisms within the Christ story.

The final events of Jesus' life, characterized by successive encounters with both heavenly and earthly forces, continue his enhancement as a special personage. During this phase of the Divine Mission—punctuated by an increased tempo of temporal conflict—Jesus undergoes transfiguration by which his countenance becomes "altered" and his raiment "white and glistening" (Luke 9:29); he is confronted by the figures of Moses and Elijah, the latter of whom Jesus indicates not only precedes the Messiah but also has already come in the person of John the Baptist (Matthew 17:3–13); sweats blood at Gethsemane (Luke 22:44); and meets his fate on Golgotha where, upon his crucifixion, the earth quakes and the bodies sleeping in the ground arise (Matthew 27:51–53).[10]

The Christ story does not end with death but with resurrection. It is in this phase of the Divine Mission that Jesus is established as a supreme metaphysical being. In his reappearance at the tomb (John 20:14), on the road to Emmaus (Luke 24:13), in the company of the disciples (John 20:19, 26; 21)—and in the ultimate ascension into heaven (Mark 16:19, Luke 24:51, Acts 1:9–11)—Jesus indicates his fulfillment of the Divine Plan, affirms his essential metaphysical nature and, in bringing to a conclusion the principal themes of the Christ story, enunciates the remaining element of the Divine Mission of the Son of Man: "Go therefore and make disciples of all nations, baptizing them in the name of the Father and of the Son and of the Holy Spirit, teaching them to observe all that I have commanded you . . . to the close of the age" (Matthew 28:19–20).

CHAPTER TWELVE

A Comparison of the Christ Story and the Horror Story

ALTHOUGH IT WOULD APPEAR THAT THE CHRIST STORY and the horror story are manifestly unlike, these two works bear remarkable similarities. The similarities extend into all categories of each of these accounts, including setting and background, characterization and plot. The similarities are in fact so substantial that, from an analytical point of view, they are in many instances identical.

Both stories take place in a setting of implied or actual antiquity, replete with incipient violence, and one in which nature can and often does go awry. Typically, the physical setting of the horror story portrays nature as being spectacularly but ominously beautiful, furiously wild and totally unpredictable:

Beyond the green swelling hills . . . rose mighty slopes of forest up to the lofty steeps. . . . Right and left they towered . . . the glorious colours of this beautiful range . . . an endless perspective of jagged rock and pointed crags . . . the snowy peaks rose grandly . . . the mountain seemed to come nearer to us . . . and to frown down on us. . . .

—*Dracula*

. . .awesome sweeps of vivid valley . . . great cliffs . . . untamed streams . . . pathless peaks . . . solid, luxuriant masses of forest . . . strange waters . . . hidden fountains . . . shadowy woods . . . breathtaking . . . greater than imagined. . . . The dense, unvisited woods on those inaccessible slopes seem to harbor alien and incredible things. . . .

—*The Whisperer in Darkness*

. . .darkness and storm . . . thunder burst . . . a terrific crash . . . flashes of lightning . . . dazzled . . . the lake . . . a vast sheet of fire . . . the tempest . . . so beautiful yet terrific.

—*Frankenstein*

These portrayals are all of natural settings, primordial, as old as the beginning itself. They are settings apart from the mainstream of life, "untrodden by the foot of man," remote, chartless, desolate and often characterized by an absence of civilization. Despite their dazzling and idyllic beauty, they hold a foreboding and the promise of ill events to come. Their legends, lore and superstitions are steeped in violence and death. They are places host to unnatural psychical and metaphysical occurrences.

The physical settings of the Christ story are also natural-like settings. The actual physical background of this story, although a real geographical place, is—like that of the horror story—a land of antiquity: it is *the* land of antiquity (Genesis), in which both idyllic and cataclysmic forces are present. It is the land of Eden and the land of Sodom, where "the smoke of the land went up like the smoke of a furnace" (Genesis 19:28). It is a place characterized by natural and historical disasters, actual and threatened. It is a place where the forces of nature go awry: "the sun . . . turn[s] to darkness; the moon . . . to blood." It, too, is a land host to psychic and metaphysical occurrences (the Red Sea divides, Jesus walks on water), a land whose metaphysical history is also steeped in violence and death.

The physical settings of both the horror story and the Christ story thus appear remarkably similar. In each case the setting imparts to the story a sense of the suspension of reason and natural law, the inevitability of fateful occurrences. Each portrays an environment over which man has seemingly little or no control.

Both the Christ story and the horror story also take place in a psychological setting. That setting imparts to each of these stories a sense of impending disaster, and serves to displace conventional time with a sense of "other" time. Such a psychological setting is contributed to by the physical settings themselves, by concepts of predestination, and by the manner in which the stories are related.

The physical settings of the horror story, whether natural or symbolic, typically imply a time of the past. The settings themselves are depicted as antiquitous, primal, remote, static, unchanging, exempt from the vicissitudes of time. These depictions of physical antiquity invoke a sense of psychological antiquity.

> . . .imprisoned amidst the ancient woods, shut in an olden land of mystery and dread . . . as if all was long ago and forgotten by the living outside . . . now and then repeating . . . evil . . . unchanged and unchangeable. . . .
> —*The Black Seal*

In such a milieu, with conventional time seemingly suspended, a state of other time becomes operative in which abnormal events associated with the metaphysical backgrounds of these settings can recur.

The concept of predestination also contributes to this sense of other time. Predestination means that future events are already known and must inevitably come to pass. In the horror story the dreadful events of the past are held in abeyance, in static suspension, until the moment when once again they can be reawakened, again embodied in the present. Predictions foreshadow their occurrence: "They've been mighty strange things a' goin' on . . . and things'll be goin' on again. . . ." Their inevitable recurrence is the fulfillment of past prophecy. Predestination renders present and future events a replay of what has happened in the past. "[They were] . . . fated to reenact . . . [the] . . . fearful tragedy. . . ." Predestination creates a sense of other time by rendering all conventional time in terms of the past; the future becomes merely the fulfillment of the past; the present is the past becoming again.

Techniques such as writing in the first person and recounting the horror story in terms of an eyewitness account also contribute to this sense of other time. The eyewitness account creates the impression that events are happening in conventional time, as if it is not known what will happen next, as if the characters can alter the events to come. However, since it *is* known what will happen next, since the characters can *not* alter events to come, and since the occurrences of the horror story *must* in general transpire in accordance with their preordained character, eyewitness narratives serve merely as windows of the present through which the past recurs. These techniques add to a sense of other time by rendering conventional time irrelevant.

The psychological setting of the Christ story is also characterized by a sense of other time, in which real time, although present, is rendered irrelevant to the story. The factors contributing to the psychological setting within the Christ story, similar to those of the horror story, include the physical setting itself, representations of predestination, apocalyptic ideas, and the manner in which the story is recounted.

The physical setting of the Christ story, the Holy Land, implies a time of the past, for it is the land of antiquity, the setting of the Beginning itself. It is a place where ancient scenes—Mount Sinai, the Red Sea, the River Jordan, Jerusalem—are imbued with metaphysical history. The depiction of such a land, with its old, immutable, eternal scenes, invokes a sense of psychological antiquity in which real or conventional time becomes unimportant, secondary, remote—in effect, suspended—and is displaced by an impression of timelessness in which the metaphysics of the setting can become operative.

Predestination contributes heavily to this sense of timelessness. The Christ story is based on the premise that its events are all preordained, part of a Divine Plan, held in abeyance from the beginning until a time of revelation.

In the beginning was the Word . . . and the Word was God. . . .
And the Word became Flesh and dwelt among us. . . .
—John 1:1, 14

Everything that happens in the Christ story is part of the Divine Plan. Its events are inevitable; they must occur in accordance with the way in which they have been laid down in the past. ". . .All this has taken place, that the scriptures of the prophets might be fulfilled" (Matthew 26:56). Predictions of events, particularly those that concern the fate of Jesus, foreshadow their occurrence:

. . .he [Jesus] began to tell them [The Twelve] what was to happen to him, saying, "Behold, we are going up to Jerusalem;

and the Son of man will be delivered to the chief priests and the
scribes, and they will condemn him to death, and deliver him to
the Gentiles; and they will mock him, and spit upon him, and
scourge him, and kill him; and after three days he will rise."

—*Mark 10:32–34*

The Christ story is in fact so rigidly cast within the framework of predestination that the very possibility that events
might be different is effectively removed: "Do you think that I
cannot appeal to my Father, and he will at once send me more
than twelve legions of angels? But how then should the
scriptures be fulfilled, that it must be so?" (Matthew 26:53–
54). Thus in the Christ story, as in the horror story, the idea of
predestination renders what happens in the present and what
happens in the future a fulfillment of what has been decreed
in the past. In this way, predestination contributes to a sense
of other time by creating a special time: a time of the past
fulfilling itself. The events of the Christ story comprise a
recounting of the past in just such terms, in which the present
and future of conventional time are reduced to an affirmation
of past prophecies.

This sense of the past becoming again is further elaborated
by the apocalyptic idea of an impending new order (Kingdom Come, the Kingdom of God, the Kingdom of Heaven
at Hand). This idea, implying a time that is *about to happen,*
courses through the Christ story, ostensibly creating a sense
of time projected toward the future. However, despite its
apparent forward thrust, the nature of this future is but the
coming true of what was long ago foretold. The idea of
Kingdom Come contributes to a sense of other time by
transforming the present into a state of imminent expecta-
tion, and by rendering the future the fulfillment of the past
that is to come. Again real time is negated. The future
becomes the projection of an inevitable past; the present is
reduced to a state of that past fulfilling itself.

The manner and style in which the Christ story is related also contributes to this sense of timelessness. The narrators of the story (the gospel writers) relate its events in the third person and in the past tense.

> And he [Jesus] went about all Galilee, teaching . . . preaching . . . and healing. . . . So his fame spread. . . . And great crowds followed him. . . .
> —*Matthew 4:23–25*

However, the recounting of past events is heavily counterbalanced by the presence of lengthy dialogue, direct conversation between the personages in the story, written in the first person and in the present tense. The major events of the story are typically presented in this fashion. The teachings, parables, healings, miracles, Jesus' struggle with the devil, his transfiguration, his admission that he is the Christ, the Last Supper, his arrest and trial, the Crucifixion and afterwards at the tomb—the events of his entire mission and fate—come alive through direct quotations. Each gospel contains running dialogues that convey the feeling of eyewitness happenings; for example, Mary Magdalen stands weeping outside Jesus' empty tomb, while Jesus, standing by the tomb but unrecognized by Mary, speaks to her:

> ". . .Woman, why are you weeping? Whom do you seek?" Supposing him to be the gardener, she said to him, "Sir, if you have carried him away, tell me where you have laid him, and I will take him away." Jesus said to her, "Mary." She turned and said to him . . . "Rabboni!" (which means Teacher). Jesus said to her, "Do not hold me, for I have not yet ascended to the Father; but go to my brethren and say to them, I am ascending to my Father and your Father, to my God and your God."
> —*John 20:15–17*

The heavy presence of direct dialogue thus creates the

impression—like first person eyewitness accounts of the horror story—that these events are occurring in conventional time. But in the Christ story these eyewitness happenings are in fact fulfillments of past prophecies. And techniques such as dialogue in this case foster the sense of timelessness in which it is possible for the past to recur or be fulfilled.

Thus, whether in the Christ story or in the horror story, the depiction of antique physical surroundings, the concept of predestination, and the use of eyewitness accounts produce a remarkably similar psychological setting in each story, in which conventional time is displaced or suspended by a sense of other time or timelessness. This sense of other time, imparted to each story by these techniques, is in reality "psychological time"—a state of mind in which metaphysics and supernaturalism are perceived as real. Psychological time in this sense may derive from the period of the mind's early development. It may be the real time of many dreams, in which conventional time in relation to events is negated. It may also be the time of religious and mystical experiences, of drug-induced states, of transcendental meditation, of "moments of eternity" related to music, the arts and the emotions. Psychological time thus appears to be the time of the unconscious mind. Under conditions of psychological time there is no logical sequence of events, no law, no order. Happenings are not bound by logic. Events occur outside nature, at random, according to no rules, regulations or ethics. Only under conditions of psychological time is it possible to convey successfully a sense of magic or supernaturalism, and only when the mind is conditioned for psychological time can the magic and supernaturalism of horror stories as well as the Christ story become plausible.[1] Thus the concept of psychological time, as a function of almost identical physical settings, narrative techniques and concepts, serves to mediate the credibility of metaphysics in each of these stories.

Characterization in both the horror story and the Christ story is based on the presence of three major figures, the triad configuration. In the horror story this triad configuration is made up of the older man, the chief metaphysical or monster figure; the younger man, the protagonist or developing metaphysical figure; and the young woman, the feminine representative of innocence and goodness. In the Christ story the triad is composed of God the Father, representative of the older man; Jesus the Son, representative of the younger man; and the Virgin Mary, the young feminine representative of purity, goodness and innocence. In their separate attributes and interrelationships one triad configuration appears to correspond analytically with the other.

In both the horror story and the Christ story the older man, the principal metaphysical figure, is presented overall as possessing two sides to his makeup: a propensity toward a manifest nature, and a propensity toward its opposite. God the Father, of the Christ story, is characterized predominantly as an ethical Being, the Giver of the Law. He is representative of righteousness, truth and justice; mercy, forgiveness and salvation. God embodies such desirable virtues as Love, Light, Truth, Beauty, Wisdom. The epitome of goodness, God is portrayed as desiring to recruit into His ranks all of mankind, both through the Old Testament Covenant and the New Testament Covenant—faith in Jesus Christ—in order to spread His dominion over the world. However, God also has another side, equal and opposite to His goodness. He is also characterized as a punishing Being, "a jealous God . . . avenging and wrathful" (Nahum). His powers can also be bent toward destructive ends: "I . . . create evil . . ." (Isaiah 45:7). For whatever reasons, God is depicted as capable of wreaking havoc. He visits plagues; sends fire and brimstone; permits a people to be carried into captivity; decrees the destruction of cities, countries and humanity. God's power to commit devastation takes the form of unleashing natural,

historic and personal disaster, in order to reaffirm His ultimate domination over all mankind.

Similarly, opposites exist in the characterization of the
older man of the horror story. In contradistinction to his
usual manifest self, he is also shown to possess a counterpart
of goodness, at least initially. He is sometimes portrayed as
charming, erudite, gentlemanly, worldly, elegant and attractive; a man of enormous ability, drive and intellect. Typically
he has had a distinguished past and a splendid beginning.
Victor Frankenstein starts out as a talented young medical
student, given to noble platitudes. Dr. Jekyll is a highly
respected physician and researcher also given to moralistic
philosophizing. Count Dracula begins as a nobleman, patriot
warrior and historian. The older man of the horror story,
however, frequently becomes the victim of his own towering
intellect, fatal curiosity, and desire for power, which lead him
beyond the border of moral or conventional law. Such an
accident invariably causes his promising beginnings to dis-
integrate into disrepute. Thus Frankenstein goes awry and
creates a monster. Dr. Jekyll concocts a potion that brings
forth the "pure evil. . ." of Edward Hyde. And Count Dracula develops an unnatural taste for blood and practices vampirism. Once fallen, the older man becomes a manifestly evil
being—ruthless, destructive and mad, committed to the
downfall of others. He forces his evil will upon his adversaries, causing personal, cultural and historic disaster. And
like his counterpart in the Christ story, he, too, desires to
recruit into his ranks all of mankind, also for the purpose of
establishing dominion over the world.

Not only do both older men share opposing manifest and
latent natures, but both achieve their similar purposes
through the same kinds of metaphysical attributes. God the
Father is depicted as the all-powerful and all-knowing
Creator of man and his world, King and Ruler of the universe. He is the possessor of ultimate knowledge and control

over the forces of life and death. The older man of the horror story, too, is depicted as an all-powerful, all-knowing meta-physician immersed in the quest for power and control over the same forces of life and death. Both have the power to suspend and transcend natural law. Both have the power of transformation—the ability to change form or appearance. God the Father can make known his presence without being seen (invisibility): His voice issues from a burning bush; from a cloud He commends His beloved Son. In the form of the Holy Spirit, He is present but unseen at major religious occasions. It is through others that He makes himself known: His words are spoken by the prophets, His messages carried by the angels, and the Holy Spirit fulfills His Will. The older man of the horror story, likewise unfettered by the laws of nature, can similarly make known his presence without being seen. Like God the Father, he can make himself entirely invisible. He can appear in a myriad of forms ("familiars")— sometimes even as a voice—and through them his words can be spoken and his messages carried. He, too, can assume the form of a spirit or ghost that carries out his will.

Both are also perceived or related to in human or an-thropomorphic terms. Most commonly, the older man of the horror story appears in human form—a part-human, part-metaphysical being, such as Count Dracula. In this respect, God, too, is characterized as the part-human, part-meta-physical being incarnated in the person of Jesus.

The older man of both stories also has the ability to effect the transformation of others. In the horror story the older man changes people into something other than what they are: while these changes are physical in nature, they always imply a psychological change as well. He can bring about abnormal aging (either no aging in many years or many years' aging in a few moments). He can cause his victim to disappear (be-come invisible). He may cause his victim to become like himself, infected with the same madness (vampirism, werewolfism, etc.). He may leave his victim physically intact but take over his mind. In like manner, God the Father effects transformations: He turns Lot's wife into a pillar of salt, causes Elisha's servant to become an instant leper, creates a woman from Adam's rib, through the Holy Spirit carries out the Miraculous Conception, and effects the transfiguration of Jesus.

Thus both older figures appear not only to share interchangeability of basic natures, but to possess like metaphysical attributes. Both have a side for the good and a side for destructiveness. Both are of a basic metaphysical nature, and in their relationships with humans both recruit others for their respective—and similar—metaphysical ends. And both use virtually identical metaphysical means to pursue their identical metaphysical ends, namely control over the forces of life and death.

The young man of the horror story and Jesus, the young man of the Christ story, also bear remarkable similarities to one another in their characterizations. Both are portrayed as being of illustrious genealogy, or of otherwise atypical origin. In the horror story the young man is often a scion of a distinguished family—of the nobility, or of respected scientists, doctors and scholars. In the Christ story Jesus is depicted as the Son of God and the Virgin Mary, a descendant of the House of David; he is named Christ the King, the Prince of Peace. Both men are also portrayed as approaching maturity. In the horror story this "youngness" is usually expressed in terms of chronological age, but may also be expressed symbolically, in terms of conveying the "time" of a young man—for example, a person about to embark on a venture or a new career. In any case, whether chronologically or symbolically young, he is always characterized as young in relation to the older man and is typically portrayed as being on the verge of manhood or of attaining identity. Similarly in the Christ story Jesus is depicted as both chronologically and symbolically young. He is the Son of God. Early in his manhood (at age thirty, according to Luke) he embarks on a ministry—a new career, underscoring Jesus' youth in relation to the older man of the Christ story, God the Father. The young men of each story are further characterized as men with a mission, a commitment, an obligation to carry out for the sake of a high and noble purpose. In the horror story the purpose of such a mission is usually associated with an effort to enlighten the world:

> "I will pioneer a new way, explore unknown powers, and unfold to the world the deepest mysteries of creation. . . . I should . . . pour a torrent of light into our dark world."
>
> —*Frankenstein*

And in the Christ story, a similar mission is depicted for Jesus:

> . . .God sent the Son into the world . . . that the world might be saved through him.
>
> —*John 3:17*

In both stories this obligation or duty is commissioned by an older figure. In the horror story the young man typically must fulfill his mission at the behest of a relative or friend, or as a last request from a parent or parent-surrogate. The adventure of the young man of *Dracula* is initiated by his employer who is "like a father" to him. The young man of *The Fall of the House of Usher* answers the dying request of a friend. In *The Shuttered Room* the young man's mission is laid down in his grandfather's will. Similarly in the Christ story, Jesus' mission is laid down by his Father's Will. In addition, both men are also hero-like, standard-bearers of truth and righteousness who must fight forces they consider to be evil and that purpose to destroy them. In *Dracula* the young man and his cohorts unite in a compact to destroy their mysterious evil enemy. In the Christ story Jesus and his disciples stand similarly against their adversaries—religious hypocrites, corrupt moneychangers, and those who attempt to politically ensnare them.

Both young men in their early careers openly espouse law, a respect for society's conventions, rationality and religiousness. In the horror story the young man is respectful of society's standards; he is religious in the sense that he adheres to establish doctrine and accepted metaphysics. He is offended by the unauthorized metaphysics of the older man. He is moral in that he knows right from wrong; he is often given to philosophic preachments. Jesus, too, presents a pragmatic, down-to-earth view of life in his parables and teachings. "It is easier for a camel to go through the eye of a needle than for a rich man to enter the kingdom of God" (Mark 10:25). He, too, evinces respect for the conventions of society. "Think not that I have come to abolish the law and the prophets; I have come not to abolish them but to fulfill them" (Matthew 5:17). He is religious, adhering to the religion of the heart, if not to all aspects of existing religious doctrine. Like his counterpart in the horror story, he, too, is moralistic; his ethics are presented in such well-known discourses as the Sermon on the Mount (Matthew 5).

As both figures proceed to their challenges, their initial rationalism fades and each begins to assume accelerating metaphysical endowments. As the young man of the horror story encounters the challenge of the older man's unauthorized metaphysics, the young man's rationalism recedes and his propensity to transcend natural law emerges. He unveils a wide array of metaphysical knowledge and power. He is portrayed as able to change himself into another person; render himself invisible; make use of metaphysical arts in an attack against the metaphysical arts of his adversary. He is likewise portrayed as able to perform the ultimate miracle—control over the forces of life and death:

> I succeeded in discovering the cause of generation and life; nay, more, I became myself capable of bestowing animation upon lifeless matter.
>
> —*Frankenstein*

Similarly, as Jesus' career unfolds, his pragmatism and obedience to convention and natural law also recede, as he becomes a clearly metaphysical figure. The gospels recount his many miracles: he turns water to wine, makes the sick well, casts out devils, walks on water, stills the storm. Like his counterpart in the horror story, Jesus also performs the ultimate miracle—raising the dead (Lazarus). Additionally, he, too, is portrayed as having a degree of control over—that is, being the embodiment of—the secrets of life and death.

> ". . .I am the resurrection and the life; he who believes in me, though he die, yet shall he live, and whoever lives and believes in me shall never die."
>
> —*John 11:25–26*

Nevertheless, the young man does not always emerge victorious from his struggle. In the horror story the young man or his proxy—for example, Quincey Morris in *Dracula*—is sometimes fated for death; even so, in his death his efforts emerge victorious. Similarly in the Christ story, Jesus is fated for death; but this fate is viewed as joyous, ending not with his death but rather with his resurrection.

In summary, the young man of each story is characterized in very similar terms. Each is reaching for maturity, comes of a distinguished ancestry, is a hero-like figure, embarks on a noble mission commissioned by a parent-figure, is at first respectful of society's conventions and natural law but in the end shows himself capable of transcending these conventions and laws. The metaphysical powers of each at first lie dormant, but after their initial expression both young men unmistakably emerge as full-blown, powerful metaphysical figures not unlike their older counterparts. And in the end, whether fated for life or for death, both young men emerge victorious in their struggle.

The young woman of the horror story and Mary, the young woman of the Christ story, also appear remarkably similar. As in the case of the other two triad members, both women also are of illustrious genealogy or of atypical origin. In the horror story the young woman is typically characterized as the offspring of a prominent family, deriving from scholars, scientists, doctors, public servants or nobility. Elizabeth, the principal young woman in *Frankenstein,* is the daughter of a Milanese nobleman. Mina, the principal young woman in *Dracula,* is an orphan who never knew her parents (atypical origin). Similarly in the Christ story, Mary's origin is as the daughter of Joachim and Ann, the former described as a religious, wealthy and charitable man. Mary is further depicted as the special child of God, exempted by Him from original sin. Additionally she is portrayed as a descendant of the House of David.[2]

Both women are young. In the horror story, feminine youth is generally expressed in chronological terms, rather than symbolically. Mina in *Dracula* is about twenty years old, as is Elizabeth in *Frankenstein*. Sarey of *The Shuttered Room* is a young woman in her teens. In the Christ story Mary is portrayed similarly. She is depicted as being about fourteen or fifteen years old when betrothed to Joseph. Popular tradition seems to place Mary's age at about sixteen when she bears Jesus. Her presentation in painting and sculpture—whether at the Crib or at Calvary—is always as a young woman. She remains ageless, despite her portrayal at varying periods of her Son's life—an eternally and perpetually young woman, unaffected by time.

Both women are also characterized as novices on the brink of maturity. They are young women ready for marriage, ready for a maternal role. In the horror story the young woman is typically about to be engaged, is engaged or is just married. Mina in *Dracula* is engaged and then newly married to Jonathan Harker, the principal young man of the story. Elizabeth in *Frankenstein* is engaged and then briefly married to Victor Frankenstein. In the Christ story Mary, similarly, is depicted as a "virgin betrothed to a man whose name was Joseph" (Luke 1:27); having "found favor with God" (Luke 1:30), she is "handmaid of the Lord" (Luke 1:38).

Both women share idealized feminine attributes. Besides young, they are depicted as beautiful, virginal and spiritually moral—their physical beauty being an outward sign of their inner goodness. In the horror story, Elizabeth in *Frankenstein* is both beautiful and saintly:

Her hair . . . the brightest living gold . . . her blue eyes cloudless . . . her face so expressive of sensibility . . . a being heaven sent, and bearing a celestial stamp in all her features.

[Her] saintly soul . . . the living spirit of love.

Mina in *Dracula* is similarly portrayed:

. . . sweet, sweet, good, good woman in all the radiant beauty of her youth and animation. . .

. . .one of God's women, fashioned by His own hand . . . so true, so sweet, so noble. . . .

In the Christ story Mary is likewise beautiful, virginal and spiritually exalted. In the arts she reflects the highest standard of prevailing beauty. Her virginity is celebrated in dogma. Her spiritual goodness—literally her spiritual perfection by virtue of her inability to sin—is made explicit in the Doctrine of the Immaculate Conception.

Both young women epitomize respect, obedience and submissiveness to the rules and roles laid down for them by society. Both are depicted as dutiful and loyal, especially toward authority and authority figures. In the horror story, the young woman is portrayed as typically attuned to what is right and proper, especially regarding the fulfillment of her feminine destiny. In *Dracula,* Mina expresses concern over the appropriate conduct of an engaged woman, aspects of courtship and marriage, and propriety in general. In *Frankenstein,* Elizabeth's entire existence is bound up in the wishes of her adoptive parents, the Frankensteins, especially as regards her adoptive mother's desire that she become Victor Frankenstein's future wife. Similarly in the Christ story Mary symbolizes respect, obedience and submissiveness to society's rules and traditionally feminine roles of wife and mother. She, too, is portrayed as dutiful and loyal, especially toward a high authority figure. Her very life revolves around her fulfilling the Divine Will. In the Annunciation, she demonstrates respect, obedience and submissiveness to the Word of the Father. In making herself an instrument of the Divine Will she fulfills her destiny by becoming the "Divine Bride" and the "Bearer of God."

Both young women represent mother figures. Their impending sexual maturity and their desire to fulfill their feminine destiny combine to cast them as prime maternal personages. Both possess qualities closely associated with motherhood, in that they are portrayed as compassionate, merciful and forgiving. The young woman of the horror story is typically depicted as a symbolic[3] mother, her maternal dimension being expressed in terms of taking care of or ministering to the sick, the less fortunate, children, animals, her role often being that of a nurse, schoolteacher, charity worker. In *Frankenstein*, Elizabeth becomes mother to the motherless Frankenstein family. In a letter to her fiancé, she alludes to his young brothers as "our . . . children." In *Dracula*, Mina is described as an assistant schoolmistress; she nurses her fiancé, Jonathan Harker, back to health. As a newlywed she envisions herself as a future mother:

> We women have something of the mother in us. . . . I felt this big sorrowing man's head resting on me, as though it were that of the baby that some day may lie on my bosom. . . . I stroked his hair as though he were my own child.

At the end of the story Mina is portrayed as a mother in fact, an atypical occurrence in horror stories. (It is through her motherhood that her salvation from vampirism is made concrete.)

In the Christ story, similarly, Mary's chief portrayal is that of the Divine Mother, *Theotokos*, the God-Bearer. Mary is depicted as the ideal mother, embodying all the virtues associated with motherhood: she is beneficent, protective, compassionate, merciful and forgiving. She is known as the Mother of Mercy and Compassion, and her characterization as the mother of Jesus has been extended to include all her "children," as a result of which Mary has emerged as the Universal Mother.

Both young women also represent heroine-like figures. They are rallying points of strength; they are pivotal in moving others into action; they are frankly inspirational. In *Dracula* Mina's signal qualities are recognized by Professor Van Helsing, who organizes a group of young men against the Count:

> "There are lights in the world and darkness; you are one of those lights."

It is Mina who inspires the group to go against the Count:

> . . .some men so loved her, that they did much for her sake.

In *Frankenstein* it is Elizabeth who is the only one capable of reaching her tormented, withdrawn and isolated fiance:

> Elizabeth alone had the power to draw me from these fits; her gentle voice would soothe me when transported by passion, and inspire me with human feeling when sunk in torpor.

Mary is portrayed similarly in the Christ story. She is a figure capable of moving men. It is at her behest at Cana that Jesus performs his first miracle and so begins his public ministry. It is Mary who initially finds favor with God. Her representation as an inspirational figure in liturgy, literature and art continues in the present day.

The young woman of the horror story and Mary of the Christ story also share an almost identical appositional relationship to the metaphysical—a relationship which extends to both the older and the young man in each of these stories. In the horror story the young woman's appositional relationship to the older man, the chief metaphysical figure, is marked by close physical as well as psychological propinquity. She is often portrayed as the object of his intentions. She may be under his spell; she may be unwillingly drawn to him; she may reside with him as his quasi-prisoner; she may be his not-quite-willing assistant; she may be related to him by blood or familial kinship. He may hold power over her, or seek to possess her. Whatever the particular circumstances, the young woman is tied to the older man. In short, her appositional relationship to the older man represents an alliance to a powerful metaphysical figure. Her appositional relationship to the young man, the emerging metaphysical figure of the horror story, is also marked by closeness. She, too, is the object of his attentions. He, also, seeks to possess her, typically through marriage. The juxtaposition of the young woman to the young man is also one approaching kinship. They are related to each other (romantically linked), the young woman commonly portrayed as betrothed, about to be betrothed or the new wife of the young man. Whatever the status of their attachment, the young woman's appositional relationship to the young man, like that to the older man, represents an alliance to a strong metaphysical figure.

Similarly in the Christ story, Mary stands in close apposition to the two most powerful metaphysical figures: God the Father and Jesus the Son. Her relationship to God the Father is also marked by kinship and direct proximity. Mary is the object of His special attention. She is His special child. She is His chosen, the favored one, destined by His Will to become the vessel of the Incarnation. In effect Mary's appositional relationship to God the Father represents an alliance to the Supreme Metaphysical Being Himself. Likewise, Mary is the Mother of Jesus and as such stands in close proximity to the powerful and emerging metaphysical figure of her Son throughout his entire career. Moreover, this appositional relationship is not only as a mother but also as a contemporary, because of her depicted perpetual youth. Mary thus shares with her counterpart in the horror story a close appositional relationship to the metaphysical, by virtue of her special alliances with the two major metaphysical figures of the story.

The young women of each story therefore appear to be strikingly similar. Both have an illustrious genealogy. Both are young, are virginal novices. Both reflect the same type of idealized feminine attributes of beauty, purity, goodness, saintliness, obedience, submissiveness. Both respect society's rules and conventions. Both are mother-figures, sharing the same maternal attributes of love, devotion, compassion, mercy, forgiveness. Both are heroine-like, are inspirational, are rallying points of strength for others. Both also have a special and similar appositional relationship to the metaphysical that places them in juxtaposition to those who would control the very forces of life and death. In essence the young woman of the horror story and the young woman of the Christ story are the same. Their individual characterization and their interrelationships with the other members of the triad configuration are virtually congruent and functionally indistinguishable from one another.

The auxiliary characters of both stories also bear strong similarities to each other. These auxiliary figures include assistants, helpers, representatives, attendants, and envoys to each of the major triad figures, as well as members of royalty and clergy, children and foreigners.

In both the horror story and the Christ story the assistant to the older man is characterized by loyalty and obedience; his function is to carry out the will of the chief metaphysical figure. In the horror story, the older man's assistant may take on several forms: he may appear as an animal (wolf, cat, snake); commonly he may come forth as a spirit or ghost. Whatever his form, human or spirit, the assistant to the older man functions as his familiar: he acts in the older man's stead; he carries out his master's bidding and performs various metaphysical feats. Similarly in the Christ story, God the Father has special representatives and envoys who are in His service. Joseph, characterized as loyal and obedient, is God's mortal representative who assumes His role by becoming husband to Mary and father to Jesus in accordance with God's Will. The angel Gabriel serves as a spiritual representative of God, acting as His spokesman and conveying His Will. A manifestation of God Himself, the Holy Spirit, a further major spiritual envoy of God, represents God at certain religious occasions (baptism, religious experiences) and serves as God's associate in such acts as forgiveness of sins.

In both the horror story and the Christ story the assistant to the young man is commonly portrayed as "the best friend." He functions as a proxy to his counterpart. In the horror story *(Frankenstein)* Henry Clerval is portrayed as Frankenstein's dearest, closest and staunchest friend. Theirs is a friendship rooted in childhood, based on a similarity of character and shared experiences. Clerval is Frankenstein's "spiritual brother." The monster, seeking revenge on his creator, murders instead the innocent Clerval. His death symbolizes a death by proxy of Frankenstein himself and serves as a foreshadow of the latter's fate. In *Dracula* the assistants to Jonathan Harker, the young man, comprise a group of helpers united in a common purpose and bound by brotherly comradeship. Outstanding in this group is Quincey Morris, Harker's courageous friend, who dies as Jonathan's substitute in a final encounter with Dracula. Similarly in the Christ story, there are several assistants to Jesus who are portrayed as spiritual brothers and who also serve as proxies to the young man. Among them is John the Baptist. A contemporary of Jesus, he is Jesus' kin (cousin), his friendship with Jesus anchored in childhood. Theirs is a particular spiritual brotherhood based on mutual esteem for their respective missions. From the beginning John the Baptist functions as a proxy to his cousin. Portrayed as six months older than Jesus, what happens to John foreshadows what will happen to Jesus. John is conceived under atypical circumstances; so is Jesus. John becomes a prophet; so does Jesus. John is fated for violent death; so is Jesus. Other assistants to Jesus include the twelve disciples. These followers are Jesus' spiritual brothers and representatives—commissioned, authorized and sent out by Jesus to carry forth his work. Among the twelve, two are especially distinguished. The first, Peter, is Jesus' first chosen disciple and Jesus' heir apparent. After Jesus' death Peter assumes the leadership of the disciples in fulfillment of Jesus' request. The second, the unnamed beloved disciple, is Jesus' "brother of the heart." Theirs is a relationship characterized by physical and psychological closeness: at the Last Supper the beloved disciple leans on Jesus' bosom; he is also portrayed as the disciple whose "testimony is true." It is to this spiritual brother that Jesus commends his mother at Calvary: "Woman, behold your Son!" And to the unnamed disciple: "Behold your mother!" (John 19:26–27).

In both the horror story and the Christ story the attendant to the young woman is also commonly portrayed as "the best friend." Her basic characterization is essentially the same—although less lustrous—as that of the young woman, and like the attendants to the other major figures in the triad, her primary function is to serve as a proxy to the young woman. What happens to the best friend foreshadows what will happen to the young woman.

In the horror story *(Dracula)* Lucy Westenra is portrayed as the best friend of Mina. Her characterization and status (like Mina, Lucy is about to be wed) are close replicas of those of the young woman. However, it is Lucy who falls victim to the Count. Her subsequent vampirism and death cast a shadow on Mina's impending fate and struggle for survival. In *Frankenstein,* Justine is portrayed as the best friend and spiritual sister of Elizabeth, to whom she bears a close resemblence of character traits. However, it is Justine who becomes the victim of Frankenstein's monster. Her unmerited execution for the monster's crime presages the fate of Elizabeth.

In the Christ story St. Elizabeth is portrayed as Mary's kinswomen (cousin) and emerges in the role of her best friend. Elizabeth's chief function is as a proxy to Mary: what happens to Elizabeth happens to Mary. In a mini-Annunciation, an angel pronounces that Elizabeth, old and barren, will transcend her physical handicap and conceive a son, John the Baptist. Later in the Annunciation, the angel tells Mary, young and virgin, that she too will transcend physical law and conceive the Son of God.

Clergy in both stories symbolize the force of established religion and authorized metaphysics. In *Dracula,* Dr. Van Helsing, a priestlike figure, uses a mixture of religion and metaphysics against the Count. In the Christ story—correspondingly, in a mirror-image reversion—the priests and scribes (Pharisees and Sadducees) use their established religious status against Jesus. In both stories members of royalty symbolize the highest and most powerful authority. In *Dracula,* Lord Godalming, Lucy's fiance and one of Jonathan's comrades, represents the power of the aristocracy. In the Christ story Caesar Augustus, emperor of the Roman Empire, is the corresponding epitome of power. The three kings from the East, the Magi, are the metaphysical representatives of this power. Children, in counterpoint, function as symbols of uncorrupted innocence: they are represented in the horror story by Mina's little boy, Quincey *(Dracula),* and Frankenstein's little brother, William *(Frankenstein)*—and in the Christ story by the multiple associations of children with "the kingdom of God" (Mark 10:13–14). Foreigners in both stories symbolize those outside the law or convention. In the horror story *(Dracula)* the American is the free spirit outside convention; Justine *(Frankenstein)* is the gypsy who is also free from convention; Punk in *The Wendigo* is the Indian possessing "the instincts of his dying race" (uncivilized). Similarly in the Christ story, sinners, the sick, the insane, the poor, criminals, a black man (Simon of Cyrene)—all represent groups outside society's conventions.

In general the presence of royalty, clergy, children, foreigners and outgroups perform the same function in both the horror story and the Christ story: they represent the contrasting ideologies of convention and freedom from convention, authorized metaphysics (religion) and unauthorized

metaphysics (monsterism), immutability and change, innocence and corruption—all of which intensify the roles and
interrelationships of the three main characters and serve to
emphasize the structural and functional integrity of the triad
configuration.

In the horror story and the Christ story, plot elements also
bear strong similarities to one another. Common to both
stories is the element of a journey, typically on the part of the
young man. Such a journey, initiated by a parent or authority
figure, is commonly portrayed as a mission for the purpose of
fulfilling a high or noble cause.

In the horror story *(Dracula)* Jonathan Harker embarks on
a trip to the Castle Dracula to fulfill a contractual obligation
of his employer. Victor Frankenstein *(Frankenstein)* responds
to the last wish of his deceased mother, journeying to medical
school where he commences what he considers to be a noble
project, the creation of a new, beneficent species of life. Later
in the story Frankenstein actually journeys to the ends of the
earth in an attempt to destroy his creation in order to save
humanity. In *Dr. Jekyll and Mr. Hyde* the doctor (representing
in this instance the young man), also driven by noble motives
of improving humanity, embarks on a venture in which he
seeks to separate the good from the evil in man. In the Christ
story Jesus, similarly embarking on a journey—both real and
symbolic—for a high, noble purpose undertaken at the behest of a parent figure, is sent into the world for the purpose
of saving humanity (i.e., to fulfill his Father's Will). The
beginning of this journey is marked by the advent of Jesus'
ministry, the start of a new venture in which he actively
travels from place to place, preaching, teaching, healing,
performing miracles—all as part of the Divine Mission. His
final journey to Jerusalem, the high point of this mission,
inaugurates the last major events of his life and represents the
last of his earthly pilgrimages. A final journey, his resurrection and ascension into heaven, concludes his mission.

In both the horror story and the Christ story, journeys are associated with foreshadowings of impending disaster. These foreshadowings are ultimately rationalized, disregarded or ignored. In *Dracula,* despite the manifestly good purpose of Jonathan's mission, the young man is plagued by premonitions of impending ill. The natural setting itself, a locale in the Carpathian mountains, contributes to this sense of doom. He is warned by some of the townspeople not to go to the Castle Dracula. Before boarding the stagecoach a woman forces him to accept a crucifix "for his mother's sake." His coach ride to the castle is punctuated by strange, extranatural happenings. However, not to be deterred, he brushes these happenings aside and proceeds with his mission. Victor Frankenstein *(Frankenstein)* and Dr. Jekyll *(Dr. Jekyll and Mr. Hyde)* are also haunted by dark forebodings concerning their noble, scientific ventures. While to some extent these forebodings are conveyed by the respective settings (the wildly beautiful mountains; the deserted, forbidden building), the source of their dark premonitions springs mainly from their conscience. Both Victor Frankenstein and Dr. Jekyll question their moral right to go beyond nature. But after a brief inner struggle both men convince themselves that their endeavors will be the Rosetta Stone to a better world. The scientists plunge forward, drowning out the inner voice which attempts to stay them from their respective missions. Similarly in the Christ story, predictions of Jesus' fate occur early. At the Presentation, Simeon the Priest prophesies that a sword will pierce Mary's soul (Luke 2:34–35)—which is taken to mean that she will suffer grief concerning her Son's mission. At Cana, Jesus seems to balk at the beginning of his mission, governed by a troublesome prediction: "My hour has not yet come" (John 2:4). During his ministry he himself makes gloomy predictions concerning his fate (Matthew 16:21).[4] At his Transfiguration (Luke 9:28–36), Jesus voices details of his upcoming ordeal. In the agony of the inevitable, however, he proceeds with his fate: ". . .not my will, but thine be done" (Luke 22:42). Both stories thus share not only the similar plot line of a journey undertaken by the young man at the behest of a parent figure for the same type of lofty purpose, but also foreshadowings of impending personal disaster associated with this journey, which are similarly ignored.

Perhaps the overriding feature of plot common to both the horror story and the Christ story, however, in contradistinction to conventional tales, is the invocation of the supernatural. In both stories the supernatural assumes the major role of plot mediation. While the horror story frequently starts out as a conventional tale, it quickly becomes an excursion into metaphysics. The Christ story, on the other hand, begins as a frankly metaphysical excursion, setting forth the fulfillment of the messianic prophecy. In both stories the advancement of the supernatural proceeds in sequential stages or periods.

The pre-encounter period includes the initial revelation of the metaphysical as well as preliminary encounters between the metaphysical and auxiliary characters. In both the horror story and the Christ story the initial revelation of the metaphysical is usually depicted through an encounter between the chief metaphysical figure and a minor auxiliary character, typically a child. For example, in the horror story *(Dracula)* Count Dracula is observed, early in the story, making off with a peasant child in a bag. In *Frankenstein* the monster first strikes Victor Frankenstein's little brother. In *Dr. Jekyll and Mr. Hyde,* Hyde's debut as a monster figure is inaugurated with his trampling of a little girl. Similarly, in the Christ story the revelation of God is initially presented through the news of the forthcoming birth of a child (an angel informs Zechariah, Elizabeth's husband, of Elizabeth's miraculous conception). Such encounters represent a first meeting between the nonearthly and the earthly, and serve to preview future encounters.

Following the initial revelation of the metaphysical, encounters of a more fateful nature begin to occur, generally between the chief metaphysical figure and major auxiliary characters. Whether for good or evil, these encounters provide a glimpse into the power of the chief metaphysical figure and serve as a primer for future conflicts with one of the other two triad characters—principally the young man. In the horror story *(Dracula)*, Dracula's encounter with a principal auxiliary figure, Lucy Westenra (the best friend of Mina Harker), not only augers Mina's fate but portends the coming, and major, confrontation between the Count and Jonathan Harker (Mina's husband, the young man of the triad). In *Frankenstein,* the monster's encounter with Henry Clerval, Victor Frankenstein's best friend, forecasts the inevitable clash between the monster and his creator. In *Dr. Jekyll and Mr. Hyde,* Hyde's encounter with the venerable and fatherly Carew foreshadows the major confrontation between Hyde and his creator. Similarly in the Christ story, God's plan for John the Baptist serves to foreshadow God's plan for Jesus; His encounter with Elizabeth likewise foreshadows His encounter with Mary.

While further encounters between the chief metaphysical figure and major auxiliary characters continue, the next stage of plot, the period of direct initial encounter, consists of the series of confrontations which occur between two of the triad figures—commonly the older man and the young man. These first direct encounters are illustrated in the horror story by Jonathan's discovery of Count Dracula in his coffin as a vampire *(Dracula)*, Frankenstein's animating the monster *(Frankenstein)* and Dr. Jekyll's first glimpse in the mirror of Mr. Hyde *(Dr. Jekyll and Mr. Hyde)*. In the Christ story the corresponding direct encounter occurs at Jesus' baptism, at which God speaks from a cloud, affirming Jesus' mission. In both stories the direct initial encounter establishes a dynamic tension between the two major triad figures in which the chief metaphysical figure, the older man, is first revealed to be more powerful than his younger counterpart. Thus in the horror story Count Dracula is at first presented as more powerful than Jonathan; while both Frankenstein and Dr. Jekyll—cast as fathers to their respective creations—believe themselves to be metaphysically superior to their sons. Similarly in the Christ story, the supremacy of the Father is made apparent to Jesus during his initial and subsequent encounters with God.

As further direct encounters ensue, the chief metaphysical figure's nature, intents and purposes are revealed; correspondingly, the metaphysical power of the young man begins to emerge. It is during these encounters that the dramatic tension between the two major triad figures increases as the young man attempts to equal or surpass the chief metaphysical figure. In the horror story *(Dracula)*, after several encounters with Dracula, Jonathan becomes expert about vampirism and associated phenomena. In *Frankenstein,* after several meetings with the monster, Frankenstein attempts to redeploy his already established metaphysical knowledge to meet the challenge. In *Dr. Jekyll and Mr. Hyde,* after discovering the nature of Mr. Hyde, Dr. Jekyll redirects his metaphysical talents in order to deal with his creation. Similarly in the Christ story, it is during this period of initial encounters between God and Jesus, in which God's purpose is made manifest to Jesus, that Jesus also gains in metaphysical stature. Jesus begins to do what God does: forgive sins, heal the sick, work miracles. At the close of the period of direct initial encounter, the two polar figures of the triad configuration, the older man and the young man, are depicted as nearly matched.

The nature of these encounters in both stories is also remarkably similar:

In each story there is an apparent ambivalence—an initial "unwillingness" yet a "willingness"—on the part of those representative of the earthly (chiefly the young man and auxiliary characters) to engage in confrontation with the nonearthly (the chief mataphysical figure). In the horror story *(Dracula)* Jonathan, although unwilling to enter a certain room, cannot resist the temptation and thereby discovers Dracula's resting place. In *Frankenstein* and *Dr. Jekyll and Mr. Hyde* both men of science, despite their manifest revulsion, are magnetically drawn to their encounters. In further horror stories a young man ostensibly refuses to look at a portrait but then stares irresistibly at the picture to elicit a ghost; another, refusing to sleep in a haunted room, finds himself drawn to the chamber. All of these characters have the power of choice; all initially say "no," but then all choose to engage in the encounter with the metaphysical. Similarly in the Christ story, Jesus initially balks at engaging in a metaphysical display at Cana, but then reconsiders and performs his first miracle.

In each story there is a denial of mental responsibility by the earthly in their encounter with the metaphysical. This denial by the earthly is rationalized as the result of an "altered state of mind," induced by various means such as alcohol, drugs, sleep, state of hypnosis, amnesia; thus they are not in full possession of their minds during these encounters. In the horror story *(Dracula)* Mina professes to have let the Count vampirize her since she was under his spell and unable to resist (she was also given a sleeping pill). Jonathan remains powerless during this encounter because he is overtaken by a strange sleep (stupor). Frankenstein *(Frankenstein)* and Dr. Jekyll *(Dr. Jekyll and Mr. Hyde)* are both psychologically entrapped in a strange mental state from which they are unable to extract themselves. Similarly in the Christ story there is a corresponding failure by the earthly to fully acknowledge their involvement in a metaphysical encounter. The disciples who witness (partake in) Jesus' transfiguration are "heavy with sleep but kept awake" (Luke 9:32). At Gethsemane the disciples fall asleep during Jesus' entreaties to God

(Luke 22:45–46, Mark 14:32–42). Jesus himself is accused of being in an altered state of mind ("beside himself") relative to his ministry (Mark 3:21). At Cana he seems to deny responsibility for an impending metaphysical encounter in which he ultimately participates (John 2:4). While reference to himself in the third person—"the Son of Man"—usually expresses acceptance of his metaphysical destiny (Matthew 16:27),[5] reference to himself in the first person does not necessarily imply that acceptance.

Each story has its own background of general violence in which the specific violence of the encounter takes place. The horror story, *Dracula,* for example, is replete with background incidents such as the presence of the violently insane, a preoccupation with the idea of blood, accounts of suicide, violent kidnappings, beheading (of a corpse) and killing (plunging of a stake through the heart of an "undead" corpse). *Frankenstein* makes reference to charnel houses, butcher shops, dissecting rooms and the carving up of human bodies for "research" purposes. *Dr. Jekyll and Mr. Hyde* portrays the milieu of a medical laboratory wherein the human spirit and the human body are violated. The Christ story contains nearly congruent accounts of background violence: the presence of the violently insane (Gadarene demoniac); allusions to the shedding of blood (the Last Supper, Gethsemane, the Crucifixion); accounts of suicide (Judas), beheading (John the Baptist), and killing (Herod's slaughter of the Innocents, crucifixion as a form of punishment).

In each story the specific violence of the encounter is associated with physical assault, the shedding of blood, and the infliction of pain and suffering—psychological as well as physical—upon the earthly figure, principally the young man. The horror story *Dracula* is replete with metaphysical encounters involving vampirism—a physical and psychological assault associated with the shedding of blood, the infliction of psychological pain and physical debilitation. In

Frankenstein strangulation is the specific physical assault as a result of the metaphysical encounter; in addition, Frankenstein suffers from "brain fever," a psychosomatic illness, as a result of his encounters with the monster. In *Dr. Jekyll and Mr. Hyde,* Dr. Jekyll is both physically and psychologically ravaged, and auxiliary characters are trampled and beaten to death in their encounters with Hyde. Similarly, in the Christ story, Jesus suffers such psychological agony that he sweats blood (Luke 22:44). At the Crucifixion, an encounter with the Divine Will, Jesus suffers physical and psychological assault associated with the shedding of blood. He is ridiculed, tormented, beaten and finally crucified.

In each story the earthly beings undergo changes or are left with physical and psychological marks after their encounter with the metaphysical. In *Dracula* earthly victims of the Count take on the appearance and psyche of vampires: their eyes harden and slant, their teeth become pointed, they begin to seek out victims of their own. A holy wafer burns a searing scar onto Mina's forehead after she is vampirized, while Jonathan's hair turns instantly white. Frankenstein *(Frankenstein)* and Dr. Jekyll *(Dr. Jekyll and Mr. Hyde)* undergo bodily and mental deterioration as a result of their encounters. In other horror stories distinctive odors, secretions, a "sympathetic" wound (a wolf is shot in the leg and a man awakes to find a bullet in his leg), remain with victims as the residue of metaphysical confrontation. Similarly, in the Christ story, Elizabeth and Mary are marked by atypical conception in the aftermath of their encounters. At baptism Jesus is psychologically changed as a result of his encounter with the Holy Spirit (Matthew 3:16). During the transfiguration Jesus' countenance is altered and his raiment becomes dazzling white (Luke 9:29). In the aftermath of his encounter with the Father at Gethsemane, Jesus is marked by sweat and blood; in his reappearance after the Crucifixion his body bears the stigmata (the marks of the nails).

While the early encounters have served to create a climate of increasing tension between the two metaphysical figures, in the third phase of plot, the period of ensuing encounters, the tension culminates with the destruction of one of them. For in both the horror story and the Christ story, as one metaphysical figure approximates the other, one must drop away, leaving only the other to survive. Thus in the horror story *(Dracula)* the hunter (Dracula) becomes the quarry and Jonathan emerges victorious. As Frankenstein *(Frankenstein)* becomes an even match for the monster, he fails in a last attempt to destroy his creation and it is he who dies. As Mr. Hyde *(Dr. Jekyll and Mr. Hyde)* approaches his final conquest of Dr. Jekyll, the doctor, in a final burst of power, destroys himself in order to destroy Mr. Hyde. Similarly in the Christ story, as Jesus approaches equality with God himself, it is he who must die.

Both stories present an atypical overcoming of death on the part of the two metaphysical figures. In *Dracula,* Jonathan escapes death by having Quincey Morris die in his place. In *Frankenstein,* Frankenstein dies but his alter ego, the monster, escapes into the wastes. In *Dr. Jekyll and Mr. Hyde,* Mr. Hyde dies but Dr. Jekyll vanishes (his body is never found). In each case the surviving metaphysical figure cheats death. Similarly in the Christ story, Jesus dies but the tomb is found empty, his body is gone, and he is pronounced "risen."

A similar period of resolution characterizes both stories. Although both the horror story and the Christ story have a sense of ending, the impression is left that the events described could happen again. This impression is the result of both stories having resolutions that take place in the metaphysical realm, in which a sense of ending and finality based on logic and natural law is missing. *In the realm of the metaphysical, death is not final.* In the horror story (Dracula), the Count, beheaded and staked through the heart, is devampirized and turns to ashes. The story is over—at least for the present. Yet the feeling persists that Dracula can return. Even the epilogue subtly suggests that not all traces of vampirism have been destroyed: "The Castle stood as before, reared high above a waste of desolation." In *Frankenstein* the resolution of the monster's disappearing in the Arctic wastes—"borne away by the waves and lost in the darkness and distance"— implies that the monster could possibly make its reappearance somewhere, sometime again. Similarly, in the Christ story, the death of Jesus is not final. In the Resurrection is the promise of his Second Coming. Thus both stories—circular in the sense that within their resolutions are contained their potential re-beginnings—have endings but do not quite end.[6]

Thus the plot of both the horror story and the plot of the Christ story are remarkably similar. Both are metaphysical stories that take place outside nature. Both are moral in tone; in both there is an attempt to distinguish between good and bad, right and wrong, moral and immoral. Both begin with a purposeful journey, a noble mission undertaken by the young man at the behest of a parent or parent figure. In both a series of violent encounters occur between the earthly and the nonearthly—at first between auxiliary characters and the chief metaphysical figure (the older man), then between a second triad figure (usually the young woman) and the older man, finally between the young man and the older man. With each encounter the young man gains in metaphysical stature, at which point a final confrontation takes place and one of the metaphysical figures drops away. In both stories there is an atypical overcoming of death by one of the metaphysical figures, and in both stories the dead ultimately make reappearances.

A further aspect of similarity between the horror story and the Christ story is that both enjoy a special credibility, despite their apparent contradiction of reality. In *Dracula* an epilogue says that there exists no proof for the events described. In

Frankenstein an eyewitness writes that the unlikely events related are nonetheless true. In *Dr. Jekyll and Mr. Hyde,* Dr. Jekyll writes a special confession to his lawyer so that the truth will ultimately be known. In each case the major metaphysical events are acknowledged as being in violation of logical, physical and natural law. Similarly, in the Christ story there exists no historical substantiation, and its major events—the Divine Conception, miracles, the Resurrection— are also in violation of logic and established physical and natural laws. The credibility of these stories is based on the belief that true reality goes beyond the manifest and rational; that true reality lies within the realm of the supernatural—a realm that can be apprehended only by means other than logic and rationality (metaphysical or religious experience, etc.); a realm in which the workings of the rational, conscious mind are held to be inapplicable or totally irrelevant. The horror story and the Christ story are credible because it is to the realm of "true reality" that both stories are beamed.

CHAPTER THIRTEEN

Horror in the Horror Story

HORROR STORIES CONTINUALLY CAPTURE AND FASCINATE
generation after generation. Old and young, rich and poor,
learned and ignorant—all respond to the mysterious message
these stories emit. With plots well-worn and characters of
faded familiarity, each story is a magnet that never loses its
power. What can be capable of so forcefully attracting individuals as diverse as the multitudinous backgrounds and
cultures from which they come? What is the horror in the
horror story?

An exploration of the precise nature of the metaphysical
encounter in the horror story may help to solve this riddle.

Such encounters take place primarily between members of
the triad configuration: between the older man, the young
man and the young woman (the chief metaphysical figure,
the protagonist and the representative of goodness or innocence, respectively). The triad configuration thus constitutes

a family constellation, the older man being a father figure, the young man a son figure and the young woman a daughter-mother figure. No matter what the encounter—whether between the older man and the young man, between the older man and the young woman, or between the older man and the auxiliary representatives of the other two—it must be perceived as taking place within this kind of family constellation.

The encounters may be subdivided into several types, depending on their nature. In the first, the psychological encounter, the earthly and nonearthly triad representatives are depicted in a contest of wills, in which the tremendous psychological power of the metaphysical—at least initially—overwhelms the earthly figure. The primary feature of this encounter is a psychological assault, the infliction of terror, fear and horror by the nonearthly upon the earthly.

In the psychological encounter, illustrated by the following examples, the earthly respond to a feeling or perception of the presence of the nonearthly, although no actual physical confrontation takes place.

A young man deliberately sets out to spend the night in a haunted house where he perceives the presence of the nonearthly:

> I strove to speak—my voice utterly failed me; . . . .I strove to rise—in vain; I felt as if weighed down by an irresistible force. . . . an immense and overwhelming Power opposed to any volition. . . . Opposed to my will was another will, as far superior to its strength as storm, fire and shark are superior in material force to the force of man.
> —*The Haunted and the Haunters*

A guide, Défago, camping in the wilderness with a companion, senses the presence of a monster that embodies the primordial spirit of the wilds. Sitting by a campfire, Défago sings an old song, the melody of which inadvertently calls up the woodland spirit:

> A curious change had come into [the guide's] voice. . . . Dé-
> fago, though still singing, was peering . . . into the Bush. . . .
> His voice grew fainter—dropped to a hush—then ceased al-
> together. The same instant, with a movement amazingly alert,
> he started to his feet and stood upright—*sniffing the air.* . . . any
> man with a pair of eyes . . . could see that [Défago] had turned
> white down to his very gills. . . . the livid hue of his face had
> turned to dirty grey. . . . nothing could explain away the livid
> terror that had dropped over his face while he stood there sniff-
> ing the air.
>
> —*The Wendigo*

A young woman pauses to glance up at the window of her brother's study and is appalled by what she perceives.

> . . . two eyes . . . glared at me . . . formless as my fear, the
> symbol and presence of all evil and all hideous corruption. . . . I
> stood shuddering and quaking . . . sick with unspeakable ago-
> nies of fear and loathing, and for five minutes I could not
> summon force of motion to my limbs.
>
> —*The White Powder*

A second type of encounter can be represented as predominantly physical. This encounter is marked majorly by a
bodily assault by the nonearthly figure upon the earthly, with
emphasis on the physical aspects of the confrontation.

> There was a Thing in the room; not a sow, nor any other
> namable creature, but a Thing. It was big as an elephant, filled
> the room to the ceiling, was shaped like a wild boar, seated on its
> haunches, with its forelegs braced stiffly in front of it. It had a
> hot, slobbering, red mouth, full of big tusks, and its jaws
> worked hungrily. It shuffled and hunched itself forward, inch by
> inch, till its vast forelegs straddled the bed. . . . The bed crushed

up like wet blotting-paper, and I felt the weight of the Thing on my feet, on my legs, on my body, on my chest. It was hungry, and I was what it was hungry for, and it meant to begin on my face. Its dripping mouth was nearer and nearer.

—The House of the Nightmare

A third gradation of encounter may be characterized as a combination of the foregoing. This encounter is marked by both a psychological and physical assault by the nonearthly upon the earthly.

. . . terror woke up in my breast. . . . bounding from my bed, I rushed to the mirror. At the sight which met my eyes, my blood . . . changed into something exquisitely thin and icy. . . . I had gone to bed Henry Jekyll, I had awakened Edward Hyde.

—The Strange Case of Dr. Jekyll and Mr. Hyde

. . . I saw the dull yellow eye of the creature open; it breathed hard, and a convulsive motion agitated its limbs. How can I describe my emotions at this catastrophe . . . ? His yellow skin scarcely covered the work of muscles and arteries beneath; his hair . . . of . . . lustrous black, and flowing; his teeth of . . . pearly whiteness; . . . [these] luxuriances only formed a more horrid contrast with his watery eyes . . . of the same colour as the dun white sockets in which they were set, his shrivelled complexion and straight black lips. . . . breathless horror and disgust filled my heart. . . . no mortal could support the horror of that countenance. A mummy again imbued with animation . . . a thing such as even Dante could not have conceived. My pulse beat . . . quickly. . . . I nearly sank to the ground. . . .

—Frankenstein

The great box was in the same place. . . . I raised the lid, and laid it back against the wall; and then I saw something which filled my very soul with horror. There lay the Count, but looking as if his youth had been half renewed, for the white hair and moustache were changed to dark iron-grey; the cheeks were fuller, and the white skin seemed ruby-red underneath; the mouth was redder than ever, for on the lips were gouts of fresh blood, which trickled from the corners of the mouth and ran over the chin and neck. Even the deep, burning eyes seemed set amongst swollen flesh, for the lids and pouches underneath were bloated. It seemed as if the whole awful creature were simply gorged with blood. He lay like a filthy leech, exhausted with his repletion. I shuddered as I bent over to touch him, and every sense . . . revolted at the contact. . . . Then I stopped and looked. . . . There was a mocking smile on the bloated face which seemed to drive me mad. . . . I seized a shovel . . . and lifting it high, struck, with the edge downward, at the hateful face. But as I did so the head turned, and the eyes fell full upon me, with all their blaze of basilisk horror.

—*Dracula*

. . . Abner made his way . . . up the stairs toward the shuttered room. He walked softly, careful to make no sound. Arriving at the door, he listened. At first he heard nothing—then. . . . Something in that room—*breathed!* Fighting back his fear, Abner put the key in the lock and turned it. He flung open the door and held the lamp high. Shock and horror paralysed him. There, squatting in the midst of the tumbled bedding from that long-abandoned bed, sat a monstrous, leathery-skinned creature that was neither frog nor man, one gorged with food, with blood still slavering from its batrachian jaws and upon its webbed fingers—a monstrous entity that had strong, powerfully long arms, grown from its bestial body like those of a frog, and tapering off into a man's hands, save for the webbing between the fingers. . . . Then with a frenzied growling sound . . . it rose up, towering, and launched itself at Abner.

—*The Shuttered Room*

There is, however, a fourth type of encounter between the nonearthly and earthly, which is of a more specific nature and which is illustrated by the following.

In the moonlight opposite me were three young women. . . . though the moonlight was behind them, they threw no shadow on the floor. They came close to me, and looked at me for some time, and then whispered together. Two were dark, and had high aquiline noses . . . and great dark piercing eyes. . . . The other was fair . . . with great wavy masses of golden hair and eyes like pale sapphires. I seemed somehow to know her face, and to know it in connection with some dreamy fear, but I could not recollect at the moment how or where. All three had brilliant white teeth that shone like pearls against the ruby of their voluptuous lips. There was something about them that made me uneasy, some longing and at the same time some deadly fear. I felt in my heart a wicked, burning desire that they would kiss me with those red lips. . . . They whispered together, and then they all three laughed—such a silvery, musical laugh, but as hard as though the sound never could have come through the softness of human lips. It was like the intolerable, tingling sweetness of water-glasses when played on by a cunning hand. The fair girl shook her head coquettishly, and the other two urged her on. One said: "Go on! You are the first, and we shall follow; yours is the right to begin." The other added:—"He is young and strong; there are kisses for us all." I lay quiet, looking out under my eyelashes in an agony of delightful anticipation. The fair girl advanced and bent over me till I could feel the movement of her breath upon me. . . . I was afraid to raise my eyelids, but looked out and saw perfectly under the lashes. The girl went on her knees, and bent over me, simply gloating. There was a deliberate voluptuousness which was both thrilling and repulsive, and as she arched her neck she actually licked her lips like an animal, till I could see in the moonlight the moisture shining on the scarlet lips and on the red tongue as it lapped the white sharp teeth. Lower and lower went her head as the lips went below the range of my mouth and chin. . . . Then she paused, and I could hear the churning sound of her tongue as it licked her teeth and lips, and I could feel the hot breath on my neck. Then the skin of my throat began to tingle as one's flesh does when the hand that is to tickle it approaches nearer—nearer. I could feel the soft, shiver-

ing touch of the lips on the super-sensitive skin . . . and the hard
dents of two sharp teeth, just touching and pausing. . . . I closed
my eyes in languorous ecstasy and waited—waited with beating
heart.

—Dracula

A young writer (Paul Oleron), entranced by his new quarters, senses them to be haunted by a female ghost. The
"beckoning fair one," as she is known, makes her presence
known to him by making a "silky . . . crackling rustle" of a
woman combing her hair, and by lying on his bed. "The
coverlets bore an impress as if somebody had lain on them."
At first Oleron is terror stricken and repelled; but quickly he
becomes irresistibly attracted, eventually possessed by a "voracious inquisitiveness" to know and to "have her sparkling
and panting in his arms. . . ." Gradually the writer allows his
life and work to slip away as he stands vigil for a ghost
"within the frame of his bedroom door." He prepares for her
as he prepares for a marriage:

> She was coming over him now; he knew by the alteration of the
> very air of the room when she was near him; and that soft thrill
> of bliss that had begun to stir in him never came unless she was
> beckoning, beckoning. . . . He let go . . . and fell back into bed
> . . . as—oh, unthinkable!—the other half of that kiss that a gnash
> of blood had interrupted was placed . . . on his lips . . . robbing
> him of very breath. . . .
>
> *—The Beckoning Fair One*

A young man's recurring nightmare comes to pass as he
chooses to sleep in a haunted room:

> . . . I sat bolt upright in bed. . . . Something I knew was in the
> room with me, and instinctively I put out my right hand, which
> was nearest the wall. . . . And my hand touched the edge of a
> picture-frame close to me. I sprang out of bed . . . a blinding

flash leaped out of the clouds, and showed me that by my bed again hung the picture of Mrs. Stone. . . . I saw . . . a figure that leaned over the end of my bed, watching me. It was dressed in some close-clinging white garment . . . and the face was that of the portrait. . . . I heard the rustle of movement coming nearer me. . . . And then a hand was laid on the side of my neck, and close beside my ear I heard quick-taken, eager breathing. . . . I knew that this thing . . . was . . . not of this earth. . . . Then a voice, already familiar . . . spoke. "I knew you would come to the room in the tower," it said. "I have been long waiting for you. At last you have come. To-night I shall feast; before long we will feast together."

—*The Room in the Tower*

It is clear that the foregoing encounters contain strong sexual overtones; that the sexual elements of these encounters are nearly overt; that they are but slightly displaced and thinly disguised. The sexual aspect of metaphysical encounters is present through all of the horror literature; although subtle and oblique in some stories, it is nevertheless there. In *The Wendigo,* for example, the monster is female, a Nature Spirit, whose call—in a voice seductive, sweet and irresistible— summons a man into a fantastic flight in which he is consumed by pangs of fire. In *Dr. Jekyll and Mr. Hyde,* Mr. Hyde's outstanding trait is his raw sensuality, his lust, and his indulgence of bestial appetites. In *Couching at the Door,* a piece of brown fluff evolves into a furry caterpillar-like creature—a symbolic representation of a woman's fur boa. The animated boa pursues the main character: it "rubs itself against" the leg of his chair ". . . in . . . affection"; he finds it "sweeping itself . . . against his hand . . . caressing . . ."; it is "in bed . . . pressed up against [him] . . . for warmth." In *The Refugee* a werewolf in the form of an extraordinarily handsome young man appears in the garden of an attractive older woman. She invites him into her house. She intends—ostensibly—to prepare a "romantic" dinner for two and seduce him. He intends to have her—literally—for dinner. While attention is focused on the rising appetite of the young werewolf-man, the woman herself is revealed as having an atypical palate. In a surprise twist, and with double entendre, the story discloses the answer to the question of who "eats" whom first.

In most horror stories the sexual nature of the encounters can be readily perceived. Consciously or unconsciously the sexuality of these encounters stands as a beacon to the mind, and to this sexuality may be ascribed at least part of the fascination these stories evoke.

Horror merges with sexuality in the metaphysical encounter of the horror story. In the typical horror tale it must be remembered that it is most commonly a member of the older generation—the older man or older woman—who intimidates a member of the younger generation: the father- or mother-figure who overtly moves against the daughter- or son-figure. In *Dracula,* for example, the Count—as the older man and chief metaphysical figure—attacks the young women, Lucy and Mina. Lucy, in turn, as a vampire (now a member of the "older" generation) goes on to attack a member of the younger generation (vampirizes a small child). In *Frankenstein* the monster as master and dominant metaphysical figure attacks a series of young people: Elizabeth (Frankenstein's bride), Justine (Elizabeth's contemporary and best friend), William (Frankenstein's little brother) and Clerval (Frankenstein's best friend). In *The Room in the Tower* the ghost of Mrs. Stone—the older woman and the mother of the young man's schoolmate—attacks the young man; in *The Wendigo* the female monster attacks the guide and vicariously the young divinity student, Simpson; in *The Refugee* the older woman attacks the young man.

Correspondingly, it is a member of the younger generation who typically "invites" the assault, who provokes the father- or mother-figure into a metaphysical encounter. For example, Celia, the young woman of *Housebound,* cannot resist calling up the ghost who inhabits her bedroom:

> She tried to keep her thoughts under control and not let them wander round the darkened room, seeking, prodding, even as a mischievous child might goad a sleeping snake, aware of the danger, but drawn to that danger. . . .

And despite the heaviest forebodings, Jonathan Harker of *Dracula,* Victor Frankenstein of *Frankenstein,* Dr. Jekyll of *Dr. Jekyll and Mr. Hyde,* Défago of *The Wendigo*—all court the metaphysical by rushing toward an encounter. The young man of *The Room in the Tower* entices the ghost by deliberately sleeping in a room where he knows he will be attacked, as does the young man of *The Haunted and the Haunters.* Paul Oleron of *The Beckoning Fair One* attempts an outright "love watch" for his ghost. While Lucy of *Dracula* keeps making fatal mistakes which result in metaphysical encounters with the vampire (she sleepwalks, forgets to lock a door, opens a window for fresh air, accidentally rips off her protective garland of garlic—all acts which invite attacks.) In every horror story the victim—consciously or unconsciously, purposely or inadvertently—issues a tacit invitation to the monster.

The assaults do not transpire only between members of the older generation and the younger. In some horror stories a contemporary can attack a member of the same generation. In *Carmilla* a female vampire attacks her closest girlfriend; in *The White Powder* a man who is transforming himself into a monster assaults his sister; in *Dracula* three young female vampires attack Jonathan Harker. Various other combinations of generational assaults from within the triad configuration are also possible. In *Dr. Jekyll and Mr. Hyde,* while Hyde—functioning as the older man—attacks a child (older generation against the younger), he also moves against Jekyll as does Jekyll against him (contemporaries against each other, son against father, and father against son).

Despite variations in the generational roles of triad participants, the victim is invariably represented as being assaulted by someone or something whose nature is primordial, of the past, *old*. Even when encounters occur between contemporaries, or when a member of the younger generation assaults a member of the older, the basic nature of these assaults is that someone or something old is attacking someone or something young or new. For example, in *The Small Assassin* the monster is a newborn baby, young, innocent, amoral, with unbridled instincts, who attacks his parents. Yet the feeling is conveyed that the baby represents something more primitive, more primordial, *older* than the parents. Likewise the monster in *The Shuttered Room* is also a baby—part-human, part-amphibian, immured for years behind locked doors, a misbegotten child of the past—older than the young man he attacks. Thus no matter what the variations in the triad configuration, symbolically it is always a member of the older generation who assaults a member of the younger.

The sexuality of the metaphysical encounter, apart from the generational nature of its triad participants, is itself not normal but aberrant. Aberrant or atypical sexuality characterizes the horror story. In its aberrancy lies a contributing core of horror—which can often be apprehended after an unmasking of sexual disguise mechanisms. These mechanisms are manifest chiefly in the two disguise forms of *displaced* sexuality and *implied* sexuality.

In *Dracula* the following encounters between the Count and Mina illustrate sexual aberrancy in the disguise form of displacement.

". . . beside the bed . . . stood a tall, thin man, all in black. . . . With a mocking smile, he placed one hand upon my shoulder and, holding me tight, bared my throat with the other . . .

strangely enough, I did not want to hinder him. I suppose it is part of the horrible curse that such is, when his touch is on his victim. . . . He placed his reeking lips upon my throat! . . . I felt my strength fading away, but I was in a half swoon. How long this horrible thing lasted I know not; but it seemed that a long time must have passed before he took his foul, awful, sneering mouth away. I saw it drip with the fresh blood!"

". . . He [the Count] pulled open his shirt, and with his long sharp nails opened a vein in his breast. When the blood began to spurt out, he took my hands in one of his, holding them tight, and with the other seized my neck and pressed my mouth to the wound, so that I must either suffocate or swallow some of the —— ——." Then she began to rub her lips as though to cleanse them from pollution.

The above scenes are illustrative of displaced sexuality, in which Mina's "throat" and the Count's "vein" are obvious displacements for genitals, and in which their mouths can also be genital displacements. In the first episode, in which the Count places his lips on Mina's throat, the disguised act involved is sexual intercourse (both Mina's throat and the Count's mouth are genital displacements); moreover, that the Count removes his mouth from Mina's throat, whereupon she sees it "drip with the fresh blood"—indicates that this is an intercourse representing the defloration of a virgin (Mina, although married, is portrayed as a virgin model throughout the story). In the event, however, that Mina's throat is the only genital displacement, a different act results: the Count "bares" Mina's "throat," placing his lips upon it for an inde-terminate time. Mina is "in a half swoon." When the Count takes his mouth away, it is dripping with "blood." This is an act of obvious cunnilingus. In like manner the second episode seems to be a clear portrayal of disguised fellatio. Mina is forced to suck on one of the Count's "veins" and she is forced to swallow some of the "—— ——". If the Count's vein is his genital, what Nina is forced to swallow is some of his ejaculate. Thus what these encounters portray is virginal defloration, cunnilingus and fellatio. However, the aberrant nature of this sexuality lies not in these practices themselves but in the fact that an older man is violently assaulting a young woman. It is *forced* virginal defloration; it is *forced* cunnilingus; it is *forced* fellatio. It is sexuality marked by sadism and cruelty on the part of the older man and by terrified compliance on the part of the young woman. But this terrified compliance itself is sexually aberrant, since it is the young woman who in many instances unconsciously invites the encounter. Mina, for example, referring to her being attacked by the Count, says: ". . . Strangely enough, I did not want to hinder him." It is not only the evident sadism of the older man that marks the aberrant nature of the sexual encounter in the horror story, it is also the less obvious but present masochism of the young woman. Each is indulged. The forced virginal defloration is invited; the forced cunnilingus is invited; the forced fellatio is invited. In the sexual encounter of the horror story, it is neither the overt sadism and cruelty of the older man or the less apparent masochism of the young woman that constitutes its aberrant nature—but the sadomasochistic totality of both.

In *Dr. Jekyll and Mr. Hyde* the aberrant sexuality is manifest in the disguise form of implication rather than of displacement. Hyde's outstanding traits are his raw sensuality, his lust, his bestial appetites and his depravity. It is implied that these basically sexual traits will be indulged and that such indulgences will result in atypical or aberrant sexual behavior.

Like the Count in *Dracula,* the expression of Hyde's traits is cloaked in cruelty. The overriding characteristic of Hyde's encounters is that they are of a cruel and monstrous nature. He brutally tramples a little girl, he savagely beats to death an elderly gentleman, he goes on rampages in which he can give vent without restraint to his nature; the expression of Hyde's implied sexuality—the result of his aberrant sexual traits—is thus one of manifest sadism.

Hyde is characterized as the exaggerated and distorted manifestation of Jekyll's latent nature. Ostensibly a pillar of society, good, respected and charitable, Jekyll is also shown to be a man given to a "certain gaiety of disposition," "wild" when young, guilty of certain "irregularities" some men "might boast about," on occasion laying aside "restraint," plunging "into shame" and participating in "undignified pleasures." While Jekyll must conceal and practice these appetites secretly, lest their indulgence arouse in him feelings of shame, disgrace, fear of public disclosure and need for penitence, Hyde is free to practice them openly. What is implicit in Jekyll becomes explicit and magnified in Hyde. In Hyde, Jekyll's "undignified pleasures" turn toward the monstrous; Jekyll's "appetites," so carefully controlled, are exercised, nourished and pampered; Jekyll's life of "restraint" becomes Hyde's life of "excesses," of "complete moral insensibility," of "leaping impulses," of "insensate readiness to evil." The irregularities of Dr. Jekyll become the assaults of Mr. Hyde. Unbridled instinct, bestial depravity, sensuality and lust—Dr. Jekyll's aberrant latency—become full-blown in Mr. Hyde and find expression most prominently in sadism.

Jekyll and Hyde are symbolic father and son figures. One is derived from the other. Dr. Jekyll is the procreator. Hyde is the "child of Hell" struggling to be born. Jekyll is the older; Hyde is young. Dr. Jekyll himself declares of their relationship that he "had more than a father's interest"; Hyde had more of a son's "indifference." Throughout the narrative the two stand in apposition to each other as father and son, exemplified by Jekyll's endless characterization as a father to Edward Hyde.

Nevertheless Hyde's sadism in the main is unleashed both physically and psychologically against his symbolic father Jekyll. In each act of transformation Hyde subjugates Dr.

Jekyll, inflicting on Jekyll tremendous physical and psychological agonies: ". . . the most racking pains . . . a grinding in the bones, deadly nausea, and a horror of the spirit that cannot be exceeded at the hour of birth or death. . . ." As the transformations become more frequent, Hyde strikes spontaneously (without benefit of an inducing potion), producing in Jekyll a state of terror. Subsequently Hyde unleashes his fury against the venerable and fatherly Carew—who closely resembles Jekyll—killing him, and thus symbolically murdering Jekyll. Thereafter the spontaneous attacks of Hyde upon Jekyll increase, Hyde torturing Jekyll without cessation. Racked by sleeplessness lest Hyde come forth, Jekyll becomes progressively ". . . eaten up and emptied by fever, languidly weak both in body and mind," until in a final confrontation with Hyde, he relinquishes his grasp on life.

Jekyll's suffering is not wholly Hyde's doing. The encounters with Hyde are in fact invited by Dr. Jekyll. It is Jekyll who voluntarily, deliberately and with conscious forethought concocts, imbibes and re-imbibes the potion which calls up Mr. Hyde. As the transformations become spontaneous, Jekyll's invitations to Hyde become unconscious: all Jekyll has to do is relax control of his conscious mind (go to sleep or allow his thoughts to wander) and Hyde emerges.

If Jekyll is latently sadistic, he is manifestly masochistic, for he knows from the first transformation that in calling up Hyde he is courting his own destruction. He is impervious to the consequences of fulfilling his desires. In addition to the physical and mental anguish he suffers from the direct emergence of Hyde, Jekyll is engulfed in a sea of guilt, torn by remorse, overwhelmed by a sense of impending doom, rent by abhorrence and self-castigation—as a result of his own actions. But like Mina in *Dracula* who "did not want to hinder" the Count in his assault against her, so, too, Jekyll, when he gets the chance to renounce Hyde, to rid himself forever of Hyde, to destroy Hyde's effects and the potion that calls him up, fails to do so, attributing his inaction (like Mina's) to some unconscious "reservation," which may well have to do with the obvious pleasures Hyde at first brings to Jekyll: "There was something strange in my sensations; indescribably new . . . indescribably sweet. I felt younger, lighter, happier in body; I was conscious of a heady recklessness . . . a current of disordered sensual images. . . ." Thus Jekyll in effect issues a standing invitation to Hyde, which ultimately results in Jekyll's being broken in body and soul and retiring to his laboratory to finally yield to the ultimate masochism of suicide.

In the disguised sexuality of *Dr. Jekyll and Mr. Hyde,* it is implied that both men engage in an aberrant sexual relationship with each other and with others. Mr. Hyde's sexuality is laced with sadism, while Dr. Jekyll—vicariously participating in Hyde's sexual excesses through his own sadistic latency—wallows in masochistic guilt and, further, invites Hyde's assaults upon himself. But it is neither Hyde's sadism nor Jekyll's masochism alone that renders the sexuality aberrant: it is the indulgence of both. In the horror story sexual aberrancy lies in the sadomasochistic totality of both characters.

In *Frankenstein* the aberrant sexuality is present in the disguise forms of both implication and displacement. Like Mr. Hyde, the monster's outstanding trait is his propensity for violence. He sets fire to a family's cottage; he unjustly incriminates an innocent girl who is sent to the gallows; he ultimately murders Frankenstein's brother, best friend and bride. It is implied that the basis of these acts is sexual in nature. The monster himself explains his acts as an expression of thwarted sexuality: "If I have no ties, and no affections, hatred and vice must be my portion. . . ." And correspondingly, the cure for his acts is also of a sexual nature: ". . . the love of another will destroy the cause of my crimes" (i.e., the monster wants a mate). Thus, like Hyde's and Count Dracula's, the monster's assaults, mediated in manifest sadism, represent an expression of disguised aberrant sexuality.

The disguise form of displacement is also operative in *Frankenstein,* as illustrated in the following encounter:

> . . . suddenly I [Frankenstein] heard a shrill and dreadful scream. . . . the scream was repeated, and I rushed into the room . . . . She [Elizabeth] was there, lifeless and inanimate, thrown across the bed . . . [her] form flung by the murderer on its bridal bier. . . . The murderous mark of the fiend's grasp was on her neck. . . .

In this scene, which takes place on the honeymoon night of Victor Frankenstein and his bride Elizabeth, an act of murder displaces an act of expected sexual communion. The bridal bed becomes a bridal bier. The "mark" that was to signify loss of virginity is displaced by a mark (on the bride's neck) which signifies loss of life. Elizabeth, instead of dying in her husband's arms on their wedding night, literally dies at the hands of his alter ego, the monster.

While this expression of aberrant sexuality—the displacement of an act of love by an act of hate—is one of clear sadism, there is also an important masochistic component that makes this action possible on the part of Elizabeth: she has willingly entered into her marriage with Frankenstein, in the face of a "presentiment of evil," a "melancholy," a feeling of impending disaster. Elizabeth feels that she should not go through with the marriage, but for various reasons she fulfills her fiance's and her adoptive parents' wishes and ignores her own forebodings. Like other willing victims in tales of horror, Elizabeth, knowingly, yet powerless to reverse her course, rushes toward her own destruction.

The suffering of Frankenstein at the hands of the monster is also not wholly the monster's doing. The assaults of the monster are in fact invited by Dr. Frankenstein. It is Frankenstein who voluntarily, deliberately, and assiduously expends his time and energy in creating the monster. And it is Frankenstein who as "father-creator" is the first to reject his offspring because he is hideous. Frankenstein's latent sadism in rejecting his "son" in turn invites the monster's expressions of overt sadism. Subsequently, Frankenstein further encourages the monster by adopting a consciously futile "wait-and-see-maybe-he-will-go-away" attitude, and by still other means: recognizing only too well the monster's antagonism to him, he fails to warn his family or friends that they may be in danger—an act which leads to his brother's death. He fails also to confess the truth in the face of Justine's unmerited death sentence, an act in support of the monster, which leads to her execution. He begins to create and then destroys the mate which he knows to be the only way of rendering the monster harmless—an act that irrevocably enrages the monster. He chooses to keep from his bride the monster's threat to strike on their wedding night, an omission that results in her murder. These acts of invitation portray Frankenstein to be, like his counterpart, Dr. Jekyll, manifestly masochistic; for the terrible assaults of the monster are in the main wreaked against his creator, bringing upon Frankenstein untold physical and mental suffering, and finally leading to his spiritual and physical dissolution.

In *Frankenstein* once again the aberrant sexuality of the metaphysical encounter is expressed in the total sadomasochism of both monster and victim alike. The sadism, unmistakably present, together with its mirror-image of masochism just under the surface, combine to produce a theater of aberrant sexual violence that typifies all tales of horror—whether or not the sexuality is readily apparent.

In the horror story sadomasochistic sexuality is aberrant because it is deathly sexuality. Sex as an act of life and pleasure is transformed into an act of pain and suffering. The sexuality of metaphysical encounters in horror stories is the sexuality of death and pain. This transformation of sexuality into an act of death and pain represents a superimposition of opposites—death upon life—itself capable of inspiring profound horror.

But if the sexual aberrancy of horror stories is a function of deathly sexuality, it is also a function of the relationships of the participants. For in tales of horror the metaphysical encounters take place between "family members," between the older man or father figure, the young man or son figure, and the young woman or daughter-mother figure. Thus the father advances against the daughter or son; the mother does likewise against the son or daughter; someone or something "older" attacks someone or something "younger." Since in reality, however, these encounters are sexual assaults, in the horror story the father is *sexually assaulting* the daughter or son; the mother is *sexually assaulting* the son or daughter; a symbolic parent is *sexually assaulting* a symbolic member of the younger generation. Metaphysical encounters of the horror story are thus sexually aberrant not only by virtue of their deathly, i.e., sadomasochistic, sexuality, but also by virtue of their incestuous sexuality.

In *Dracula* an incestuous configuration relates the Count, the "father" and chief metaphysical figure, to Mina, the "daughter." During the encounter in which the Count sucks Mina's throat and he forces her to suck the opened vein in his chest, he affirms the close "familial" nature of their relationship by declaring: ". . . you . . . are now to me, flesh of my flesh; blood of my blood; kin of my kin. . . ." Incestuous encounters are also represented between the Count and Lucy. For example, Mina has discovered that Lucy has walked in her sleep to a meeting with Dracula in an old graveyard. The incestuous nature of the attack by the Count (an older man assaulting the young) is underscored by the fact that Lucy is symbolically seeking her own deceased father, who was also a sleepwalker and who would be in a graveyard.

Lucy eventually becomes a vampire and as such returns as a metaphysical figure to attack a little boy. The incestuousness of this encounter is implied not only by the respective ages of the participants, but also by the direct characterization of Lucy as a "carnal and unspiritual" being assaulting the child in a "voluptuous, wanton and cruel," i.e., "sexual," fashion: "The sweetness of Lucy was turned to adamantine, heartless cruelty and the purity to voluptuous wantonness. . . . the lips were crimson with fresh blood. . . . her eyes blazed with unholy light, and the face became wreathed with a voluptuous smile. With a careless motion, she flung to the ground . . . the child . . . growling over it. . . . The child gave a sharp cry and lay there moaning."

An incestuous configuration is also represented between Lucy, as a vampire, and her earthly fiance, Arthur, the incestuous nature of the encounter being achieved through the fact that Lucy is "dead" and death represents the primordial. Lucy thus represents the "old"—the "mother"— attacking Arthur, no longer her contemporary but in juxtaposition to her immortality, a member of the younger generation (the "son"): ". . . she advanced to him with outstretched arms and a wanton smile . . . he fell back and hid his face in his hands. She still advanced . . . and with a languorous, voluptuous grace said: 'Come to me, Arthur. . . . My arms are hungry for you. Come, we can rest together. Come, my husband, come.' There was something diabolically sweet in her tones. . . . Arthur . . . seemed under a spell; moving his hands from his face, he opened wide his arms. She was leaping for them. . . ."

A symbolic incestuous configuration even develops between Mina and her husband, Jonathan, as she relates to him the events of the Count's attack on her. During the narrative Jonathan begins to age, his hair turning white. Jonathan's abnormal aging thus projects him as a father figure to Mina, rather than her husband.

In *Frankenstein* the primary incestuous configuration is between Frankenstein and his symbolic mother. In Frankenstein's psyche his fiancee Elizabeth is psychologically interchangeable with his mother. (In Frankenstein's dream Elizabeth becomes his mother.) Elizabeth is in fact cast as a substitute mother to the Frankenstein family: she takes care of the children, performs motherly duties for the family, and ministers to Frankenstein's father. On their wedding night Frankenstein is to engage in sexual relations with his surrogate mother, Elizabeth. The sexual act, ostensibly between bride and groom, thus becomes a symbolically incestuous act between mother and son. The incestuous nature of this scene is underscored by the fact that it is the monster, Frankenstein's alter ego but also his "offspring" and "son," with whom this scene is consummated.

Justine, Elizabeth's contemporary and best friend, also functions as a symbolic mother to Frankenstein (Justine is nursemaid to Frankenstein's little brother). Coming upon her sleeping form, Frankenstein, through his alter ego, the monster—his "son" or "offspring"—wishes to make love to her, thus placing the two in an incestuous configuration. In addition, at this time he places the picture of Frankenstein's real mother on Justine's body, further reinforcing this configuration.

The incestuous sexuality between the triad figures is also manifest in: *The Wendigo* (an animistic mother assaults the guide Défago); *The Beckoning Fair One* (a female ghost equated with the young man's grandmother sexually attacks the young man); *The Room in the Tower* (the mother of an acquaintance sexually attacks the young man); *An Account of Some Strange Disturbances in Aungier Street* (the uncle as father surrogate attacks the young man); *The White Powder* (the brother assaults the sister); *Carmilla* (the adoptive sister attacks the younger sister).

In summary, the sexuality of metaphysical encounters in tales of horror is both deathly and incestuous, the sexual assaults taking place between members of the family triad. Monster attack is incest assault, primarily between parent and child, expressed in the sadomasochism of death, pain and destruction. It is this deathly sexuality vectored toward the destruction of life and the life force that defines and gives meaning to the horror in the horror story.

CHAPTER FOURTEEN

Horror in the Christ Story

LIKE THE HORROR STORY, THE CHRIST STORY APPEALS TO diverse segments of civilized societies. Its attraction transcends broad socioeconomic, cultural and even religious groups. Rich and poor, learned and ignorant, young and old, generation after generation respond to its powerful drama, sweeping action and memorable personalities, to its miracles, metaphysics and supernaturalism. Despite seeming differences, the Christ story and the horror story are remarkably parallel, sharing similarities of structure, function and content. Their physical and psychological settings are similar; their characterizations are similar; their elements of plot are similar. Moreover, both have irresistible appeal. In the horror story the appeal lies in its horror. Is there a similar element in the Christ story?

An exploration into the nature of the metaphysical encounter represented by the Christ story may reveal an answer to this question.

Encounters in the Christ story take place principally between members of the triad configuration—between God the Father, Jesus the Son and the Virgin Mary (the older man or chief metaphysical figure, the young man or developing metaphysical figure and the young woman, the representative of goodness and innocence). In the Christ story the triad participants comprise a family constellation, God being the father figure, Jesus the son figure and the Virgin Mary the daughter-mother figure. No matter what the encounter—whether between God and Jesus, between God and Mary, between Mary and Jesus, or their auxiliaries—it is clear that the episode takes place within this Holy Family.

Encounters in the Christ story may, as in the horror story, take place between the earthly and nonearthly and may be characterized into several types or gradations. In the first or psychological encounter, a contest of wills takes place in which psychological pain is inflicted by the nonearthly figure upon the earthly figure.

Illustrative of this type of encounter is Jesus' temptation by the devil (Matthew 4:1–11). In this episode God the Father sends His messenger, the Holy Spirit, to bring Jesus into contact with the devil: "Then Jesus was led . . . into the wilderness to be tempted by the devil." After Jesus' fast of forty days and forty nights, the devil appears and attempts to entice him with three temptations—riches, fame and power.

> . . . the devil took him [Jesus] to a very high mountain and showed him all the kingdoms of the world . . . and he said . . . "All these I will give you, if you fall down and worship me."

In this scene the powerful nonearthly figure (the devil) psychologically assaults the earthly figure (Jesus) through the temptations he puts before his victim. After a struggle of wills, however, Jesus emerges victorious, declaring to his attacker: "Begone, Satan! for it is written, 'You shall worship the Lord your God and him only shall you serve.'" Even so, Jesus suffers psychological pain from this encounter, as evidenced by the fact that after the devil left him ". . . angels came and ministered to him."

A psychological encounter occurs between Jesus and his mother, Mary, at Cana (John 2:1–11). Mary initiates events by informing her Son that the wedding feast is out of wine. Implicit in her remark is the demand that Jesus do something about it. Jesus responds sharply and negatively: "Woman, what have you to do with me?" Jesus finally acquiesces to Mary's request by performing "the first of his signs." In this encounter Jesus is caused apparent psychological stress, reflected not only in his initial reluctance to accede to his Mother's wishes ("My hour has not yet come"), but in his apparent grasp of his ultimate fate once "the first of his signs" launches him on his course.

A second kind of encounter, the physical encounter, is illustrated by the baptism of Jesus (Matthew 3:13–17), in which the physical immersion of Jesus takes place in the River Jordan under metaphysical circumstances. The baptism itself is initiated by Jesus' accession to the Will of the Father. "Let it be so now; for thus it is fitting for us to fulfil all righteousness," declares Jesus. Immediately after immersion there is an exchange between him and his Father in which he is portrayed as being actually physically touched by God's special envoy, the Holy Spirit, in the form of a dove: ". . . [Jesus] saw the Spirit of God descending like a dove, and alighting on him. . . ." And the voice of God issues from heaven: "This is my beloved Son, with whom I am well pleased." At face value this encounter seems to level no malevolence at Jesus—quite the contrary: God is "well pleased" with Jesus' baptism, the symbol of Jesus' willingness to go forth with his mission. But the end of Jesus' mission, in accordance with the Divine Plan (God's Will)—is his violent physical destruction at Calvary. Thus the encounter in which

God is pleased with Jesus' baptism ultimately implies a corresponding pleasure in the unfolding of his ministry, which ends with Jesus' physical torture and death. As in the horror story, the physical encounter with the nonearthly ends in the wreaking of physical violence upon the earthly.

The Transfiguration of Jesus (Luke 9:28–32) represents a third kind of encounter in the Christ story, characterized by a combination of the foregoing. In this encounter Jesus comes into both physical and psychological contact with God and with the ghosts of Moses and Elijah. Jesus, taking with him the disciples Peter, John and James, goes "up on the mountain to pray." And while in prayer, an act that invokes the presence of his Father, Jesus becomes physically transformed: ". . . the appearance of his countenance was altered, and his raiment became dazzling white." The spirits of Moses and Elijah convey to Jesus his impending fate (his suffering and death) which "he was to accomplish at Jerusalem." This fate, moreover, is emphasized by God Himself as Jesus and his disciples are enveloped by the heavenly cloud in which the Father reaffirms the final events of His Son's Divine Mission. Thus, as in the horror story, the combined physical and psychological encounter portrays the emerging metaphysical figure—Jesus is designated by Peter as the Messiah at the Transfiguration—in a kind of double jeopardy: Jesus is both physically marked as a result of his confrontation with the non-earthly and psychologically imperiled by the prophecy of his coming destruction.[1]

Yet a further kind of encounter is illustrated by the following:

And there appeared to him [Zechariah] an angel of the Lord. . . . And Zechariah was troubled when he saw him, and fear fell upon him. But the angel said to him, "Do not be afraid, Zechariah, for your prayer is heard, and your wife Elizabeth will bear you a son, and you shall call his name John." . . . And

Zechariah said to the angel, "How shall I know this? For I am an old man, and my wife is advanced in years." And the angel answered him, "I am Gabriel, who stand in the presence of God; and I was sent to speak to you, and to bring you this good news." . . . After these days his wife Elizabeth conceived . . . saying, "Thus the Lord has done to me . . . to take away my reproach among men."

—*Luke 1:11–25*

And [the angel Gabriel] came to her [Mary] and said, "Hail, O favored one, the Lord is with you!" . . . "Do not be afraid, Mary, for you have found favor with God. And behold, you will conceive in your womb and bear a son, and you shall call his name Jesus." . . .And Mary said to the angel, "How can this be, since I have no husband?" And the angel said to her, "The Holy Spirit will come upon you, and the power of the Most High will overshadow you; therefore the child to be born will be called holy, the Son of God."

—*Luke 1:28–35*

The above two depictions can be characterized as metaphysical encounters of a "sexual" nature, since each involves the conception of a child as a result of the intervention of the chief metaphysical figure (through His principal representative, the Holy Spirit). The element of sexuality, here nearly overt, is depicted in other metaphysical encounters of the Christ story as a love relationship. Whether disguised, oblique, subtle or more concrete, this love relationship between triad members of the Holy Family—between God the Father and Mary, between God the Father and Jesus, between Mary and Jesus—is omnipresent. Its expression, conscious or unconscious, provides for a degree of the fascination of the Christ story.

But disquietude merges with the expression of love in the metaphysical encounter of the Christ story. For, as in the horror story, it must be remembered that it is a member of the older generation—the older man or older woman—who advances toward a member of the younger generation. For example, it is God the Father who in the Annunciation approaches Mary the daughter; it is God the Father who draws near to Jesus the Son—at Jesus' baptism, in his encounter with the devil, at his Transfiguration, at Gethsemane and at Calvary. It is Mary the Mother who, as the older figure, presses upon her Son at Cana.

And, as in the horror story, it is typically a member of the younger generation who invites the older figure into a metaphysical encounter. Thus Mary in the Annunciation finds favor with God. Jesus, despite the most onerous forebodings, actively pursues the fulfillment of the Divine Will. And again at Cana Jesus performs his miracle, despite his manifest reluctance.

Variation in the generational roles of the triad participants is also a feature of the Christ story. Mary is both daughter (in the Annunciation) and mother (at Cana). Her agelessness and perpetual youth cast her also as a contemporary of Jesus. Jesus, as God Incarnate, functions also as a contemporary of his Father. As a child, held in abeyance since the beginning of time (representing the primordial), Jesus functions additionally as an older figure to Mary. However, despite the apparent age changes, the earthly figure of the triad is invariably presented as the younger, less metaphysically powerful and limited by earthly laws and time, as opposed to the nonearthly figure who is metaphysically all-powerful, unlimited and timeless. Thus in the Christ story, as in the horror story, no matter what the apparent generational configurations within the triad, symbolically it is always a member of the older generation who advances toward a member of the younger generation.

Apart from the generational nature of its participants, the love relationship of the metaphysical encounter of the Christ story is also not normal. It is aberrant, in the same way that sexuality is aberrant in the horror story. And it contains the same core of misgiving. The aberrant sexuality of the Christ story can be glimpsed only when the love relationship of the metaphysical encounter is divested of its disguise mechanisms and is viewed in the context of related metaphysical encounters.

In the Christ story the Annunciation constitutes an aberrant love relationship. The basic sexuality of this passage (it recounts the conception of the Son of God) is atypical in view of its participants. Yet this atypical feature merely masks a more fundamental aberrancy, inherent in the admixture of anxiety and acceptance on the part of the earthly figure, to the event thrust upon her by the nonearthly figure. The aberrant dynamics of this encounter, though subtle, are rendered obvious in their comparison to the very same mechanisms at work in the horror story. For example, in Mary's encounter with God in the Annunciation and Mina's encounter with Dracula (in *Dracula*) the following similitudes emerge:

Both young women are virginal, engaged or wed to another at the time of their encounter with the chief metaphysical figure. Mina is a young virgin model wed to Jonathan Harker at the time of her metaphysical encounter with Dracula. Mary is a young virgin betrothed to a man named Joseph at the time of her metaphysical encounter with God.

In both instances it is the metaphysical figure who is attracted to the young woman. Mina first captures the Count's attention in one of her recurrent visits to a churchyard. Likewise, the angel Gabriel informs Mary that she has "found favor with God."

The sexual nature of both encounters is atypical. Mina's encounter with Dracula is disguised by corporeal displacement, Mary's encounter with God, by incorporeal displacement ("The Holy Spirit will come upon you . . . "). The encounters are additionally atypical in that they represent sexuality between a mortal and a supernatural being (Mina and Count Dracula, Mary and God the Father).

Both young women react to their encounters with fear. Mina suffers a "great fear"; she is "terrified." Mary is "greatly troubled." (She is told by the angel Gabriel, "Do not be afraid.")

The fear of both women is compounded by reminders issued to them by the chief metaphysical figure, which serve to emphasize his power. Mina is reminded by the Count of the fate of "the others," including her best friend, Lucy (they were vampirized). Mary is reminded by the angel Gabriel of the fate of her cousin and contemporary, Elizabeth (she becomes miraculously pregnant).

In the aftermath of their encounters, both women are portrayed as physically marked: Mina bears a scar, Mary bears a child. Both are wed to father figures: Mina is married to the "older man," Jonathan (his hair has turned white); Mary is married to Joseph, who in fact is an older man. Both are mothers of extraordinary personages: Mina's son Quincey is the embodiment of Jonathan's "god-like" comrades; Mary's son Jesus is the embodiment of God.

The equivalency of Mary and Mina becomes discernible through this comparison. Even the metaphysical encounters themselves are seen to be functional equivalents. But it is in the outstanding psychological response of each young woman—fear—that the aberrant psychodynamics underlying one encounter, are seen also to underlie the other.

In his reminder to Mina of the fate of "the others," the Count makes clear that unless she complies with his wishes, a similar or worse fate will befall her. No such enjoinder is apparent in Gabriel's reminder to Mary as it applies to her cousin Elizabeth (i.e., Elizabeth's conception did not result from noncompliance with the angel's wishes). But in his reminder to Mary of the fate of Elizabeth, the angel also (indirectly) alludes to the fate of Elizabeth's husband (Zechariah)—who was struck dumb, "silent and unable to speak," simply because he "did not believe [in the angel's] words" (Luke 1:20). Thus reminded of the outcome of Zechariah's mere doubts concerning the angel's pronouncements—(Zechariah's fate was common knowledge [Luke 1:21–22,65] and therefore well known to Mary at the time of the angel's visitation to her)—Mary is made pointedly aware of the possible consequences to herself of a similar noncompliance. Effectively, she is given the same kind of choice as Mina, or Zechariah, as she declares to the angel: "Let it be to me. . . ."

The psychodynamics of the Annunciation accordingly reveal the presence of an irresistible force, represented by the angel Gabriel, and the fear-ridden ("afraid," "greatly troubled") earthly figure of the young woman who is quite aware of the alternative to compliance with the angel's wishes. Mary's consent to the angel is given under these circumstances, in the virtual absence of any freedom of choice, or recourse. Thus, in a very real sense, the Will of the Father is forced upon Mary. Her compliance, obedience and submission are forced compliance, forced obedience, forced submission—and the resultant sexuality, forced sexuality. However, like her counterpart Mina who is masochistic in allowing herself to be used for Dracula's purposes, Mary exhibits a similar idiosyncrasy of character in allowing herself to become an instrument of God's purposes, no matter what the circumstances. In so doing she destroys a part of her human[2] self.

In essence the same devices of a forced sexual act and its willing acceptance which are at the core of aberrant sexuality in the horror story are also present in Annunciation. Specifically, the powerful demand of the Father, although disguised by displacement, and the fearful, though willing, compliance of the young virgin constitute the underlying dynamics of this metaphysical encounter. The sexuality of the Annunciation, atypical by virtue of its disguise mechanisms and its participants, is also aberrant by virtue of the subtle sadomasochistic interplay between the partners.

The love relationship between God the Father and Jesus the Son also finds atypical expression within their metaphysical encounters. In the New Testament, God is recurrently depicted as referring to His Son as "beloved," while Jesus reciprocates in his espousal of what he terms "the first" commandment: ". . . and you shall love the Lord your God with all your heart, and with all your soul. . . ." (Mark 12:30). The gospels thus depict the relationship between the Father and the Son as one of mutual love. However, in the implementation of the Divine Plan as revealed in encounters between Father and Son, it is the Will of the Father that repeatedly initiates the infliction of physical and psychological pain and suffering upon the Son. It is God the Father, via the Holy Spirit, who calls Jesus to his mission of self-sacrifice at his baptism; who leads Jesus into the wilderness to suffer the psychological assaults of the devil; who transfigures Jesus, concomitantly marking him for death. And it is God the Father, for whom "all things are possible," who stands unbending to the pleas of His Son at Gethsemane, and at Calvary when Jesus cries, "My God, my God, why hast thou forsaken me?" (Matthew 27:46). In each successive encounter it is the Will of the Father that causes Jesus' increasing suffering and pain—which finally culminates in his violent death.

Correspondingly, in the willing pursuit of his mission of self-sacrifice, Jesus actively seeks out his own dissolution. He consents to baptism, follows the Holy Spirit into the wilderness in a confrontation with the devil, repeatedly and deliberately invokes the irreversible Will of his Father in prayer—in the process calling down upon himself physical and psychological privation (fasting, sweating blood)—in the knowledge that his every attempt to fulfill the Divine Will will result in pain, suffering and eventual death. In assenting to be an accessory to every aspect and detail of his doom, Jesus in effect aids and abets his own destruction.

Thus in the Christ story the love relationship between Jesus and God finds manifest expression in an accelerating exchange of pain inflicted and suffering received. The imposition of pain by the Father and its willing acceptance by the Son, render this relationship of "fidelity and devotion" aberrant and deathly in the same manner as within the horror story: namely, in the sadomasochistic expression of love.

The love relationship[3] between Mary and Jesus, celebrated throughout the New Testament, the New Testament Apocrypha, and the arts as the epitome of perfect love, likewise finds atypical expression within the two gospel encounters in which both Mary and her Son are portrayed as adults: at Cana where Jesus emerges as a metaphysical figure; and at Calvary where Jesus is the crucified God. At Cana Mary assumes her prerogative as Mother of God and, by implication, requests that Jesus do something about the wine that has failed. But Jesus responds with negativity and initial noncompliance: ". . . woman, what have you to do with me?" Taking no heed of his apparent painful state of mind that her request has occasioned in her Son, Mary nevertheless persists: she in effect recognizes no choice but that her Son comply with her wishes. At Cana, it becomes the Will of the Mother which, out of love, compels the Son to perform publicly the first of his signs, thereby launching him on his subsequent ministry of progressive pain and suffering. Moreoever, what Mary helps to initiate at Cana, she helps end at Calvary. As Co-Redemptress of mankind, Mary becomes an active participant in her Son's death: ". . . she . . . was . . . entrusted with the task of tendering and nourishing this Victim [Jesus] and even offering it on the altar at the appointed time" (Pope Pius X); ". . . [she] offer[ed Christ] at the foot of the Cross as Victim for our sins . . ." (Pope Pius XI); "She offered up her

Son to the divine Justice dying with Him in her heart" (Pope Leo XIII). Thus in both instances of their adult exchanges, Mary's love for her Son finds expression in the ultimate infliction upon him of pain, suffering and death.

And as Jesus must accede to the Will of the Father in order to fulfill the Divine Plan, for the same reason he must also accede to the Will of the Mother. At Cana, despite the apparent inclination toward self-preservation in his initial refusal, Jesus obediently yields to his Mother's Will, overtly sanctioning his course of pain and suffering. At Calvary, as pain is inflicted upon Jesus in the presence of Mary, Jesus accepts even this fate in love—commending his mother to the unnamed disciple.

Thus at Cana and at Calvary the love relationship between Mary and Jesus finds atypical expression in the same manner as the love relationship between God the Father and Jesus: in an exchange of pain inflicted and suffering received. At Cana, out of love Mary initiates Jesus to his fateful mission; out of love he complies. At Calvary, out of love Mary "immolate[s] the Son" (Benedict XV); while out of love Jesus responds with willing acceptance. The expression of love between Mary and Jesus, like that between God the Father and Jesus, becomes a relationship of pain and death—a relationship that turns aberrant in the same manner as the relationship of sexuality in the horror story: that is, through sadomasochism within the family constellation of the triad.

In effect, the three triad relationships of the Christ story—between God the Father and Mary, between God the Father and Jesus, between Mary the Mother and Jesus—all take place in a context of love, the expression of which becomes aberrant by virtue of its sadomasochistic content.

But if the aberrancy of the Christ story is a function of the love relationship turned toward death through sadomasochism, it is also a function of the kin-relationships of the participants. In the Christ story, as in the horror story, the metaphysical encounters take place between family members. God the Father "approaches" Mary the daughter; God the Father "approaches" Jesus the Son; Mary the Mother "approaches" Jesus the Son. These encounters between triad members of the Holy Family are in reality acts of assault, for in moving toward the younger member, the older member wreaks fear, suffering and death. Thus encounters within the Christ story, as in the horror story, represent primal assaults of parent against child. The father figure assaults the daughter or son figure, the mother figure assaults the son figure (the older figure assaults the younger figure), such assaults occuring with the context of a love relationship. In the Christ story, as in the horror story, the relationship between triad members is one of incest and death.

Thus the metaphysical encounters of the Christ story, directly congruent to those of the horror story, are at heart incestuous and deathly, manifest in sadomasochistic assaults taking place among family members of the Holy Family. Mary's encounter with God in the Annunciation, Jesus' multiple encounters with his Father and his adult encounters with his Mother constitute confrontations between parent and child, expressed in terms of pain, destruction and death. It is this deathly love, leading toward the destruction of life and the life force, that is the essence of horror in both stories.

CHAPTER FIFTEEN

Incest

BIOLOGY TEACHES THAT AS ALL LIVING THINGS DEVELOP they repeat their ancestral evolution. This means that many of the primitive systems of lower animals in the chain of life are temporarily re-created during the development of the embryo. A human embryo passes through fish-like, amphibian and reptilian phases before attaining its definitive state. In a sense each individual relives in a microcosm of time an evolutionary process that took millions of year. For example, at a certain point in development the human embryo has a tail—a temporary survival from our ancestral past—which dissolves. At another point gills of the embryo give rise to the thymus and parathyroid glands. A new individual is born with old organs—organs that no longer serve their original purpose and have fallen into apparent disuse. Yet these vestigial organs (the tonsils, the appendix and nearly two hundred others within the human body) persist. Sometimes, too, features normally dropped during development suddenly reappear due to peculiar genetic factors ("ancestral reversions").

The theory of physical recapitulation of our ancestry may

also hold true in the psychological realm. Perhaps an individual must ascend his family tree not only physically but psychologically, too. It may be that in the embryo's psychological development it relives the evolutionary process of the mind's development, recapitulating the psychological history of the species. As a result of this process a new individual might be left with a psychological memory of his ancestral past. Further, just as every human being has vestigal, nonfunctioning organs, so too may an individual have vestigal patterns of behavior that are latent rather than manifest—primitive, atavistic traits no longer serving their original purposes, repressed but still present—which, as in ancestral reversion, can become overt under special conditions.

The primal sexuality of our first forebears was of necessity incestuous in nature, probably a pattern repeated over long periods of time and becoming indelible in the psyche of early man. With the passage of time this first sexuality became unnecessary to human survival, and as human beings multiplied and diversified into groups—tribes and families—incest became anathema to its original purposes and to the very foundations of social structure and order.

In the course of evolution the first sexuality of man's conscious mind has become disused and repressed, and is now the sexuality of the unconscious mind. But like a vestigial organ that still persists, this ancestral pattern of behavior also endures. Its almost universal presence is attested to by its almost universal taboo. The very potency of the incest taboo suggests that the psychological circuits of this ancient sexuality are still open, sometimes running in peculiar channels of disguise, and sometimes, under special conditions, reverting to overt expression.

Incest today is defined as sexual intercourse between persons related by blood within degrees in which marriage is prohibited. This includes sexual relations between father and daughter, mother and son, brother and sister, half-siblings who share a common parent, grandparent-grandchild, uncle-niece, aunt-nephew and, in some instances, first cousins. Incest is also commonly extended to include the sexuality of persons who are perceived to be in immediate familial relationship to one another. This includes overt sexuality between stepparent and stepchild, guardian and ward, persons raised as brother and sister—in short, sexual relations between any parent figure and child figure who are in close familial configuration.

Incest may find psychological, rather than physical, expression. In the wake of maturation the primal sexuality of incest may remain repressed and unresolved to varying degrees, rather than be resolved and deflected outside the immediate family. In psychological incest the physical possession of overt sexuality becomes the psychological possession of one family (triad) member by another. In this instance, sexual union between kin becomes replaced by psychological bondage between these family members. Some examples of psychological incest are: the mother who seeks to possess her son, to isolate him, to make him dependent on her, to make herself the central woman in his life while systematically excluding the father; the father who is attracted to his daughter, is domineering, is jealous of and rude to his daughter's beaux—or overly permissive, her indiscriminate ally, indulgent of her every desire, seeking to become the man in his daughter's life by making her "his" girl while systematically excluding the mother. Configurations of psychological incest also include two female figures in the family triad who are in competition for the male (one female seeks to destroy the other by various psychological means); two male triad figures in competition for the female (one male seeks to destroy the other); a brother and sister, deserted by the parents, clinging to each other for affection and security; a divorced or widowed parent looking upon the child as a substitute mate; the overly attached or self-sacrificing orientation of a child to parent (or parent to child). Psychological incest is charged with conflict—with fear, guilt, anxiety, feelings of inner imprisonment, irresistible attraction, unbreakable ties, comminglings of love and hate, dependency and rejection. In psychological incest, incest desire is countered by incest repression; incest pursuit is countered by incest flight.

Incest is also defined by its taboo. In societies literate and nonliterate the injunction against sexual relations between close family members represents one of the most powerful and prevalent prohibitions of man. Though lost to antiquity, the origins of this prohibition are thought to be more than man-made. *Taboo* refers to the forbidden, and in this case to the sacredly forbidden. Its origins are therefore associated with the metaphysical, with a proscription from the gods, with a proscription from God. Scriptural prohibition against incest occurs in the Old Testament—principally in Leviticus 18. Extensive church interdictions, particularly during the fifteenth century, have reinforced the taboo against incest. Today, although a criminal offense punishable by law, incest has retained its aura of metaphysical prohibition: it is regarded as a crime of special enormity, a moral crime, a crime outside nature, against natural law, against God Himself. In an age where some traditional concepts of sin have been eroded away, the taboo against incest still remains unchallenged: it is still the archetypal sin, and those who partake of this sin are regarded as spiritual lepers.

Incest evokes retribution. Freud, in his use of Sophocle's *Oedipux Rex,* describes the personal disaster attendant upon violation of the incest taboo:

Oedipus falls in love and weds Jocasta, unaware she is his natural mother. As a result of this union the country is struck by blight and misfortune. When Oedipus finally discovers he is the "heir to his father's bed, shedder of his father's blood," blindness and banishment become his fate, while his mother kills herself.

The consequences of incest are death. Suicide, murder, blight, sterility, blindness, banishment—physical and spiritual death—have long been associated with the incest taboo.

The power of any taboo indicates the strength of the urge it seeks to suppress. The urge to commit incest must be regarded as powerful, for despite the strength of the incest taboo and the consequences of its violation, its expression in contemporary society has endured without interruption.[1]

Perhaps nowhere is the expression of incest more evident than in two of the most popular literary forms, forms that maintain the association between incest and death: the horror story and the Christ story. The theme of incest is present in virtually every aspect of these stories. It is woven into the fabric of their settings and characterizations, their incidents, their action and function. Ubiquitous and amorphous, incest lies at the very heart of the horror story and the Christ story.

The backgrounds and settings of both stories, for example, recreate a time of the beginning—a time of the primal sexuality of incest. The Edenesque settings of the horror story endow the main character (the hero, usually the young man) with a "first-man"-like quality as he enters their domain; while against similar backgrounds of the Christ story, Jesus likewise presides as the New Adam. These settings, primordial, eternal, cut off from civilization and law, serve to recreate the psychological time of the unconscious mind, within which the memory of ancestral sexuality—immutable, intact, compelling—lies ready to manifest itself again.

These settings, moreover, are menacing. In the horror story they are natural (or symbolically natural)—wild, destructive, ominous, ruled by forces over which man has no control and to which he is prey. The apocalyptic settings of the Christ story are equally threatening, portraying a nature that can and does go awry, disastrous upheavals and—with the advent of Kingdom Come—the metaphysical cataclysm of the Day of Destruction.

Thus the backgrounds of both stories, by setting the stage for the reenactment of early ancestral sexuality, are not only in themselves incest-laden but make the association between incest and death, an association that becomes overt within the metaphysical encounter of each of these stories.

Characterization also figures substantially in incest expression. The chief characters of both stories are set in a classical incest configuration: the family triad of father, mother and child. This triad, despite variations, is present throughout the horror literature—as well as represented in the Christ story by the Holy Family of God the Father, Jesus the Son and Mary the Mother. Moreover, incest is represented by these figures not only in their incest configuration but also in that they belong to groups which are traditionally exempt from the incest taboo: namely, the gods, royalty and the specially privileged.

Historically, incest was the special prerogative of the gods and royal personages. The mythology and primitive religions of ancient time recount the many incestuous unions between deities: Kronus and Rhea (father-daughter), Ishtar and Tammuz (mother-son) and Isis and Osiris (sister-brother). Incest as a religious expression was often made obligatory in the rites of fertility religions, especially upon those individuals who reenacted the roles of the central deities of these cults. For example, in ancient Rome the Vestal Virgins, among whom were often the king's daughters (or members of his household), engaged in a marriage ceremony with the king when he masqueraded as the god. Likewise, in ancient Egypt it was often the king's sister who married her brother when he appeared as the god-incarnate. In ancient Africa the king of Gabon married his daughters, while the queen wed her eldest son; in South America Incan princesses married their brothers; in ancient Persia incestuous unions within royal families were required; in ancient Egypt the Ptolemaic dynasty produced every type of incestuous union; incest marriages between siblings were also practices in ancient Greece and Rome.

Incest has also been sanctioned to certain individuals for special reasons: the perpetuation of the race (Lot and his daughters, Genesis 19:30); the insurance of victory in battle (Derri warriors of ancient Africa with their mothers and sisters); a cure for sterility and venereal disease (among the peasantry in parts of Eastern Europe); a means of keeping the blood lines pure (among royalty and privileged classes); for holy purposes (within the context of ancient religion).

In the horror story and the Christ story the major triad figures—godlike characters, royalty and others—are similarly indicated as being incest exempt (they belong to a privileged class, they have an illustrious genealogy often associated with special parentage, and so forth). In the horror story these figures are generally represented by those who have control over life and death: doctors, scientists, clergy, as well as others (Dr. Van Helsing, a priestlike metaphysician of *Dracula;* Drs. Frankenstein and Jekyll; Count Dracula; Mina, an orphan [person of special genealogy]). In the Christ story the three major triad figures fulfill every criterion of those traditionally associated with incest: all are godlike (God Himself; Jesus, Son of God; Mary, Mother of God), and all are members of royalty and have an illustrious genealogy (King of the Universe, Prince of Peace, Queen of Heaven, House of David).

Auxiliary characters, too, mediate incest in both stories by functioning as proxies, substitutes and surrogates for the major triad figures: Doctor Seward, entitled Lord Godalming (godlike), John the Baptist (special genealogy), the Apostles (privileged, godlike). A special variant of auxiliary character—the foreigner, the outsider, sinners, the sick, the insane, criminals, those who are different—additionally underscores incest by embodying a freedom that is deviant with respect to social conventions. Quincey Morris, the American, represents freedom of spirit; the gypsy Justine embodies freedom from inhibition; Mary Magdalen suggests (reformed) sexual freedom. This deviance of psychological and physical freedom in itself acts as a surrogate for the archetypal deviation of incest, distinguishing the auxiliary characters, like their proxies, as being outside the confines of conventionality and likewise immune from the incest taboo.

Auxiliary characters serve to foreshadow the consequences of incest which ultimately overtake the major triad figures. In *Frankenstein,* Elizabeth's surrogate, Justine, is executed; in *Dracula,* Mina's surrogate, Lucy, is vampirized; in *Dr. Jekyll and Mr. Hyde,* the murder of the fatherly Carew presages the fate of Jekyll himself. Likewise in the Christ story, Mary's surrogate, Saint Elizabeth, becomes miraculously pregnant.

The auxiliary character of a child also serves to herald the results of incest. Whether in the form of unusual offspring (gods, kings, atypically good or evil beings) or of symbolic or actual pregnancy, the child serves as an embodiment and reminder that incest has occurred. For example, in *The Shuttered Room* an incestuous union between cousins results in a batrachian baby monster. Little William of *Frankenstein,* an atypically good child, is the symbolic incestuous offspring of Dr. Frankenstein and his mother surrogate, Elizabeth. Lucy in *Dracula* is shown with child ("cradling"—in reality vampirizing—a baby) after her encounter with her "father" (the Count); Mina conceives after Jonathan's hair turns white (symbolically, he becomes her father). And in the Christ story both Elizabeth and Mary deliver an unusual child after their encounter with the Father.

The expression of incest in both stories is a function of the triad characterization and interrelationships. Within a context of love or disguised sexuality the older parent figure advances upon or toward the younger child figure. In the horror story the incestuous nature of the assault upon a family member is easily perceived once the disguise mechanisms of displacement and implication are removed; such an incestuous assault is perhaps best exemplifed in *Dracula,* in which the Count as the older man physically forces Mina as the young woman to engage in acts (cf. Chapter 13) which are at once both sexual and deviant.

In the Christ story the incestuous nature of the encounters between generational triad members is more difficult to apprehend because of the complex nature of the disguise forms. While the sexuality of the Holy Spirit's coming upon Mary and thus causing her to conceive may be to an extent obvious, there is a more pertinent relationship of incest within this story—that which involves the two earthly members of the triad, Mother Mary and Son Jesus. Hidden in shifted frames of allegorical reference, this relationship—once uncovered—imparts to the Christ story a virtual core of incest.

An insight into the relationship between Mother and Son is provided by a most intriguing yet puzzling and atypical event in the Christ story, the wedding at Cana. A source of extensive commentary as to its possible significance, it continues to inspire various theological interpretations. It is atypical in that it is recounted only in John (2:1–11), being entirely and singularly absent in the synoptic gospels of Matthew, Mark and Luke (i.e., no parallel accounts). It is puzzling because taken at face value it fails to reconcile certain difficulties: the somber rather than joyous mood of the occasion ("My hour has not yet come"); the portrayal of the main figures seemingly out of character ("O woman, what have you to do with me?"); the curious omission of detail. Indeed, at face value the language of the Cana passage conveys the impression of elements of a dream—censored, jumbled, incomplete—with dialogue correspondingly out of character, uttered as though in code. Cana is intriguing because in its enigmas lies the possibility of resolution. Cana is intriguing because, seen in a particular light, questions previously unanswerable—Who were the bride and bridegroom? What were Jesus and his mother doing there? Why is Mary able to give orders to someone else's servants at someone else's wedding?—suggest a new and very different relationship between Mary, Queen of Heaven, and her Son.

The curtain obscuring Cana can be penetrated by a consideration of its chief miraculous event, the turning of water into wine. This feature of Cana, presented in the Gospel of John as a Christian phenomenon, in reality relates to an earlier religious ideology prevalent at the time, namely, that of the fertility religions. This relation has not been missed by some scholars, who have perceived in Cana a strong pagan influence. Indeed, Bultmann[2] identifies this distinctive transformation of water into wine as belonging specifically to fertility cult ideology and ascribes Cana as a "story . . . taken over from heathen legend."[3] In John 2:1–11 representation of this miracle has thus undergone a shift in frames of reference—from fertility cult ideology to Christian. By reversing this shift—from Christian back to pagan—the wedding at Cana and the nature of the relationship of its participants may be more precisely defined.

The pagan fertility cult specifically identified by the turning of water into wine was that of Dionysus. Its festivals (called Bacchanalias), both wild and licentious in character as well as sorrowful and lamentive, reenacted the life cycle of the young god of the vine: his springtime reawakening or return from the land of the dead, his marriage to the mother goddess Ariadne, his violent death (usually by dismemberment), and again in the spring his reawakening—all aimed at ensuring the propagation of the vine and the continuity of the cycle of nature. The heart of these rites was the miraculous transformation of water into wine. This important event signified the "showing forth" of the god (Dionysus) in person at his festival, the arrival of the "hour of the god," at which all laws were thought to lose their power and to become invalid. So characteristic was this miracle of Dionysian ideology, predating any other ideological context, that it was marked by a multiplicity of variations: on the islands of Andros and Ters the temple springs poured fourth wine instead of water (on the island of Naxos this same yearly phenomenon was said to commemorate the miracle of its first occurrence at the marriage of Dionysus and Ariadne); in Elis and Thyia three empty jars set up on the eve of the feast were found full of wine the next morning; and at Parnassus vines flowered and bore fruit during the hour of the appearance of the god (the miracle of the "one-day" vines), an event alluded to in Eurypides, Sophocles, Homer and Euphorion.

The turning of water into wine—the first of Jesus' signs—is thus conspicuous in its pertinence to the cult of Dionysus. However, there is a further connection which this miracle makes, linking the events at Cana to Dionysian relevance. In ancient times the epiphany (the showing forth, the appearance) of Dionysus was celebrated on January 6; in contemporary times this same date marks the showing forth of Jesus—the Christian celebration of Epiphany,[4] commemorating the event of the turning of water into wine by which Jesus manifested his glory. On this date, January 6, the Cana liturgy is read.

Cana is thus linked by the miraculous transformation of water into wine with Dionysian rite on more than a single level. This link, moreover, serves to portray the remarkably similar nature of these separate occurrences. For against the backdrop of a wedding ceremony the epiphany of Dionysus takes place, marked by the miracle of water turning into wine; and against a backdrop of a wedding ceremony the epiphany of Jesus takes place, marked by the same miracle.

That the sign of Dionysus—the turning of water into wine—is also the first of Jesus' signs; that the miracle of turning water into wine which marks the epiphany of Dionysus also marks the epiphany of Jesus; that the Dionysian epiphany and the Christian Epiphany both occur on the same date; that both take place against the backdrop of a wedding ceremony—indelibly stamp Cana with the "imprint of Dionysus." These parallelisms, etching Cana in pagan influence, inescapably imply that the events at Cana *may well have been a fertility cult occasion.*

In the context of a Dionysian festival the events at Cana become clear, yielding to a straightforward interpretation. The enigmas disappear. The vagueness dissolves. The hidden elements emerge. John 2:1–11 becomes transformed into a highly literal account.

This new rendering makes immediately obvious the chief hidden element of Cana: the identity of the bride and bridegroom. The wedding is the chief reason for the gathering of the parties—the central theme of the occasion; yet the Cana passage does not specify who the marriage participants are. However, their identity is known. They are, as in any fertility cult wedding, the great Mother Goddess and her son, the young God. The two main personages who have come together to reenact the sacred rite that will ensure the perpetuation of nature. Can the presence at Cana of mother and son be accounted for? John 2:1–11 indicates affirmatively: "On the third day there was a marriage at Cana in Galilee and the mother of Jesus was there; Jesus also was invited." But the mother of Jesus is the Virgin Mother of God, a metaphysical representation investing her with the credentials of the great Mother Goddess. And Jesus is the Son of God, which likewise reveals him in the image of the young deity. Thus the answer to Cana's fundamental question, "Who are the bride and bridegroom?" becomes immediately apparent: they are, in fact, Mary and Jesus.

The portrayal of Cana as a bridal festival for the Mother Goddess and deity Son indeed discloses a line by line correspondence of the entire passage to Dionysian ritual and drama:

On the third day there was a marriage at Cana. . . . This opening allusion in John 2:1–11 to a three-day event has no logical precedent; there is no prior mention of the first or second day. However, its specific attribution of a wedding on the third day calls attention to a Dionysian setting. For Dionysian festivals commonly lasted three days[5] and typically included a marriage ceremony. The expression "on the third day" identifies the Dionysian character of the event.

When the wine failed, the mother of Jesus said to him, "They have no wine." In expressing this concern to her Son, Mary, as a Mother Goddess figure, is in effect attempting to ensure that the central theme of Cana, the marriage, takes place. For the wine was the symbol of the showing forth of the young god; the "miracle of the wine," its bountiful flow, signalled the god's epiphany. Without the wine there would be no showing forth of the god, no epiphany, no marriage, no reenactment of the fertility rite. If "the wine failed," the god failed, the wedding failed, and so too would nature fail.

Mary's exhortation to the servants to "do whatever he [Jesus] tells you" reflects this same concern. In this same way she tells them to make ready for their part in the coming miracle. Her order to these servants both recognizes their ritual importance and indicates her special relationship with them. For these are not someone else's servants, and she and her Son are not guests, at someone else's wedding. These are the Maenads who ladle out the wine, the female servants or attendants of the young god, whose presence is a ritual necessity in the forthcoming rite. In attempting to expedite the marriage, Mary's command to the servants, "Do whatever he tells you," in a sense becomes a command to her Son: "Do whatever I tell you," i.e., perform the miracle.

O woman, what have you to do with me?[6] My hour has not yet come." This response—one of the most disputed and puzzling of New Testament passages (its unexpected and undeniable negativity raises the question of relationship between Jesus and his mother)—portrays Jesus' reluctance in the face of the Mother Goddess' advances. He denies what is being pressed upon him: the hour of his epiphany. The hour when he must show forth as the young god. The key hour of the festival. The hour consonant with his marriage to the Mother Goddess figure. The hour of his subsequent death and resurrection, according to ritual. It is to this fateful, pluralistic hour that Jesus' expression of reluctance relates.

Yet it is the marriage that is the pivotal event at Cana. *The marriage on the third day* is the reason why the characters have come together. The marriage is the central theme of the entire passage. And it is the marriage to which Jesus' hour of epiphany most immediately and specifically relates. For Jesus' response at Cana, although it may have relevance to his eventual death and resurrection,[7] is to the Mother Goddess' concern about the wine: her concern about the marriage. In replying "My hour has not yet come," Jesus indicates it is the hour of his marriage[8] of which he speaks.

His preface, "O woman, what have you to do with me?" thus rejects out of hand his hour of marriage—and yet at the same time anticipates it. For the term "O woman" is an appellation that renders the mother-son relationship secondary, that acts to put social distance[9,10] between himself and his mother. It is an appellation of Greek precedence used to disguise a prior or existing closeness of relationship. Thus King Odysseus (Ulysses) addresses his wife Penelope after an absence of twelve years with this expression (he is in actual physical disguise); Oedipus the King makes use of this same expression in addressing his wife Jocasta (Oedipus is in psychological disguise, not consciously aware that Jocasta is his mother). In calling up this same expression Jesus seeks to accomplish the same purpose: to nullify the closeness of relationship between himself and his mother; to extricate himself from the hour of incest confronting him. *Now six stone jars were standing there, for the Jewish rite of purification, each holding twenty or thirty gallons. Jesus said to them* [the servants], *"Fill the jars with water." And they filled them up to the brim. He said to them, "Now draw some out, and take it to the steward of the feast." So they took it.* The association of six stone jars with a "Jewish [marriage] rite of purification" is erroneous. On the contrary, stone jars standing empty at a wedding ceremony were a feature of Dionysian—not Jewish—weddings, as exemplified in Elis and Thyia. Nor in Jewish weddings was there a "steward of the feast"; this personage "who supervises the drinking" is typically identified with non-Jewish (Gentile) custom.[11] Attribution of the stone jars and the "steward" to Judaic practice serves to disguise the non-Jewish[12] character of the events described.

When the steward of the feast tasted the water now become wine, and did not know where it came from (although the servants who had drawn the water knew), the steward of the feast called the bridegroom. . . . The steward, although he does not know where the wine "came from," nevertheless makes the connection between its source and the bridegroom. He addresses the bridegroom as though he were the author of the miracle. In so doing he makes the cardinal association of a Dionysian wedding, the identity of the miracle-worker (the god) with the bridegroom. The steward's action thus emphasizes the Dionysian element of the wedding at Cana and, in addition, indicates Jesus, the author of the miracle, to be the actual bridegroom.

"Every man serves the good wine first; and when men have drunk freely, then the poor wine; but you have kept the good wine until now." The steward's statement concerns the order of events; he implies that there has been something out of order, something not right, at this wedding feast. In allegorical fashion he relates what has been wrong: ". . . You have kept the good

wine until now." He tells the bridegroom that he has kept himself back, that he has withheld himself, that he has been a reluctant bridegroom—an accurate portrayal in light of Jesus' earlier reticence with his mother. With the restoration of order—the appearance of the good wine—the allegorical implication is that the wedding feast can proceed, the marriage at Cana can now take place.

Cana, unveiled, reveals the nature of the relationship between Jesus and Mary. The core of incest that links these figures together. The coherent drama of a wedding in which the two earthly triad members of the Christ story are the main participants. With flawless fidelity John 2:1–11 presents this startling tableau, the reenactment of the ancient rite whose purpose is to maintain the very fount of life. The wedding festival for Mother and Son, in which the mother goddess asks her son to show forth, to engage with her in the archetypal sexual rite of the sacred marriage ceremony. The inaugural event of a fertility drama in which the son, hesitant and reluctant, ultimately accedes to his mother's wish.

Jesus' incestuous relationship with his mother is underscored by the episode of the cleansing of the temple (John 2:13–22) which is the couplet-passage of Cana.[13] This incident describes Jesus' clash with those who conducted commerce at the temple—the sale of sacrificial animals and the changing of money for religious pilgrims who journeyed to Jerusalem for the Passover holiday.

> In the temple he [Jesus] found those who were selling oxen and sheep and pigeons, and the money changers at their business. And making a whip of cords, he drove them all . . . out of the temple; . . . he poured out the coins . . . overturned their tables. . . . "Take these things away; you shall not make my Father's house a house of trade."

Scholars have pointed out that the sale of sacrificial animals and the changing of money were essential legitimate services performed by members of the temple priesthood within the area of the temple. Jewish law required the sacrifice of special animals without blemish, while imperial coins brought by the pilgrims, bearing the graven image of the Roman emperor, were forbidden within the temple confines and had to be changed into temple coins. What then was the basis for Jesus' rash actions? Even in the face of corrupt money-changing practices[14] Jesus' violence is out of character (Matthew 5:39).

The episode of the cleansing in reality continues the theme of the fertility drama. Jesus, the bridegroom of his mother, is shown at his Father's house in the wake of his wedding at Cana. It is the time of the "Passover of the Jews," a holiday commemorating the occasion when the angel of death *passed over* the Jewish people, smiting the firstborn of each non-Jewish household (Jesus is the firstborn Son of God). Jesus' purpose is ostensibly to cleanse the temple. But the allegory of John clearly equates the temple with the "temple of his [Jesus'] body" ("But he spoke of the temple of his body"). Thus Jesus' actions become clear: he comes to his Father's house in the aftermath of incestuous union with his mother to cleanse "the temple of his body."

But the allegory of the passage extends also to the "time of the Passover." Jesus is in the non-Jewish role of the young deity of Cana, subject to the angel of death. The cleansing thus becomes a portent of Jesus' ultimate fate. For as the temple itself is cleansed by Jesus' violence, so too is the symbolic temple of his body to be cleansed by his Father's violence. (That Jesus is not exempt from the angel of death is made abundantly clear in his, and the passage's, non-Jewish characterization: it is the Passover *of the Jews;* Jesus does not speak of our Father's house, but my Father's house; it is they [the Jews] and he [Jesus]. Jesus and the Jews are separate; he is not of them. Jesus is asked Jewish questions: "What sign have you to show us for doing this?" [They have not recognized the first of his signs at Cana because of its non-Jewish nature.] To which Jesus gives a non-Jewish reply: "Destroy this temple and I will raise it up in three days." They do not perceive this classical fertility cult allusion to the coming death and resurrection of the god. Instead, their Jewish rejoinder emphasizes the ideological difference between them and him: "It has taken forty-six years to build this temple, and will you raise it up in three days?")

Thus John 2:13–22 portrays a continuing fertility drama, set in Jewish symbolism, in which the events at Cana are extended to a foreview of their ideological conclusion: the death and resurrection of the young god. In its coupling of incest and death the passage underlines the nature of the relationship between Jesus and his mother.

Calvary sustains this relationship. Against a backdrop of Passover[15] the motif of the cleansing is continued as the passage (John 19) extends the fertility drama to its cyclical conclusion. Again the configuration of Mother and Son surfaces:

> So they took Jesus. . . . they crucified him. . . . standing by the cross of Jesus were his mother . . . and Mary Magdalen.
>
> —*John 19:17–18, 25*

The "Woman of Cana" reappears with the destruction of the god.

> When Jesus saw his mother, and the disciple whom he loved standing near, he said to his mother, "Woman, behold your son!" Then he said to the disciple, "Behold your mother!" And from that hour the disciple took her to his home.
>
> —*John 19:26, 27*

In this final exchange on Calvary[16] Jesus addresses his mother with the same appellation of social distance used at Cana. The use of this appellation of disguise, carrying forward their closeness of relationship, indicates Mary's presence at the Crucifixion to be a continuation of her role at Cana. The appellation "woman" thus links the incest of Cana with the death of the Son on Calvary—and reiterates the essence of the relationship between Mother and Son.[17]

Both the fertility drama and the Christ story end and begin with the resurrection of the God. In this final chapter the incest of the mother-son relationship comes full circle with the reappearance of the Mother Goddess who, grieving, goes to reawaken the sleeping god. In lamentation and sorrow she journeys to the land of the dead (the tomb) to retrieve the crucified Jesus; she stands at the tomb, wishing to know where they have laid him, wishing to take him away.

". . . they have taken away my Lord and I do not know where they have laid him."

—*John 20:13*

". . . Sir, if you have carried him away, tell me where you have laid him and I will take him away."

—*John 20:15*

In the person of Mary Magdalen[18] the incest of the Mother Goddess is thus carried into the resurrection. With her return the expression of incest also returns, as the Risen Son—now in actual disguise[19]—addresses his Mother as he did at Cana and Calvary:

". . . Woman, why are you weeping? Whom do you seek?"

Thus the resurrection faultlessly expresses the concluding event of the fertility drama: the mission of the Mother to the regions below, the reappearance of the Son; the recurrence of the "appellation of relationship." In its recapitulation of the tableau of Cana and Calvary, this ending chapter once again affirms the nature of the relationship between the two earthly members of the Christ story.

The core of incest within the Christ story is further reinforced and made explicit in the doctrinal recognition of Mary as an incest figure. In her promulgation as Madonna, each attribute that Mary acquires acts to call attention to her incest image, whether by accentuating or attenuating the characterization. The Doctrine of the Incarnation (declared to be dogma in 449 A.D.), in stating that God the Father incarnated Himself as God the Son in the womb of the virgin Mary (Father and Son are thus One), portrays Mary not only as "Bride of the Father" but also "Bride of the Son"—a characterization not materially different from that of the mother goddesses who were also bride and mother of the god and typically were also represented by a young virgin, who, with the god-surrogates, conceived their divine sons under religious and holy circumstances. Her designation *Theotokos* (declared to be dogma in 431 A.D.) underlines this mother goddess characterization by expressly revealing her as "God-Bearer" (the mother goddesses commonly were "god-bearers"). Succeeding doctrines call special attention to Mary's incest configuration by divesting of incestuous content the very Mother Goddess image they augment. The Doctrine of Perpetual Virginity (declared to be dogma in 649 A.D.) denies that any sexuality (and therefore incest) has ever occurred; but in doing so, it portrays Mary as having transcended physical law (maternity in the face of virginity), which relegates her to Mother Goddess status. The Doctrine of the Immaculate Conception (declared to be dogma in 1854) declares Mary incapable of sin, and thus absolves her from any possibility of the sin of incest; however, in her exemption from all sin (the Doctrine of the Immaculate Conception proclaims that sin never has and never can take

place in Mary) she transcends—becomes also exempt from—
human nature, again attaining Mother Goddess stature. The
Doctrine of the Assumption (declared to be dogma in 1950)
rules out any incestuous component in Mary, since she
is declared to have been assumed to heaven as a complete
person—"bodily inviolate" (incest is rendered a physical im-
possibility); yet in her corporeal assumption she transcends
human death, becoming Co-Ruler, with her Son, of heaven
and earth, which firmly establishes her in the exact image of
Mother Goddess. Thus, whether in promulgating Mary in
the same incest image as the Magna Mothers of old (Divine
Spouse and Mother) or in asserting the nonpresence of
Mary's sexuality, all of these doctrines address Mary's incest
content; they all recognize its presence. By characterizing
Mary as the perpetually virgin, immaculately conceived,
physically inviolate Mother Goddess, these doctrines give
theological substance to her scriptural portrait as the Woman
of Cana.

It is thus within the gospel of John that the relationship
between the two earthly figures of the Christ story, Jesus and
his Mother, becomes apprehensible. That the wedding at
Cana, the cleansing of the temple, the death and resurrection
of the God become identifiable as fertility cult proceedings.
That the link between Mother Goddess and deity Son becomes defined. A link, moreover, that is given substance by
its theological conformity to doctrine.

Like the horror story, the Christ story is an incest tale. A
fertility cult drama with Judaistic facade. With backgrounds,
settings and characterizations congruent with those of the
horror story. Both suggest that in the unconscious mind
incest is a psychological inevitability. Both transmit their
incest message to the realm of the unconscious, activating
primeval circuits in apparent disuse, reawakening vestigal
channels of ancient sexuality, giving expression to primordial
patterns of behavior. And unleashing surprising social forces.

CHAPTER SIXTEEN

Pornography

". . . Beside the bed . . . stood a tall, thin man, all in black. . . . With a mocking smile, he placed one hand upon my shoulder and, holding me tight, bared my throat with the other, saying as he did so, 'First, a little refreshment to reward my exertions. You may as well be quiet; it is not the first time, or the second, that your veins have appeased my thirst!' I was bewildered, and, strangely enough, I did not want to hinder him. I suppose it is part of the horrible curse that such is, when his touch is on his victim. . . . He placed his reeking lips upon my throat! . . . I felt my strength fading away, and I was in a half swoon. How long this horrible thing lasted I know not; but it seemed that a long time must have passed before he took his foul, awful, sneering mouth away. I saw it drip with . . . fresh blood!"

AS DESCRIBED PREVIOUSLY, THE ABOVE PASSAGE FROM *Dracula,* unmasked of its disguise mechanism of sexual displacement—in which Mina's throat, the Count's vein and both their mouths are displacments for genitals—reveals the sexuality of virginal defloration, cunnilingus and fellatio. The horror of this passage is represented by an older man forcing these acts on a young woman. However, when this passage is substituted by word, concept, and mirror-image equivalents, its horror disappears, and in its place is a residue of pornography, as is likewise apparent in the remainder of this passage:

> " '. . . flesh of my flesh; blood of my blood; kin of my kin; my bountiful wine-press . . . When my brain says "Come!" . . . you shall . . . do my bidding . . .' With that he pulled open his shirt, and with his long sharp nails opened a vein in his breast. When the blood began to spurt out, he took my hands in one of his, holding them tight, and with the other seized my neck and pressed my mouth to the wound, so that I must . . . swallow some of the—Oh my God! My God! . . ."

Like the horror story, pornography cuts across all social, economic and religious groups and enjoys the same wide audience—old, young, rich, poor, learned, ignorant, social misfit, community pillar. Both are of antique origin,[1] extending in an unbroken line into contemporary times, especially reinforced during the mid-Victorian era. (It was this era that gave rise to the classics of pornography and the horror story alike, upon which most of the modern-day genres are based.) Both stories have attracted writers of high caliber: Edgar Allen Poe, Robert Louis Stevenson, Bram Stoker, Mary Shelley in the horror story; Frank Harris, Henry Miller, D. H. Lawrence, James Joyce and Mark Twain in works which at one time or another have been deemed pornographic. However, the kinship between pornography and horror does not lie primarily in common historical and social roots, but rather in the basic similarities of their structure and content.

Structure and content of horror and pornography are often interrelated and therefore difficult to separate; however, certain features of structure are shared by both stories. Pornography is commonly written in the first person. So is horror. Pornography is intensely voyeuristic. So is horror. Both stories employ diaries, letters, stories within stories, journals, reportage, vivid descriptions, abundant dialogue— which convey the impression of eyewitness accounts. Both stories employ a special vocabulary: pornography uses "dirty" words to arouse and heighten sexual interaction; horror uses "magic" words (the gibberish of abracadabra) to heighten the metaphysical encounter. In both stories conventional time is negated; the sequence of cause and effect, deed and consequence, which mark real time, is totally disordered. In pornography events happen in an open-ended milieu of free will, unrestrained by law, order or logic. In the horror story events occur in a close-ended milieu of destiny, similarly unaffected by law, order or logic. The plot of pornography is sometimes as nonexistent as the plot of horror is predictable. Pornography propels the viewer from one sexual escapade to the next, building up erotic tension that finally culminates in a grand orgy in which all the major characters participate. Horror propels the viewer from one encounter to the next, building up suspense and tension, which also culminate in a grand climax involving the main characters.

The content of both stories is also remarkably similar. Both portray action that is essentially taboo in nature. Pornography depicts homosexuality, fellatio, cunnilingus, bestiality, masturbation, unusual couplings; the horror story depicts the "kissing" of the victim *(Dracula)*, the "eating" of a young handsome werewolf *(The Refugee)*, the indulgence of a frog-like creature's taste for humans and other mammals *(The Shuttered Room)*. In pornography the encounter is uncensored and undisguised; the story reflects the suspension of morality. In the horror story the encounter is censored; its sexual content is submerged in a psychological context likewise free of moral restraint.

Both stories are chiefly fantasy—their principal events occur outside natural law. Pornography deals with supersexual powers—perpetual penile erections, uninterrupted series of earthshaking orgasms, prodigious ejaculations, sexual feats that typically defy human physiology and psychology; horror deals with supernatural powers—raising the dead, creating life, transformations—also in defiance of natural and physical law.

In both stories that which is considered holy is juxtaposed to the profane. In pornography sex and religion are irreverently mixed; members of the clergy and sacred sites are often used sacrilegiously. Pornographic tales relate an adulterous liaison in a choir loft, the sexual escapades of a flagellant priest, sexual orgies that take place in a convent, sexual encounters held in a churchyard.[2] In horror, characters stalk graveyard and bedchamber hunting vampires with crucifixes, a monster attack takes place on a churchyard bench, a holy wafer is applied to the forehead of a victim *(Dracula)*, construction of a monster is accompanied by lofty thoughts of the Creator *(Frankenstein)*, a scientist's excursion into monsterism is followed by reading his mother's Bible *(Dr. Jekyll and Mr. Hyde)*. In both stories profanation of the sacred serves to intensify the morally forbidden nature of the encounter.

Major elements of sadomasochism occur in both stories.[3] In pornography flagellation and associative torture achieve a special prominence in conjunction with encounters; characters commonly enjoy a wide variety of sexual experiences while whipping, being whipped or watching others being whipped, raped or creatively tormented. In horror, encounters similarly involve the infliction of pleasure and pain: Jonathan of *Dracula* lies in "agony" as three girls prepare to "suck" him, while Dr. Jekyll *(Dr. Jekyll and Mr. Hyde)* marinates masochistically in the newfound pleasures of Mr. Hyde's debauchery. Both types of stories exemplify that peculiar inversion of pleasure and pain, which acts as an aphrodisiac to the sexual encounter of pornography, and an intensifier to the monster attack of horror.

Seduction, defloration and rape give prominent expression to both stories. Seduction is consummated with the aid of a willing victim. In pornography the seducer reveals his intentions; the victim may register some perfunctory protest; the seduced is a quick and willing collaborator. In horror the seducer (monster) makes known his intentions; the victim becomes irresistibly attracted, giving but perfunctory attention to his forebodings; the seduced is an unconsciously willing collaborator. Defloration and rape typically involve a virgin. In pornography *(The Lascivious Hypocrite)* the lovely Eugenie lies drugged in her bed as the fatherly St. Geraud steals into her bedroom to commit "the blackest of all outrages"[4]. The blood on the bedsheet reveals what has occurred. Likewise in horror, Mina of *Dracula* lies in a drugged stupor while the Count steals into her bedroom, his ruthless hands holding her in "that terrible and horrid position." Again the trickle of blood—on Mina's chin—signifies what has happened.

Similar consequences befall the victims of sadomasochism in both stories. In pornography the characters, once initiated, become sexually charged, seeking nothing more than to express their newfound power in a series of never-ending conquests. (The lovely Eugenie, for example, cannot wait to repeat "the blackest of all outrages.") In horror the characters, once initiated, become metaphysically charged, acquiring monster tastes, seeking out conquests of their own.

Characterization in both stories in similarly unique. In horror the characters are idealized representations of right and wrong: metaphysics, in all its variations, is their particular forte. In pornography the characters are idealized sex objects: sex, in all its variations, is their particular forte.

The characters of pornography are represented as little more than animated genitalia. In this respect there is a "transposition" of major figures in the two stories. The hairy, hungry, voracious, insatiable monster of horror becomes the hairy, hungry, voracious, insatiable genitals of pornography. Like the monster, the genitals possess remarkable and marvelous attributes. They, too, have the power of transformation. From the invisible they grow to a thing of prodigious strength and power, or to a vibrating, pulsating, carnivorous man-eater. Like the monster, they, too, entice their victims, bewitching them with their power, intoxicating them with overpowering odors, strange perfumes, fascinating imagery. Like the monster, they, too, torture their victims in fires of passion, engulfing them physically and psychologically, bumping, grinding and thrashing their victims to frenzied ecstasy. Covering their victims with copious discharges and telltale marks. Plunging them into exhausted unconsciousness, from which they awake to begin again.

Yet the similarities of structure and content, which relate one story to the other, are themselves expressions of a deeper root, one which more than any other distinguishes these two stories and establishes their fundamental congruency.

Both are incest stories. In each, the use of eyewitness accounts, nonsequential cause and effect, concepts of predestination and free will, serve to disorder or negate real time, invoking a sense of time ungoverned by civilization, law or order. Thus the settings of pornography, like those of horror, recreate a time of the beginning, a time reminiscent of man's first sexuality, the time of incest.[5]

Incest characters appear in both stories. Doctors, clergy, persons of special genealogy (those exempt from the incest taboo) are integral to each story. Blacks, orientals, foreigners, outsiders (prominent incest symbols) are also conspicuously present.

Incest relationships characterize each story. In horror the major characters compose a family triad, in which the older member advances against the younger member in a series of escalating sexual assaults. A secondary characterization occurs in the form of a permissive parent figure who unwittingly commissions the young for subsequent encounters. In pornography the same situation prevails. The interrelationships of the family triad are replaced by frank sexual unions between family members—between brother-sister, father-daughter and mother-son. In pornography permissive parent figures are also present—fathers, mothers, aunts, uncles and guardians—who not only commission their children for sexual encounters, but actively join them.

Incest plots typify both stories. In each a series of events outside nature, supernatural or supersexual, sets forth and attempts to reconcile the inherent incestuous sexuality of the triad relationships.

In effect the configuration of pornography is an incest configuration. Whether manifest in similarities of structure or content, or of settings, characterization or plot, it is this theme—the expression of primal sexuality—which imparts to pornography its similarity to horror, which allows for the latency of pornography in horror, which accounts for the congruency of these two stories. Philosophical elixir or tasteless spiritual depressant, pornography is incest expression. It is this expression which renders these two stories alike.

CHAPTER SEVENTEEN

Anti-Semitism

ANTI-SEMITISM IS INCEST FEAR.

Immune to social, economic, political and religious restraints, equally endemic among the ignorant and the intelligent, the loathing and hatred of Jews and Jewishness crosses all barriers of human society. Subtle, blatant, clever, crude. Printed or spoken. Finding expression in the rabble of a street mob, in the innuendoes of the drawing room. In quota systems, racial laws, economic boycotts, political disenfranchisement, ghettoization, vandalized shops, burned synagogues, pogroms, refugees. Ending in a mountain of human ash. From country club to concentration camp, whatever its variations, anti-Semitism is the univeral recognition of the Jew as a monster figure.

Ruthless, deviant, destructive, mad, committed to the downfall of others, forcing his evil will upon society for the express purpose of establishing dominion over the world, the Jew as a classic monster figure derives from his portrayal as a practitioner of unauthorized metaphysics. The purveyor of atypical ideology, the bearer of contrary supernaturalism, the agent of unconventional occultism, the author of sorcery, magic and nefarious rites, he is in effect cast by his religion in the very image of a monster: a figure outside authorized religion.

In the bitter schism that divided Judaism and Christianity—a schism formalized in A.D. 394 when the Roman Empire adopted Christianity as the state religion—the stubborn root that would neither die nor bend in its belief, gave mute testimony to the recurrent presence of the monster. For in the dissociation of the two religions, Christian ascendancy gave impetus to Jewish decline. Christianity had captured the imagination and allegiance of the myriad fertility cults of the Graeco-Roman world and, in emerging as the dominant religion, cast its shadow upon Jewish precedence. Under pressure, the religion of the Jew receded. The Jew became the representative of the minority faith, the unaccepted faith, a figure thrust outside authorized religion. In his denial of Christ, in his refusal to enter the Christian fold, in his adherence to Judaism, the Jew was the infidel, the unbeliever, the accursed.

He was in fact a monster.

For with the advent of Christianity the monster portrait of the Jew came alive. Through doctrine and dictums, teaching and tradition, through art and literature the image of Jewish monsterism materialized into flesh and blood.

"You [Jews] are of your father the devil, and your will is to do your father's desires."

—*John 8:44*

". . . one of you [twelve disciples] is a devil. . . ." He spoke of Judas. . . .

—*John 6:70–71*

". . . the devil comes and takes away the word from their hearts, that they may not believe and be saved."

—*Luke 8:12*

Throughout the gospels devil and Jew merge in scriptural paradigm. It is the devil who is characterized as the chief adversary of Jesus; it is also the Jews. It is the devil with whom Jesus engages in constant struggle (his temptation, his casting out of demons and unclean spirits, and so forth); it is also with the Jews (his troubles with the Pharisees, his casting out of the money changers). It is the devil who is outside and opposed to the true religion of the heart; it is also the Jews. In the fusion of these duplicate figures the gospels themselves give recognition to the devil-portrait of the Jew; whether by inference or explicit portrayal the Jew emerges from the Scriptures as a monster incarnate.

The Patristic Fathers—the early Church theologians of the second through seventh centuries A.D. who shaped and formulated the basic doctrines of the Christian faith—were swift to apprehend the monster configuration of the Jew and bring it to life. Irenaeus[1] declared: ". . . those who do not believe and do not obey His Will, are sons . . . of the devil".[2] "The Bible itself says that the Jews are an accursed people . . . the devil is the father of the Jews," specified St. Cyprian.[3,4] "Companions of the devil, race of vipers . . . Sanhedrin of demons, accursed . . ." Gregory of Nyssa[5] wrote of the Jews.[6] "Serpents," concluded St. Jerome[7,8] ". . . Possessed by the devil . . . they murder their offspring and immolate them to the devil . . . they worship the devil . . ." inveighed St. John Chrysostom;[9] ". . . [their synagogue is] the domicile of the devil . . . a cavern of devils, an abyss of perdition."[10]

The Patristics were given papal reinforcement in their characterization of the Jew. Pope Gelasius I (492–496), explaining that in biblical symbolism "the whole is often named from the part," extended the devil-image of Judas to all Jews in general:

Judas, concerning whom it is said "One of you is a devil" (John 6:71) . . . without any doubt gives his name to all the race.[11]

And in 1080 Pope Gregory VII, in a letter to Alphonso VI, King of Spain, depicted Jewry as "the Synagogue of Satan"[12,13] while Innocent III, one century later, labeled the Jews "demons" whose king was the devil.[14]

The theological equation of devil and Jew found full expression in the art and graphic depictions of the Middle Ages. In portals and frescoes, in stained glass windows of churches and cathedrals, on monuments and public buildings, in illustrated Bibles and prayer books, even in secular household items such as china and bric-a-brac, the Jew was commonly portrayed as devil-like, with misshapen body, tapered hands and feet, fitted with horns, a serpent's tail, a goat's beard, having an inordinately long nose, head frequently topped with pointed hat, clothes adorned with representations of scorpions—symbol of the devil.[15]

Medieval folklore also contributed to the Jew's portrayal as demonic. Like the devil, Jews purportedly emanated a terrible odor, whose nature became the subject of scholarly dissertations. Jews also suffered from strange diseases and congenital defects, one of the most bizarre of which being that Jewish males, as well as females menstruated. Jews were in general held to be feminized beings, i.e., physically weak (many depictions portray Jews in a cringing, subservient posture). Yet what the Jew lacked in physical strength, he made up for in psychological power. He was a sorcerer, a magician, a practitioner of the black school whose rites, like the devil's, included a celebration of the Sabbath, enacted in collusion with the Satanic Master.

Theater, religious and secular tracts, prose and poetry also added medieval impact to the communion of Jew and devil. Especially noteworthy were the thunderings of Martin Luther (1483–1564). Stunning innovator, religious rebel, founder of a new Christianity—when it came to the Jews, Luther could only reiterate what had been said centuries before:

> . . . they are children of the Devil, condemned to the flames of hell. . . . they have a God . . . he is called the Devil. . . . [16]

Passion plays, dramas that emphasized the suffering and death of Jesus, produced in an atmosphere of violent carnival, made similar representations. In the ever-popular *Mystery of the Sacred Host,* the Jew addresses his god as he is burned alive at the stake:

> O Devil, I feel I am burning
> Devils, devils burn and flame
> I flare and flame in every limb
> I perish now in fire and flame
> My body, mind and soul
> Burn now and fiercely consume
> Devils come speedily
> And carry me off. . . .[17]

Even Shakespearean drama bore witness to this same imagery. In the celebrated *Merchant of Venice,* Solano observes:

> Let me say amen . . . lest the devil cross my prayer; for here he comes now in the likeness of a Jew."[18]

Nor was the perception of the Jew altered by the advent of the modern era. A scene from the late nineteenth-century anti-Semitic tract, *The Jewish Cemetery in Prague and the Council of Representatives of the Twelve Tribes of Israel,*[19] illustrates that what the gospels had conceived, the Patristics nourished, the popes made explicit and the Middle Ages amplified, was to prove impervious to the Age of Reason.

The scene begins:

. . . At any moment, these tombs, overgrown with shrubbery, are ready to open, these stones growing for thousands of years are ready to raise themselves, and to let . . . into the world the restless wanderer with a pack upon his shoulder, with a staff in his hand. . . .

Two witnesses (one a converted Jew with face pale, of waxen color, without the slightest natural red in the cheeks) lie hidden in the darkness of night. They are about to discover the secret of the Caballah, an evil Jewish rite that takes place every hundred years.

The gates [to the cemetery] creaked softly; the rustling of long coats was heard, touching the stones and shrubbery. Finally a vague white figure appeared and slipped like a shadow along the pathway. . . . This figure knelt before one of the tombstones; three times it touched the stone with its forehead and softly whispered a prayer. . . . Thirteen times this was repeated. Thirteen old men came over to the tombstone. The doctor [the second witness] counted them, but he could not understand whether they were alive or dead. A shiver crept down his back, his heart began to beat faster from fright. . . . It seemed to him that the prayer shawls had fallen off the heads of the praying old men, and a row of dead skulls appeared. At that moment the clock struck twelve. . . .

The apparitional figures—the "heads of the twelve tribes of Israel" plus the "tall impressive figure" of the devil—come to order: ("We greet you, son of the accursed"). Whereupon the Wise Men of Zion begin their recitation. As the devil calls the roll, each proceeds to lay out the Jewish plan for the next hundred years.

To concentrate . . . all the capital of the nations of all lands; to secure possession of all the land, railroads, mines, houses; to be at the head of all organizations, to paralyze commerce and industry everywhere, to seize the press, to direct legislation, public opinion and national movements . . . for the purpose of subjugating all nations on earth. . . .

The Jewish Cemetery in Prague is significant in that it contains the nucleus of the infamous twentieth century "Bible" of the anti-Semites, *The Protocols of the Elders of Zion,*[20] a tract that outlines the point-by-point strategy of a Jewish plot aiming at world domination. It is also significant in that it indicates the immutability of the Jewish portrait. For in this remarkable exposition the monster that roamed the medieval world is captured in the context of a horror story and made modern. The Jew is once again revealed in the exact image of his predecessors, as a figure of atypical metaphysics, associate of the devil and sower of ever-contemporary havoc. In conveying its message of anti-Semitism—and in subtle fashion reiterating the doctrine "once a Jew, always a a monster" (even conversion fails to dispel the Jew's monster-like physiognomy)—*Cemetery* recognizes the psychological reality of the Jew as an agent of archetypal monsterism. In *Cemetery* the Jew steps into the twentieth century, the ageless figure, committed to the downfall of others, forcing his evil will upon society for the express purpose of establishing dominion over the world.

As a monster figure the Jew was the possessor of classic monster attributes.

"You are of your father. . . . He was a murderer from the beginning. . . ."

—*John 8:44*

All four gospels recognize the Jew's propensity for violence, in particular his authorship of the ultimate crime—deicide—the slaying of God Himself. "Crucify him. Crucify him," Matthew, Mark, Luke and John cite the Jews in their fury as

the killers of Christ. But it is not those Jews alone who cry
out for the life of Jesus who are murderers—it is all Jews: "His
blood be on us and on our children" (Matthew 27:25).[21] The
Patristics repeated, reinforced and elaborated this characterization. Irenaeus, St. Justin Martyr, St. Cyprian, St. Hip-
polytus, Origen, Tertullian, Eusebius, St. Jerome, St. Ambrose, St. Cyril of Alexandria—all held the Jews to be:
"Slayers of the Lord, assassins of the prophets,"[22] "cru-
cifiers,"[23] "Christ-killing . . . murderers,"[24] "inveterate murderers, destroyers [who] . . . know only to kill"[25]—a view
echoed even by St. Augustine:

> The Jews held him, the Jews insulted him, the Jews bound him,
> they crowned him with thorns, dishonored him by spitting upon
> him, they scourged him, they heaped abuses upon him, they
> hung him upon a tree, they pierced him with a lance.[26]

Following suit, New Testament Apocryphal writings, the
"Passion Gospels" (particulary the "Gospel of Peter"), as well
as Church law and liturgy[27] established the Jew as a mur-
derous being. The Middle Ages saw the Jew escape his religious confines and hurtle into the realm of secular society.
Poets, pamphleteers, playwrights, roving entertainers travel-
ing from castle to castle, from town to town, juggling,
singing, dancing, acting in plays and in mime, let loose their
version of the Christ killer. In particular the Passion Play at
Oberammergau,[28] performed today essentially intact, with a
cast of hundreds, an audience of thousands, has renewed
every ten years the image of the Jew as the murderer of God,
the nefarious agent of Satan:

> The people [the Jews] cried wildly,
> "Up to Golgotha, to the Cross with him!
> To the Cross! Let him die on the Cross!"

He hangs . . . upon the Cross,
And Belial's [Satan's] sons, in godless triumph,
Gloat joyful o'er His pain and loss. . . .

Secular tracts further elaborated:

Infamous murderers,
Detestable nation
Abhorred by men,
Everywhere rejected,
Must you today
Renew the effort
Of your horrid cruelties
Which put to death
The God by whom we live?[29]

Hovering menacingly in the consciousness of Christendom, the murderer of God strode down through the centuries—to be addressed again in Vatican II (1965). The Council's original concluding statement (The Declaration on the Relationship of the Church to Non-Christian Religions) asserted:

Although the Church is the new people of God, the Jews should not be presented as repudiated or cursed by God or guilty of deicide as if such views followed from holy scriptures.[30]

However, in the final vote the words "or guilty of deicide" were deleted from this text. The Council thus let stand the ancient charge of deicide—and with it the connotation of the Jew as an ever-present murderer.

While Vatican II repudiated the collective guilt[31] of the Jews for the death of Jesus, a guilt that demands perpetual retribution, the Council's repudiation is moot in the face of its retention of the deicide charge and therefore of prior Church theology:

. . . The blood of Jesus falls not only on the Jews of that time, but on all generations of Jews up to the end of the world. (Origen)[32]

The Jews are dispersed throughout all nations, as witness of their iniquity. . . . (St. Augustine)[33]

. . . The Jews, against whom the blood of Jesus Christ calls out . . . must remain vagabonds upon the earth, until their faces be covered with shame and they seek the name of Jesus Christ the Lord. (Innocent III)[34]

It would be licit, according to law, to hold the Jews, on account of their crime, in perpetual servitude. . . . (St. Thomas Aquinas)[35]

In effect, Vatican II, in failing to rescind the deicide charge without qualification, reaffirms it. Jewish guilt, like a classic monster trait, is implied to be inheritable, genetically transmissible, extending to all Jews in all times.

Insatiable in his homicidal inclinations, the Jew's thirst for blood found expression also in ritual murder. Kidnapping and murdering Christian children during the Easter season in a re-creation of the Crucifixion, the Jew drank the blood of his victim, incorporating it into the unleavened bread of Passover, ingested the victim's organs or used them in the brewing of love potions, magic elixirs and medicine.[36,37] Little William of Norwich (St. William) fell victim to the monster's proclivity for the young in A.D. 1144. The slaying of little Simon of Trent (St. Simon) was immortalized in an engraving carved at the entrance to a public bridge in Frankfurt, *The Judensau*. The ritual murder of little Hugh (St. Hugh) of Lincoln[38] was set to rhyme. And on the stages of the medieval theater the monster committed his act repeatedly and in dramatic detail.[39] Trials, expulsion, massacre and official proclamations of Jewish innocence[40] failed to stop the monster's crimes, his presence as a ritual murderer being chronicled well into the nineteenth century,[41] even into the twentieth century.[42] (Vatican II also aided in the recognition of the Jew as a ritual murderer; for in banning the veneration only of Simon of Trent—the Council found that little Simon was probably killed by non-Jews—it let stand the veneration of victims of other ritual murders.)

A master of satanic pharmacopoeia, the Jew was also a poisoner of body and mind. Privy to the secret of magic recipes of death, the monster—with a concoction of human blood, urine, herbs and the ground-up Host—killed cattle, blighted crops, inflicted sterility and pestilence on man and beast. So widespread were his activities that legislation was enacted prohibiting Christians from buying certain footstuffs, while two popes found it necessary when massacres of revenge got out of hand to issue official denials of these activities.[43] His most notable achievement, however, was the poisoning of all the wells of Europe, which caused the Black Death (the bubonic plague of 1347–1349), purportedly killing one-half to two-thirds of those affected.

In particular the Jewish physician, an unauthorized metaphysician who controlled the forces of life and death, who might as easily kill as cure, was singled out as a poisoner. Allegedly required to poison a certain number of patients per year—in 1610 the medical faculty of Vienna solemnly confirmed that Jewish physicians were bound by their medical oath to "kill every tenth Christian patient by means of drugs"[44]—the Jewish physician was forbidden by law to treat Christians.[45] Nevertheless, like the monster kept by his masters, the Jewish doctor was kept by members of the nobility, clergy and upper classes to perform his Jewish magic in treating the otherwise untreatable.

The Jew was also perceived as a spiritual killer, a corrupter, a darkener of the mind,[46] a creature to be separated from the rest of society lest his contagion[47] overspread the Christian peoples:

> The worst of it is they [the Jews] seduce a great many imprudent and weak persons with their satanic illusions, their fortune-telling, their charms and magic tricks and witcheries, and make them believe that the future can be foretold, that stolen goods and hidden treasures can be recovered, and much else can be revealed.[48]

Recognition of the monster's fascination led to laws that forbade Jewish-Christian marriages; banned close relations between Jewish and Christian communities; prohibited Jews from blessing the fields of Christians;[49] prohibited Christians from celebrating Passover with the Jews;[50] forbade Christians to keep the Sabbath or receive gifts from Jewish festivals;[51] banned conversion to Judaism; made Jewish proselytism criminal; forbade Jews to hold Christian slaves; barred Jews from public functions, certain public offices and professions; denied Jews the right of asylum by the Church;[52] and stripped Judaism of its legality.[53] His rites criminal and his religion a disease,[54] the Jew extended his sorcery by means of his books. The *Talmud*—his handbook of monsterim—directed his subversive acts in all fields of behavior and endeavor.[55] The *Caballah (Kaballah),* guarding the magic formulas by which he practiced the black arts of alchemy, necromancy and healing, wreaked similar havoc.[56]

A special case of the Jew's poisoning of the mind was his practice of usury. A quarry constantly on the move, barred from many occupations by the law, excluded from trade unions, the monster preyed on Christian victims, financially entrapping them in a vise of interest. Though put to good use (Jewish money-lenders became the special property of the upper classes, kept and traded by baron, king, and clergy for the purpose of advancing capital[57]), the avaricious drive of the Jew identified its owner as a greedy, heartless fiend, ever ready to cut a "pound of flesh" from the body of his hapless victim.

Innately aberrant, the Jew was also characterized by another attribute:

"You [who would receive circumcision[58]] are severed from Christ."

—*Galatians 5:4*

His fleshly[59] mark the symbol of his inner nature, the monster was likewise noted as carnal (St. Augustine[60]), wicked (St. Justin Martyr[61]), perpetually perverse (St. Hilary of Poitiers[62]), lustful, rapacious (St. John Chrysostom[63]); his place of worship a house of prostitution (St. John Chrysostom[64]), a harlot (St. Ephraim[65]), a house of impiety (St. Ambrose[66]), a whorehouse (Roman Imperial Law[67]). The author of seduction,[68] driven only by what the sense perceives (Pope Innocent III[69]), he was also chronicled in later generations: "The Jews sent their servants with plates of silver and pots of gold to gather up Judas' piss . . . and then they ate and drank his offal" (Luther[70]). His likeness decorated urinals;[71] his women gave birth to piglets;[72] his exploits—reading the Talmud while fornicating and sucking a beast—were legend.[73] Law forbade him Christian union:[74] "coition with a [Jew] is the same as . . . copulat[ion] with a dog";[75] it was recognized that "more than two-thirds" of his women were "fallen",[76] that it was his influence which stood "behind the amazing degeneracy of the modern [arts and his presence which] served . . . to dry up the sound serum of Anglo-Saxon morality."[77] To him was accorded the universal epithet "dirty Jew," paying homage to his representation as the immutable figure of psychosexual aberration.

Murderer, poisoner, associate of the devil. Corrupter and force of evil. A figure untouched by the passing centuries.

From Golgotha to the cemetery in Prague, from the Scriptures to the Protocols, from medieval art to contemporary literature—the Jew is in every respect indistinguishable from the archetypal monster.

Even in pre-Christian times the Jew was regarded as different. Surrounded by the rich polytheism of gods and goddesses, the Jews held to One God. The God of the Covenant. Inspired and sustained by the prophets, they resisted the celebration of foreign gods, the orgiastic rites and pageantry, the tangible, accessible images, the potent psychosexual drama that fused sex and religion, and held fast to the Law. From a Judaic point of view, the core of fertility religions— the worship of deities in sexual rites and ceremonies—was an abomination. Fertility cult ideology was spiritual whoredom.

But fertility cult ideology dominated the ancient world. And worship of deities through sexual expression was the rule. The Jews' rejection of this ideology (Jewish sexuality was tightly prescribed by law and precept) thus cast them as not only religiously different but sexually different as well. This difference found expression in the distinguishing religio-sexual mark of the Jew, circumcision—what the Greeks regarded as a deformity and the Romans a mutilation.[78]

Thus from earliest biblical times the Jew was cast as religiously and sexually different from his neighbors. "I am the Lord your God, who have separated you from the peoples" (Leviticus 20:24). "And you shall not walk in the customs of the nation which I am casting out before you; for they did all these things, and therefore I abhorred them" (Leviticus 20:23).[79] Within the context of fertility cult ideology, it was the Jew who, in deviating from the religious norm, deviated from the sexual norm. Whether conscious or unconscious, the first outlines of the Jew as a sexually atypical figure began to form.

The religious difference of the Jew implied yet a further

difference. In the ancient world, church and state commingled and were often one. Greek city-states were built on a religious-political system bonded together by the worship and celebration of common gods. (The Roman Empire was similarly united by emperor worship.) Although the Jews were exempt from laws and obligations that violated their religious precepts under the Greeks and Romans, their rejection of foreign gods elicited from the Greeks the charge of impiety, and was construed as an attack upon established government. To the Greeks and their Roman successors impiety gave way to disloyalty and treason. (Ironically, the Jew was charged with credulity, the gullibility to believe in an imageless God.) In reprisal the Syrian-Greek king, Antiochus Epiphanes IV, answered with, "Hellenize or Die," a policy indicating the lack of distinction between the religious and political differences of the Jew. And Rome, in its brutal assault upon Jewish messianism, equally assessed the religion of the Jew in frankly political terms.

Thus in the context of Graeco-Roman paganism the Jew, not only religiously and sexually different but also politically different by virtue of his faith, was early regarded as a figure outside the norm of society's conventions. To this primary yet shadowy portrait other attributes were readily attached:

The Jews were an inferior race—the mongrel offspring of criminal outcasts, a band of traitors led by the leprous Moses, a people who worshiped an ass (Egyptian symbol of the devil).[80] The Jews were "Syrians," a term of contempt applied to a non-aggressive, submissive people,[81] members of the slave race, cunning, cringing, low, lacking in self-respect, afflicted with the vices of slavery.[82] The Jews were held to be descendants of Hindu philosophers, Persian magi, related to magicians, sorcerers, fortune-tellers, a superstitious caste inclined toward mysterious and occult practices.[83]

The Jew was unsociable, aloof from civilized society, engaging in inhospitable[84] and inhuman acts, a creature hateful to gods and men alike. (Particularly odious was his observation of the Jewish dietary laws and the Sabbath, severely restricting his fellowship and withdrawing him from the milieu of the Saturnalias.) The Jew was xenophobic, ill-using strangers. On special occasions he engaged in cannibalism.[85] At other times he was the agent of ritual murder, being given to capturing young Greek males and sacrificing them for religious purposes.[86]

With the advent of the Romans, the proto-monsterism of the Jew, laid down by the Egyptians and the Greeks, was refined from crude legend and folktale to the sophistication of poetry, wit, the theater and satire. Fueled by such luminaries as Horace, Martial and Petronius, the new elitism was perhaps best expressed by the famed orator Cicero in his otherwise uneventful defense of a Roman prefect accused[87] of maladministration. Cicero's speech[88] is remarkable in that it brings forward the same elements of the Jew's aberrant profile as were expressed two thousand years later in the editorials of the American newspaper, *The Dearborn Independent*.

<table>
<tr><td>*Cicero:*</td><td>*The Dearborn Independent*</td></tr>
</table>

(A figure outside convention . . .)

. . . There was little in common between the religious customs of which their [Jewish] rites are examples and those which befit an empire as splendid as ours. . . .	Into the camp of [the American] race . . . comes a people that has no civilization . . . no aspiring religion, no universal speech, no great achievement in any realm. . . . (May 21, 1921)

(. . . transcending law . . .)

Because of Flaccus' [the Roman prefect's] vigorous administration [i.e., upholding a law repugnant to Jews] . . . he dared defy . . . the furious mass of Jews. . . .

"Any law which appears to be obnoxious to the self-centered Jewish element, is deliberately . . . opposed [by them] with a stubborn resistance. . . ." (December 10, 1921)

(. . . accursed . . .)

. . . the [Jewish nation] . . . has made clear how far it has enjoyed divine protection by the fact that it has been conquered, scattered and enslaved.[89]

"But enough of the 'chosen people.' Someday they will reap what they have sown. . . ." Moses is their judge, and . . . will be their destroyer. . . . (August 27, 1921; January 7, 1922)

(. . . committed to the downfall of others . . .)

[The Jews are members of] a foreign superstition . . . recently in arms against Rome. . . .

[The Jews are arms merchants] . . . their traditional loyalty being to the Jewish nation, rather than to any other nation. . . . (October 8, 1921)

(. . . forcing his evil will upon society . . .)

. . . mischief-makers . . .

[The Jews] have stirred up the people in all countries, have incited them to wars, revolution and communism. . . . (August 27, 1921)

(. . . with the intent of seeking world dominion.)

... how numerous [the Jewish class] is, with what unanimity they act, and what strength they exhibit in the political meetings. . . .

International Jews today occupy literally every controlling level of power. . . . (January 14, 1922)

Thus by the time of Jesus a distinctly anomalous blueprint of the Jew had been drawn. To be sure this pre-Christian prototype was sketchy and incomplete, yet its major components were unmistakably in evidence: the Jew was a creature of unorthodox metaphysics, belonging to an inferior race, inhuman, unsociable, inhospitable, a member of a powerful conspiracy, socially, politically and sexually different.

By what quirk did the Jew become the anti-hero of the New Religion?

How was the sketchy Graeco-Roman portrait transformed into a coherent picture? How did Christianity come to perceive the Jew no longer as a figure of simple religious difference—but in the image of the devil? From what scriptural clues did the Patristic Fathers apprehend the configuration of the demon and bring it to theological life? How did the Middle and subsequent Modern Ages emphasize—in the idiom of art and drama, literature and rhetoric—the continuity of the disciple of Satan?

Contemporary anti-Semitism is nearly two thousand years old. What has accounted for this peculiar phenomenon? By what means has the New Testament come to identify the Jew as *persona non grata* in the Christian era?

How does the Christ story fuel anti-Semitism?

The answer lies in the apprehension of the Christ story as a fertility drama. In the ancient theme of rite and pageantry, manifest in the duality of Jesus as God and as man. In the visibility of the sacred marriage ceremony for the propitiation of the life force—immured within the Gospel of John. For in setting forth an account of birth, death and resurrection, in the specific imagery of a "wedding on the third day," the Christ story invokes the reality of its inner voice. The marriage of the Mother Goddess and the young deity, the relationship of incest between Mother and Son. It is in this relationship—within the dialectics of the unconscious mind—that Christian anti-Semitism is born:

For as God, Jesus is absolved of earthly transgression, exempt from the incest taboo. But as man, Jesus is bound by the incest taboo. He is subject to retribution.

As God, Jesus is privileged, innocent by reason of his Divine Prerogative. As man, Jesus is culpable, in violation by virtue of his human condition.

As God, Jesus is Christian: the emerging Deity of Cana, the offspring of Father and Virgin, the Firstborn to be Sacrificed, the suffering, dying God of Calvary. As man, Jesus is a Jew.

Correlatively, Christians—who believe in the divinity of Jesus, who follow him, who are part of him—are also incest free, absolved by virtue of their membership in Jesus the God. Those who are outside the Christian God, who remain living representatives of Jesus' earthly counterpart, are guilty of incest by virtue of their kinship in Jesus the Jew.

It is thus in the "verification" of the Christ story's latent incest drama that a credible mechanism for Christian anti-Semitism emerges. In the dual nature of Jesus the Divine Prerogative of the God becomes the mortal error of man. The religious incest of the Son becomes the sacrilegious act of the Jew.

It is by this mechanism that the Jew is transformed into a "monster," and that the Christ story transmits its message of Christian anti-Semitism;[90] also that a story that teaches love, brotherhood, sacrifice, salvation and redemption can convey hate and loathing for the very people, the very religion from which it historically derives; that a story whose central character—himself Jewish—can be anti-Jewish.

And it is for this reason that Jews are hated. That Jews have been persecuted, murdered and massacred. The Christ story transmits the Jew as guilty. Of incest. Of being a "monster." At the end of a cruader's sword or a modern bayonet, the target of "special missions" or "special handling," the anti-Semite has seen only the monster.

From Inquisition to Holocaust, good, sane men and women acting in the name of God, have merely done what they have been programmed to do: kill. Kill the monster. By tens, hundreds, thousands. By six millions.

Notes

Chapter 5

[1] Jastrow, Morris, Jr "The Gilgamesh Epic," in *The Religion of Babylonia and Assyria,* Ginn and Company: Boston, 1898, pp. 467–517.

[2] Kapelrud, Arvid S. *Ras Shamra Discoveries and the Old Testament* (G. W. Anderson, trans.), Basil Blackwell: Oxford, 1965, pp. 62–63.

[3] The religion of the Canaanites was apparently the principal fertility cult with which the Hebrews contended throughout the Old Testament. Despite the constant polemic against the cult of Baal, especially on the part of the prophets, Baalism did influence to some extent the language, rites and practices of the religion of the Israelites.

[4] Frankfort, Henri. *Kingship and the Gods,* The University of Chicago Press: Chicago, 1948, p. 40.

[5] The name *Virgo,* the Virgin, sixth constellation in the zodiac, is of ancient origin and has always been associated with the planting and harvest.

[6] Old Testament accounts of such practices include the king of Moab who burnt his eldest son as an offering to the fertility god (2

Kings 3:27), and the Israelites themselves who, despite contrary tradition, were sometimes corrupted by the practice of child sacrifice to the fertility god Molech: "And they caused their sons and daughters to pass through the fire . . ." (2 Kings 17:17).

[7] Sayce, Archibald H. *The Religion of Ancient Egypt,* T. & T. Clark: Edinburgh, 1913, pp. 249–250.

[8] The name given to the temple prostitutes among the Babylonians meant "the sacred one," attesting to the religious nature of their rite.

[9] Herodotus, Book I (Clio), paragraphs 181, 182, in *Herodotus* (William Beloe, trans.), F. C. and J. Rivington (et al.): London, 1821.

[10] Charles, R. H. Herodotus, Book I, paragraph 199, in *The Apocrypha and Pseudepigrapha of the Old Testament,* Clarendon Press: Oxford, 1913, Vol. I, Apocrypha: Epistle of Jeremy, note 43.

[11] Matthew answers the skeptics by portraying the miracle of the Divine Conception from Joseph's point of view, in which the husband's doubts are put to rest by the words of the angel.

[12] The Transitus literature includes the gospels of *Pseudo-Melito, Pseudo-John* and a tract by the sixth-century Archbishop Theodosius, *The Falling Asleep of Mary.*

[13] In contradistinction, the New Testament itself presents certain challenges and apparent inconsistencies to the virgin motherhood of Mary. For example, various passages refer to Jesus' parents and to Joseph as Jesus' father (Luke 2:27, 41, 43, 48). Other passages refer to Jesus' brothers and sisters (Mark 3:31, 6:3). Matthew and Luke trace the genealogy of Jesus to the House of David through his father, Joseph (Matthew 1:1–16, Luke 3:23–38). Matthew remarks that "Joseph . . . took his wife, but knew her not until she had born a son" (Matthew 1:24–25), implying challenge to the concept of the perpetual virginity of Mary.

Another inconsistency is found in the Old Testament passage Matthew quotes as being a prediction of the virgin motherhood of Mary: "Behold, a virgin shall conceive and bear a son, and his name shall be called Emmanuel" (Isaiah 7:14, Matthew 1:23). In this passage the word "virgin" is translated from the Hebrew word, *almah,* which means "young woman, girl or maiden"—but not necessarily a virgin. The word *almah* is translated as the equivalent of "young woman" in Exodus 2:8 and Psalms 68:25. It is the feminine form of "elem," meaning "young man" as translated in 1 Samuel 17:56 and 20:22. Not until the *Septagint,* the Greek translation of the Hebrew Bible dated about 300 B.C., did the Hebrew word *almah* become translated into the Greek *parthenos,* which does indeed mean virgin. Whatever the reasons behind the rendering of *almah* (young woman) as *parthenos* (virgin), subsequent translations from the original Old Testament Hebrew and from the Septuagint tended to perpetuate the new rendering. In short, the word "virgin" has been challenged as a misreading which should read "young woman," as do Jewish and liberal Protestant translations.

The most significant challenge to the doctrine of the virgin motherhood of Mary in the New Testament is the complete absence of such a doctrine from the Epistles of Paul, the very architect of the Christian faith. Paul's only reference to Mary is found in Galatians 4:4: "God sent forth his Son, born of woman . . ." The absence of the doctrine of the virgin birth is echoed in the Epistles of Peter. Neither Mark nor John laid down any formal doctrine of the virgin motherhood of Mary. In Mark 3:32, Mary appears incidentally: "Your mother and your brothers are outside . . ." a crowd announces. In John, Mary appears at two significant events in Jesus' life: at the wedding at Cana where, at her request, Jesus performs his first miracle; and at Calvary, where he commends his mother to the unnamed beloved disciple.

These challenges and inconsistencies are answered in general by implication. Throughout the New Testament, Jesus is always portrayed as a divine being, the Son of God. A grouping of God as the Father with Jesus as the Son of God, would suggest that Jesus' mother, "the handmaid of the Lord," is also an extraordinary personage.

[14] Palmer, Paul F. A Mother's Song to Her Son (St. Ephrem: Hymns on Blessed Mary), in *Mary in the Documents of the Church,* The Newman Press: Westminister, Maryland, 1952, p. 18, vs. 6.

[15] In final rebuttal to the Nestorian heresy.

[16] Miegge, Giovanni. *The Virgin Mary, The Roman Catholic Marian Doctrine* (Waldo Smith, trans.), Luttleworth Press: London, 1950, p. 61.

[17] Palmer, *op. cit.*, p. 52 (Theodotus of Ancyra: Mary Immaculate).

[18] Carol, Juniper B. (ed.). *Mariology,* The Bruce Publishing Company: Milwaukee, 1955, Vol. 1, p. 394.

[19] Palmer, *op. cit.*, p. 63 (St. John of Damascus: On the Nativity of the Mother of God). See also: Carol (ed.), *op. cit.*, p. 356.

[20] Sheed, Francis J. (ed.). *The Mary Book,* Sheed and Ward: New York, 1950, p. 220.

[21] The doctrine of Mary's perpetual virginity was not easily accepted, and it became a subject of dispute among the early church fathers, even among some of Mary's champions. This dispute and related challenges were in part answered by the Protoevangelium (Gospel of James) and allied writings, in which the absolute and perpetual virginity of Mary were defended.

[22] Carol (ed.), *op. cit.*, p. 13. See also: Palmer, *op. cit.*, pp. 31–32.

[23] This primal sin is transmitted from generation to generation through sexual intercourse. To this sin are ascribed all the troubles of mankind associated with the "fall from grace."

[24] The Doctrine of the Immaculate Conception holds that although Mary was conceived in intercourse, God intervened and preserved her from original sin. See Carol (ed.), *op. cit.* (Pope Pius IX: *Ineffabilis Deus*), pp. 22–23. See also Palmer, *op. cit.*, pp. 86–87.

[25] Especially the *Transitus Literature*. See James, Montague Rhodes (ed.): The Discourse of Theodosius, in *The Apocryphal New Testament,* Clarendon Press: Oxford, 1972, pp. 199–200; *ibid.,* Pseudo-Melito: The Assumption, p. 216. See also Carol (ed.), *op. cit.*, pp. 164–175.

[26] Carol (ed.), *op. cit.*, pp. 24–25 (Pope Pius XII: *Munificentissimus Deus*). See also: Palmer, *op. cit.*, p. 113.

[27] These phenomena are principally manifest in apparitions of the Virgin. Such apparitions have reputedly occurred at many times and in many places: in Lourdes and La Sallette (France), in Banneux and Beaurang (Belgium), in Fatima (Portugal), etc. Typically the apparitions take place in a pastoral setting, in the countryside, away from civilization (remote, natural setting) or in or near a church, and are witnessed by children as well as adults. Invariably the Virgin delivers a message to the world through these witnesses, and

the locales in which she is seen often become shrines to which the sick make pilgrimage. Statues, paintings, relics and various depictions of the Madonna have also allegedly become animated: in Hungary a painting shed tears and blood on St. Patrick's Day in 1697; in Syracuse, Sicily, a terra-cotta bust of the Virgin wept in 1953. Paintings, statues, medals, relics, which have come alive and replicas thereof, are regarded as being endowed with miraculous powers associated with the Virgin.

[28] This portrayal is based on her purity, which obliterates the sin of the first mother of mankind. The seduction, disobedience and death represented by the original Eve, are negated by the virginity, obedience and life of the New Eve.

[29] Carol (ed.), *op. cit.*, p. 46 *(Magnae Dei Matris)*.

[30] *Ibid.*, p. 39 *(Ad diem illum)*. See also: Palmer, *op. cit.*, p. 95.

[31] Carol (ed.), *op. cit.*, p. 39 (Pope Benedict XV: *Inter Sodalicia*). See also: Palmer, *op. cit.*, pp. 96–97. See also: *Acta Apostolicae Sedis*, Vol. 10, 1918, p. 182.

[32] Ishtar, principal mother-goddess of the ancient Babylonian religion, was accorded similar appellations. She was the queen of heaven, the glorious lady, the lady of heaven and earth, Associate of the [sun-god], ". . . who receives prayer, who harkens to the petition . . ." See Jastrow, op. cit., pp. 310, 325.

[33] Mary is portrayed as an active participant in her Son's Crucifixion: *Iucunda Semper,* Pope Leo XIII, *in* Carol (ed.), *op. cit.,* p. 37; *Ad diem illum,* Pope Pius X, *in* Carol (ed.), *op. cit.,* p. 36; Apostolic Letter, *Inter Sodalicia,* Pope Benedict XV, *in* Carol (ed.), *op. cit.,* p. 37 (see also Palmer, *op. cit.,* pp. 96–97); *Miserentissimus Redemptor,* Pope Pius XI, in Carol (ed.), *op. cit.,* p. 37 (see also: Palmer, *op. cit.,* p. 98; *Acta Apostolicae Sedis,* Vol. 20, 1928, p. 178); Encyclical *Mystici Corporis,* Pope Pius XII, *in* Carol (ed.), *op. cit.,* p. 37 (see also: Palmer, *op. cit.,* p. 99; *Acta Apostolicae Sedis,* Vol. 35, 1943, pp. 247–248).

Chapter 6

[1] See Old Testament Apocrypha, 1 Maccabees.

[2] The relationship between the Jews and Rome prior to 63 B.C. was one of geniality, characterized by mutual respect and admira-

tion. In *1 Maccabees* (c. 100 B.C.) the Jews are proclaimed by the Romans as "friends, confederates and brethren . . ." (14:40). The Jewish view of the Romans was also similar:

> And Judas [Maccabee] heard of the fame of the Romans . . . that they were friendly disposed towards all who attached themselves to them, and they offered friendship to as many as came unto them . . . that they were valiant men.
>
> —*1 Maccabees 8:1*

Partly as a result of the Hasmonean policy of making Judaism a missionary religion and extensive propaganda, Jewish rituals and beliefs were observed by many Romans, who on the whole exhibited a marked interest in Jewish culture (several major Roman synagogues date from this period). Converts and followers, adding to the already significant Jewish population in Rome, were commonplace, the former including many women; for men, circumcision tended to remain a deterrent to full conversion. The period of mutual respect and admiration came to an end in 63 B.C. with the Roman presence in Palestine.

[3] Jesus was indicated to be of Davidic lineage (Matthew 1:1).

[4] So sustained was the Roman reaction to the threat of Jewish messianism that even after the death of Jesus, at the time of Paul, the "prophet" Theudas who promised to divide the Jordan river was beheaded by the Romans, his followers murdered by Roman cavalry.

Chapter 7

[1] The Pharisees were responsible for the moral leadership of the Jewish people and for promulgating democratic principles among them. It is essentially because of Pharisaic tenacity that normative Judaism survives today.

[2] One doctrine held that the Messiah would be a military leader who would throw off the yoke of Sadducean oligarchy as well as that of paganism.

[3] Josephus: Wars of the Jews, Book II, Chapt. VIII, 5, in *The Works of Flavius Josephus* (William Whiston, trans.), George Virtue: London, 1844.

[4] Dupont-Sommer, Andre. *The Jewish Sect of Qumran and the Essenes*, The Macmillan Company: New York, 1956, pp. 98–99; see also Josephus, *op. cit.*, Book II, Chapt. VIII, 5. John the Baptist has been linked with the Essenes (Burrows, Millar: *More Light on the Dead Sea Scrolls*, The Viking Press: New York, 1958, pp. 56–63; see also Dupont-Sommer, *op. cit.*, pp. 149, 154).

[5] Dupont-Sommer, *op. cit.*, pp. 99–101; see also Josephus, *op. cit.*, Book II, Chapt. VIII, 5. Josephus likens the Essene dining room to a "holy temple" (see also Dupont-Sommer, *op. cit.*, p. 100). The Last Supper is sometimes described to be an Essene meal (Dupont-Sommer, *op. cit.*, p. 152).

[6] Josephus, *op. cit.*, Book II, Chapt. VIII, 6.

[7] *Ibid.*, Chapter VIII,5.

[8] *Ibid.*, Chapter VIII,12.

[9] Pliny the Elder, A. D. 23–79; in Wilson, Edmund, *The Dead Sea Scrolls*, Oxford University Press: New York, 1969, p. 26.

[10] Burrows, Millar. *The Dead Sea Scrolls*, The Viking Press: New York, 1955, pp. 390–399; see also Wilson, Edmund, *op. cit.*, pp. 64–65.

[11] The fate of the Essenes after the Revolt of 66–70 A.D. is unknown. They may have fled into exile or become absorbed into other groups bearing different names. However, their ideas survived as did their writings—the Dead Sea Scrolls representing one of the most significant archeological finds of the twentieth century.

[12] The Zealots disappeared entirely with the Bar Kochba rebellion in 132 A.D.

[13] In the gospels Pharisaic doctrine and the Pharisees were to be depicted in an unsympathetic manner, being portrayed as antagonistic to Jesus and ready to ensnare him with ambiguous religious questions. Yet their relationship is also one of commonality. As a youth Jesus sits in the Temple "among the teachers [Pharisees], listening to them and asking questions" (Luke 2:46). As an adult Jesus accepts the Written Law (Torah), the prophets and eschatological ideas, emphasizing: "Think not that I have come to abolish the law" (Matthew 5:17). He admonishes his disciples: ". . . practice and observe whatever they [the Pharisees] tell you" (Matthew 23:3). He is called "Rabbi" (John 3:2), preaching in the syn-

agogues without encumbrance: "And they went into Capernaum; and immediately on the Sabbath he entered the synagogue and taught" (Mark 1:21). Jesus employs Pharisaic techniques; questioned on points of law, he renders an interpretation (Matthew 22:17,21). Since the Pharisees were ultimately to become synonymous with "the Jews"—being the only party to survive Roman-Jewish conflicts and carry on Judaism—their unflattering depiction in the gospels was to have far-reaching consequences for the Jewish people in general.

[14] The Sadducean view and the Sadducees were also to be distinguished in the gospels by their conflict with the architect of this theme. Jesus is arrested by Sadducean (Temple) police; he is arraigned before a Sadducean High Priest (Annas); he is tried before a Sadducean court (the Sanhedrin, presided over by an appointee of Pontius Pilate), and he is remanded by Pilate to elements of a Sudducean mob (chief priests) who cry for his death. As with the Pharisees—Pharisees, Sadducees, chief priests, High Priests, scribes, elders all being synonyms for the "Jews"—the gospels' portrayal of this group was to have fateful consequences for all Jews.

[15] Because much of Essenism was "a foretaste of Christianity" (Ernest Renan), many attempts have been made to inferentially associate Jesus directly with the Essenes. However, the association is conjectural, since nowhere in the gospels is there any mention of the Essenes, and nowhere in those documents which do reference the Essenes is there any mention of Jesus. Indirect evidence supporting an Essene link with Jesus includes the following: Essene-like references have been detected in such New Testament works as the teachings of Paul, the Gospel of John, the Epistle of James, the Epistle of Barnabus, the Epistle to the Hebrews and in one of the Dead Sea Scrolls; Essenic sects were widespread at the time of Jesus; John the Baptist preached the Essenic doctrine of baptism for the remission of sins; Jesus' brother, James, established the first Christian Church (Primitive Church) in Jerusalem along Essene organizational lines; Jesus' values, as expressed in the Sermon on the Mount (Matthew 5), indicate a common reservoir of beliefs with the Essenes. Whether Jesus and the Essenes did have a relationship,

and the nature of this relationship, is a manifestation of what has been called "the quest for the historical Jesus" (Albert Schweitzer) and as such awaits documentation still pending discovery.

[16] Although the gospels were to make but a single reference to the Zealots—"Simon the Zealot" (Luke 6:15; also Acts 1:13)—the question arises, Was Jesus an adherent of this group? In effect, Was Jesus a Zealot? Jesus declares: "Do not think I have come to bring peace . . . I have come not to bring peace, but a sword" (Matthew 10:34). He employs parables and symbols in answering queries put to those of specific Zealot leanings (Matthew 22:17, John 18:33). He is accused of Zealot offenses: "Perverting the nation . . . forbidding to give tribute to Caesar, saying that he himself is Christ" (Luke 23:2). He is prosecuted as a "Galilean" (revolutionary). And he is crucified as a Jewish subject of Rome. A Pharisee by tradition, a Sadducee by exception (his rejection of the Oral Law), an Essene by inclination, Jesus is charged, tried and dies a Zealot.

[17] The Zealots were to underline the primacy of Roman interests in the political affairs of Palestine. Pilate, characterized as an indecisive, basically good fellow, upon learning that the prisoner Jesus is a "Galilean" (synonym for Zealot), apparently changes his mind about finding "no fault" in him. With the revelation that the accused—a messianic figure, a man who has violently attacked the existing order (money changers), who has rejected the "crown," who has a following—comes from a province of insurrections, the interest of Rome is rekindled in the prisoner. Jesus is sent to Herod Antipas, who returns him to Pilate. Thereupon the death sentence is pronounced.

Chapter 8
[1] However, the ancient Jews did believe that in death under certain circumstances the spirit *(nephesh)* was set free from its envelope of flesh, that it could assume an identical preexisting body, that it was not uncommon for "the double" to make public appearances after death.

[2] "In the beginning was the Word . . . and the Word was God" (John 1:1).

[3] Gr., *knowledge:* "Divine Enlightenment."

[4] Based on the myth of Persephone and Hades.

[5] In a rendering of the drama of Cybele and Attis, Attis—son and lover of Cybele—castrates himself under a pine tree (after intercourse) and bleeds to death. Lamenting her lover's (son's) death, the grieving goddess, Cybele, in order to ensure his resurrection and rebirth, designates the pine tree—ever-green—as the symbol of his eternal life.

[6] As originally celebrated, a real man, usually a priest, was tied to the tree.

[7] Frazer, Sir James George. *The Golden Bough,* Macmillan Company: London (St. Martin's Press: New York), 1955, Vol. 5, pp. 267–273.

[8] The gods were in general amoral beings, themselves given to extremes in vice, demanding little from their respective worshippers.

[9] Because the life forces of the world were perceived to be a function of the sexual relationships of the gods, under fertility cult auspices sexual expression became religious expression; sexual practices—in all their manifestations—became religious rite. It was this aspect of pagan ritual with which religious propagandists and writers contended both before and immediately after the advent of the Christian era.

[10] Similar accounts appear in many Near Eastern religions.

[11] In contradistinction to the dualistic scheme, the final dwelling place for the dead in pre-Exilic Judaism was *Sheol*—a netherworld deep in the earth, a place of darkness and silence where "[the dead] . . . sleep a perpetual sleep, and not wake" (Jeremiah 51:39,57).

[12] Guignebert, Charles. *The Jewish World in the Time of Jesus,* E. P. Dutton & Co.: New York, 1939, p. 109. See also: Josephus, Antiquities of the Jews, Book XVIII, Chapter I,3, in *The Works of Flavius Josephus* (William Whiston, trans.), George Virtue: London, 1844.

[13] Viewed as sexuality outside God's Law, intermarriage was equated with the taking of foreign gods, the direct cause of the Babylonian Exile and resulting Dispersion: "We have trespassed against our God, and have taken strange wives of the people of the land. . . . Now therefore let us make a covenant with our God to put away all the wives, and such as are born of them. . . ." (Ezra 10:2,3)

Chapter 9

[1] From the Greek, meaning *hidden, difficult to comprehend*.

[2] Charles, R. H. *The Apocrypha and Pseudepigrapha of the Old Testament*, Clarendon Press: Oxford, 1913, Vol. 1, Apocrypha: 1 and 2 Maccabees.

[3] *Ibid.*, 1 Esdras.

[4] *Ibid.*, Ecclesiasticus (Sirach), Wisdom of Solomon.

[5] *Ibid.*, Epistle of Jeremy, Bel and the Dragon.

[6] *Ibid.*, 1 Baruch.

[7] This theme was mirrored in the pseudepigraphical book, the Fragments of a Zadokite Work (also known as the Damascus Document of the Dead Sea Scrolls).

[8] Charles, *op. cit.*, Vol. II, Pseudepigrapha: The Book of Jubilees, The Books of Adam and Eve, The Martydom of Isaiah, The Assumption of Moses.

[9] *Ibid.*, The Sibylline Oracles.

[10] *Ibid.*, The Psalms of Solomon.

[11] *Ibid.*, *Pirke Aboth:* The Sayings of the Fathers.

[12] *Ibid.*, 4 Maccabees.

[13] *Ibid.*, The Letter of Aristeas.

[14] Gaster, Theodor H. Thanksgiving Psalms XIV, 1–27, in *The Dead Sea Scriptures*, Doubleday & Co.: New York, 1956, p. 188.

[15] In 1986 a manuscript—the Fragments of a Zadokite Work—was discovered in a Cairo *genizah*, a room in which discarded scripture is "buried" (stored), since it is against Jewish law to destroy holy books. The manuscript, thought to date from the Middle Ages, was translated in 1910 by Solomon Schechter. Over fifty years later the syncretistic content of this manuscript, puzzling to many scholars at the time of its discovery, would become clear. Among the Dead Sea Scrolls was the Damascus Document, containing the Fragments of a Zadokite Work: The Damascus Document of Qumran was the manuscript of the Cairo *genizah*. The document relates the migration of the Sect of the Covenant to the "land of Damascus"—the real geographical location of which is still uncertain—spelling out in detail the Order's teachings on sacrifices, dietary rules, procedures for enrolling adherents, penal and urban codes, and rules concerning the observance of the Sabbath.

[16] The Isaiah Scroll, the first of the Dead Sea Scrolls to be discovered, was initially recognized by E. L. Sukenik of Hebrew University to be at least one thousand years older than any previously known copy of the same book.

[17] Charles, *op. cit.*, Vols. I and II, Apocrypha and Pseudepigrapha: Tobit, The Book of Jubilees, I Enoch.

[18] *Ibid.*, Ecclesiasticus, The Sibylline Oracles, The Book of the Heavenly Luminaries (I Enoch).

[19] *Ibid*, The Widom of Solomon, The Testament of Levi.

[20] Gaster, *op. cit.*, The Manual of Discipline, pp. 39–60.

[21] *Ibid.*

[22] Charles, *op. cit.*, Vols. I and II, Apocrypha and Pseudepigrapha: The Wisdom of Solomon, 2 Enoch.

[23] *Ibid.*, 2 Maccabees, Fragments of a Zadokite Work.

[24] Gaster, *op. cit.*, The Manual of Discipline, pp. 39–60.

[25] *Ibid.*, Thanksgiving Psalms XII, 35, p. 183.

[26] Dupont-Sommer, André. The Manual of Discipline X, 8–17, in *The Jewish Sect of Qumran and the Essenes,* The Macmillan Co.: New York, 1956, p. 141.

[27] Charles, *op. cit.*, Vols. I and II, Apocrypha and Pseudepigrapha: The Wisdom of Solomon, The Assumption of Moses.

[28] Gaster, *op. cit.*, The War of the Sons of Light and the Sons of Darkness, pp. 281–306.

[29] Ibid., The Manual of Discipline, pp. 39–60.

[30] Charles, *op. cit.*, Vols. I and II, Apocrypha and Pseudepigrapha: Ecclesiasticus, the Letter of Aristeas.

[31] *Ibid.*, The Wisdom of Solomon, IV Maccabees.

[32] Gaster, *op. cit.*, The Manual of Discipline, pp. 39–60.

[33] Dupont-Sommer, André. The Manual of Discipline iii, 4–9, in *The Jewish Sect of Qumran and the Essenes, op. cit.,* p. 99.

[34] Charles, *op. cit.*, Vol. I, Apocrypha: The Wisdom of Solomon 8:2.

[35] "For my memorial is sweeter than honey, And the possession of me [sweeter] than the honey-comb" (Ecclesiasticus 24:20). See also Charles, *op. cit.*, Vol. 1, Ecclesiasticus (Sirach) 24:19.

[36] Esdras asks the question, Which is the strongest: wine, the

king, women or truth? Following a lengthly dissertation on the power of women, Truth, although later idealized in the form of woman, is given as the ultimate victor: "Women are the strongest: but above all things Truth beareth away the victory" (1 Esdras 3:12). See also Charles, *op. cit.*, Vol. I, Esdras 4:40.

37 Charles, *op. cit.*, Vol. II, Pseudepigrapha: The Letter to Aristeas 250.

38 *Ibid.*, Vol. I, Apocrypha: Ecclesiasticus 25:24.

39 *Ibid.*, Vol. II, Pseudepigrapha: The Books of Adam and Eve, iii, 2.

40 *Ibid.*, The Testaments of the Twelve Patriarchs: The Testament of Reuben 5:1–6:2. See also: The Testament of Judah 17:1; The Testament of Issachar 4:4.

Chapter 10

1 Isaiah 45:1.

2 Haggai 2:20–23.

3 Daniel 9.

4 Various scholars have described the "suffering servant" of Isaiah 53 as an allegorical allusion to Israel's suffering at the hands of the Gentiles (in Isaiah 49:3, antecedent to Isaiah 53, Israel appears as the personified servant of God).

5 The concept of expiatory suffering is more complex than that of the scapegoat as expressed in Leviticus 16:8–10, in which the goat merely relieves others of their sins.

6 Various scholars believe Isaiah to have been composed over a period of several centuries.

7 Frazer, Sir James George. Laments for Tammuz, in *The Golden Bough*, The Macmillan Co.: London (St. Martin's Press: New York), 1955, Vol. 5, p. 9.

8 *Ibid.*, Vol. 9, p. 371.

9 This quotation represents part of Ezekiel's reactions to the practices (sun worship, idolatry, human sacrifice) of fertility cults prevalent at the time.

10 Charles, R. H. *The Apocrypha and Pseudepigrapha of the Old Testament*, Clarendon Press: Oxford, 1913, Vol. II, Pseudepigrapha: Enoch 48:10.

[11] *Ibid.*, Enoch 53:6.

[12] *Ibid.*, Enoch 69:27.

[13] *Ibid.*, Enoch 51:2.

[14] *Ibid.*, Enoch 48:4.

[15] *Ibid.*, Enoch 49:2.

[16] *Ibid.*, Enoch 71:15.

[17] *Ibid.*, Enoch 48:3.

[18] *Ibid.*, Enoch 48:7.

[19] *Ibid.*, Enoch 51:3.

[20] The appellation, Son of Man, connoting a closeness of relationship with God, appears in the late Old Testament Book of Daniel, written in the intertestamental period in 165 B.C., in the context of a Messiah figure: ". . . and, behold, one like the Son of man came with the clouds of heaven. . . . And there w.s given him dominion, and glory, and a kingdom, that all people, nations, and languages, should serve him. . . ." (Daniel 7:13,14).

[21] Charles, *op. cit.*, Vol. II, Pseudepigrapha: Enoch 46:1–4.

[22] *Ibid.*, Enoch 48:5; 62:9.

[23] Features of this Messiah, relating to the fall of Jerusalem to the Roman general Pompey in 63 B.C., may date somewhat later and represent subsequent insertions to the Testament of Levi.

[24] The Messiah from the House of Levi incorporates the attributes of the Messiahs from the House of Judah (king) and from the House of Aaron (prophet).

[25] Charles, *op. cit.*, Vol. II, Pseudepigrapha: The Testament of Levi 18:9,10. See also: Dupont-Sommer, André. The Testament of Levi, in *The Jewish Sect of Qumran and the Essenes,* The Macmillan Co.: New York, 1956, p. 42.

[26] Charles, *op. cit.*, The Testament of Judah 24:1.

[27] "And in the New Jerusalem shall the righteous rejoice. . . ." See Charles, *op. cit.*, The Testament of Dan 5:12.

[28] The Teacher of Righteousness appears prominently in the Habakkuk Commentary of the Dead Sea Scrolls. He is also mentioned directly in the Damascus Document (Fragments of a Zadokite Work), Commentary on Psalm 37 and the Micah Commentary. Allusions to this personage may likewise occur in The Testament of Levi, The Assumption of Moses and the Nahum Commentary.

²⁹ The Teacher of Righteousness may antedate the Messiah from the House of Levi, as presented in The Testament of Levi 18, 19.

³⁰ A clear-cut portrayal of the Teacher of Righteousness is lacking, owing in part to the deliberate obscurity of the principal writings, *pesherim,* which describe his activities. Constructed of a series of veiled historical allusions, the *pesher*—a history in disguise—uses names of historical people, places and events of time past to represent contemporary people, places and happenings; the purpose of such disguises was most likely to protect the authors from political and religious reprisal. A portrayal of this figure is further complicated by scholarly differences in translation and the restoration of pertinent fragmentary and missing pages. Significant events of the Teacher's life are known principally as they relate to his chief adversary, the Wicked Priest (Habakkuk Commentary). Thought to be synonymous with the Prophet of the Untruth, Preacher of Falsehood, Preacher of the Lie, Man of the Lie, this antagonist—one of the last of the Hasmonean priest-kings (portrayed as corrupt plunderers of the people)—is characterized as an idolatrous drunkard who ". . . took the wealth of the people," wrought ways of "abomination" and reigned "in all impurity and uncleanness". Victims of treachery on the part of the Man of the Lie and his faction, the Teacher of Righteousness and his followers are persecuted, and subsequently imprisoned, exiled or executed—their exact crime remaining obscure. Although the "men of the House of Absalom" are also indicted for having "kept silence at the chastisement of the Teacher of Righteousness", the fate of this major historical Messiah figure is essentially unknown. See: Wilson, Edmund, *The Dead Sea Scrolls,* Oxford University Press: New York, 1969, p. 66. See also: Burrows, Millar, Habakkuk Commentary in *The Dead Sea Scrolls,* The Viking Press: New York, 1955, pp. 367, 368.

³¹ Burrows, *op. cit.,* Habakkuk Commentary 1:5, p. 365.

³² Referring to undeserved suffering, the Thanksgiving Psalms thematically resemble Babylonian Penitential hymns. See Burrows, *op. cit.,* Thanksgiving Psalms II (ii.8–13,16–19), p. 401.

³³ *Ibid.,* Thanksgiving Psalms XI (vii.6–9,11–15), P. 409.

³⁴ Gaster, Theodor H. Thanksgiving Psalms XIII, 1–21, in *The Dead Sea Scriptures,* Doubleday & Co.: New York, 1956, p. 187.

[35] *Ibid.*, Thanksgiving Psalms III, 19–36, p. 140.

[36] *Ibid.*, Thanksgiving Psalms XII, 35, pp. 182–183.

[37] *Ibid.*, Thanksgiving Psalms II, 2–19, p. 129.

[38] *Ibid.*, Thanksgiving Psalms III, 3–18, p. 136.

[39] Dupont-Sommer, *op. cit.*, Habakkuk Commentary viii, 3, p. 55.

[40] *Ibid.*, The Testament of Levi XVI, p. 48. See also: Charles, *op. cit.*, The Testament of Levi 16. The events related in The Testament of Levi may comprise the same story presented in the Habbakuk Commentary. The central character of the Testament of Levi—"the man who reneweth the law . . . the Savior of the world"—may be identical to the central character of the Habbakuk Commentary, the Teacher of Righteousness. See Dupont-Sommer, *op. cit*, pp. 14–57 and Wilson, *op. cit.*, pp. 55–77.

Chapter 11

[1] Opinions vary as to the date of the birth of Jesus, ranging from 20 B.C. to A.D. 4.

[2] Scholarly consensus generally puts Jesus' crucifixion in A.D. 30.

[3] Thirty-five miracles are attributed to Jesus in the Scriptures, with allusions to three others.

[4] Luke 1:34.

[5,6] Jesus responds to his mother in kind. When as a twelve-year old boy she discovers him in the temple, he replies: "How is it you sought me? Did you not know that I must be in my father's house?" (Luke 2:49). Upon hearing from his mother at Cana, "They have no wine," he replies, vexed: "My hour has not yet come" (John 2:3,4). Similarly, when a crowd announces, "Your mother and brothers are outside asking for you," he retorts: "Who are my mother and brothers?" (Mark 3:32,33; Matthew 12:47,48; Luke 8:20,21); when a woman in the crowd cries, "Blessed is the womb that bore you and the breasts that you sucked," he replies only: "Blessed rather are those who hear the word of God and keep it" (Luke 11:27,28); when upon returning home from a successful healing campaign and being declared by his family to be deranged ("He is beside himself"—Mark 3:21), he comments: ". . . a man's foes will be those of

his own household" (Matthew 10:36). The theological rationales for these incidents which portray a mother and son in seeming dissension, are many. Jesus' apparent lack of warmth for his mother is explained not as a matter of rudeness but of priority: even at a young age he is aware of the all-encompassing nature of his religious mission, which precludes special treatment for family members. When Jesus asks: "Who is my mother, and who are my brethren?" he is not rejecting his family, but merely alluding to the motif that all mankind is a holy family and that there are larger obligations than those of blood ties. His response to the woman commending his mother is likewise indicative of religious priorities, rather than evasion. Even the incident at Cana—in which both mother and son appear distinctly out of characer—illustrates not "contention" but rather the concept of Mary as a powerful Intercessor: the Son will not deny his Mother's wishes. Nevertheless, Jesus' rejection for his mother may well be genuine, as evidenced by his repeated renunciation of family: "If anyone comes to me and does not hate his own father and mother and wife and children and brothers and sisters . . . he cannot be my disciple" (Luke 14:26, Matthew 10:37).

[7]John is executed by King Herod Antipas as a result of his criticizing the king's marriage to Herodias, the former wife of Antipas' brother. At the king's birthday party, Herodias' daughter (Salome) danced and the king promised to fulfill her any wish. Consulting her mother, Salome is told to ask for the head of John the Baptist on a platter. The king, reluctant, but true to his word, complies.

[8]Royalty in the Christ story is further manifested in the serious attempt to crown Jesus king (John 6:15)—which is the fatal charge leveled against him: "This is Jesus the King of the Jews" (Matthew 27:37).

[9]Mary Magdalen displays the loyalty, devotion and love for Jesus characteristic of his outgroup followers. Frequently depicted in the arts as young and beautiful, she is held to be the woman who in each gospel anoints Jesus. She is depicted as being his devotee throughout his ministry, at Calvary and at the tomb where, after his crucifixion, he appears to her first (Mark 16:9), carries on a poig-

nant conversation with her, instructing her to go to his disciples, to whom she relates: "I have seen the Lord" . . . (John 20:18).

[10] ". . . many bodies of the saints which slept arose."

Chapter 12

[1] Year after year the horror story and the Christ story have been among the most successful publications in Western culture.

[2] Paul affirms several times that Mary's child, Jesus, is the seed of David according to the flesh (Romans 1:3) which would make Mary, Jesus' earthly parent, of Davidic lineage.

[3] The classic horror story frequently contains allusions to the idea of birth and motherhood. But in most of these stories it is the *male* who is portrayed as the creator: Frankenstein creates his "son" (the monster); Dr. Jekyll creates his "son" (Mr. Hyde); Dracula "vampirizes" his "children." The young woman is thus cast as a symbolic mother by being placed in proximity to the male, and therefore in proximity to the concepts of birth and the creation of new life forms.

[4] See also: Mark 9:31, 10:33; Luke 18:31–33; John 13:21.

[5] See also Matthew 10:23, Mark 10:45, Luke 5:24, John 3:14.

[6] Because death is not final in a metaphysical tale, the characters of both the horror story and the Christ story have the potential for reappearance after death. The characters of classic tales of horror (Dracula, Frankenstein and his monster, Dr. Jekyll and Mr. Hyde) are revived in an endless flow of continuing sequels. Similarly, in the Christ story Jesus makes several reappearances after death (to Mary Magdalen: Matthew 28:9, John 20:14; on the road to Emmaus: Luke 25:15; to the disciples: Matthew 28:17, Luke 24:36, John 21). And the figures of Jesus and the Virgin Mary continue to appear to living persons in religious experiences and visions.

Chapter 14

[1] Jesus is also both physically and psychologically marked as a result of his encounter with God at Gethsemane. ". . . greatly distressed and troubled . . . [his] soul sorrowful even unto death," Jesus calls upon his father in fervent prayer to reverse his fate: ". . . that . . . the hour might pass from him. . . ." In agony, Jesus

"sweats blood," but in the end realizes his fate must proceed unaltered: ". . . the hour has come. . . ." (Mark 14:32–42, Luke 22:39–44).

² In Mary's consent to the Father, she disavows her humanity (she conceives outside the laws of nature) and becomes a metaphysical being. As a result she must abdicate that part of her earthly condition which would otherwise participate in the fellowship of man. She must in effect relinquish the human dimension of her mortality.

³ Despite the fact that the relationship between Mary and Jesus has evolved into a model of mother-son love, gospel exchanges between Mary and Jesus (as an adult) are devoid of warmth, tenderness or affection. In these exchanges Mary typically moves in the direction of her Son, who in turn rejects her advances. For example, in Luke 2:42–49, Jesus, even as a boy of twelve, lost in the Temple, seems indifferent to the anxieties of his worried mother when he is found; in Mark 3:31–33 Jesus declines to meet with his mother and his family; in Luke 11:27–28 Jesus fails to take the opportunity to commend his mother under appropriate circumstances. (Jesus is repeatedly negative about family relationships in general: Mark 3:31–35; Matthew 10:35–37, 12:46–50; Luke 8:19–21, 14:26; John 7:5.) The relationship between Mary and Jesus has been rendered "loving" by interpretations of gospel exchanges and by commentaries outside Scripture.

Chapter 15

¹ Incest as an overt act occurs with surprising frequency, as evidenced in daily media accounts, court cases and sociological studies. It has been portrayed artistically in contemporary literature (W. Somerset Maugham, Thomas Mann, Nathaniel Hawthorne, Maxim Gorky, etc.) It is the subject of Old Testament episodes (Genesis 19:30–38; 2 Samuel 13:1–14). It is likewise expressed in the fairy tales, mythology and folklore of all modern societies.

² Bultmann, Rudolf. *The Gospel of John: A Commentary*, Basil Blackwell: Oxford, 1971, p. 118.

³ The gospel of John is generally regarded to have been deeply influenced by Greek metaphysics and religion.

[4] Epiphany also commemorates the Day of the Magi, the Feast of Christ's Baptism, and is celebrated in the Eastern Church as Old Christmas Day.

[5] Dionysian festivals were contemporary and widespread at the time of Jesus. Their celebration is alluded to in 2 Maccabees 6:7.

[6] Alternative translation: "O woman, what have I to do with you?"

[7] As in the traditional Christian view.

[8] Jesus indeed alludes to himself in the role of a bridegroom at a wedding feast (Mark 2:19–20). He asserts that as long as the bridegroom is with his wedding guests they cannot fast. But once the bridegroom is removed (taken away), on that day they will fast. While this passage is usually taken metaphorically, its exact correspondence to fertility cult ideology cannot be ignored: namely, that as long as the god is present the wedding guests cannot fast, the festival must go on; but when the god suffers and dies, fasting and lamentation must ensue.

[9] Bultmann, *op. cit.*, p. 116.

[10] Schnackenburg, Rudolf. *The Gospel According to St. John*, Vol. 1, The Seabury Press: New York, 1980, p. 328.

[11] *Ibid.*, p. 333.

[12] The six stone jars, each holding "twenty or thirty gallons," indicate a maximum of one hundred eighty gallons of wine which result from Jesus' miracle. But this is the "good" wine. It is served only after the "poor" wine has failed. The total quantity of wine, poor plus good, is thus excessive—but quite consistent with the needs of a Dionysian wedding, in which the bountiful flow of wine was the prerequisite to the continuation of the proceedings. This quantity of wine thus suggests the non-Jewish character of the event.

[13] The two passages together constitute a *diptych*. They are inseparable, each an extension of the same motif. See Bultmann, *op. cit.*, p. 112.

[14] Alluded to in Zechariah 14:21.

[15] In deciding who shall be passed over, Pontius Pilate assumes the symbolic role of the angel of death: "But you have a custom that I should release one man for you at the Passover; will you have me release for you the King of the Jews?" (John 18:39).

[16] This exchange occurs only in John.

[17] The maintenance of this quintessential relationship of the fertility drama is implied in the establishment of a proxy mother-son relationship—in which the beloved disciple becomes the *new* Son; he is Jesus' "spiritual brother"; he bears witness to all of Jesus' acts; his "testimony is true." Jesus indicates: ". . . it is my will that he [the disciple] remain until I come"—a statement interpreted "among the brethren [to mean] that this disciple was not to die" (John 21:22,23). The beloved disciple is thereby suggested as the new deity who will sustain the cycle of the fertility drama.

[18] The "sameness" of the two figures—Mary Magdalen and Mother Mary—is implied in their dual representation at the Crucifixion, in the equivalence of their mirror-image attributes.

[19] Mary "suppos[es] him to be the gardener" (John 20:15).

Chapter 16

[1] Sexually explicit representations and writings have been found in the ruins of ancient Greece, Rome, South America and Africa; these include the giant phallic representations of the Mayans, the vase paintings of Dionysian erotica, statues of the fertility god Priapus (upon whose giant stone penis virgins sacrificed their hymens), erotic drawings depicted on the excavated buildings of Old Pompeii, and other representations generally associated with fertility cults, in which worship of the genitals was part of the religious ritual by which the powers of procreation were supplicated.

[2] Kronhausen, Eberhard and Phyllis. *Pornography and the Law,* Ballantine Books: New York, 1964. The Oxford Professor, p. 260. Dialogues of Luisa Sigea, pp. 279–280; Confessions of Lady Beatrice, p. 259.

[3] In medieval times flagellation and torture became popular religious expressions; nuns and priests whipped each other and eager penitents in the name of God. During the witch hunts of the fourteenth, fifteenth and sixteenth centuries that swept Europe and later spread to the New World, those accused of intercourse with the devil were stripped by inquisitors, who proceeded to whip and pinprick the genitals of the accused in search of the "devil's mark."

In Victorian times houses of prostitution specializing in sadomasochism sprang up in Europe and have persisted in contemporary times.

[4] Kronhausen, *op. cit.*, The Lascivious Hypocrite, pp. 221–222.

[5] This sense of time is reinforced by major elements of content. Sadomasochism represents primitive and unorthodox sexuality, unrefined, of a time early in man's psychosexual development. Dirty and magic words symbolize a primal language, devoid of restraints and taboos. Profanation of the sacred recalls a time before the development of codes of behavior, of ethics, when the profane *was* the sacred (when sexuality was the heart of religious expression).

Chapter 17

[1] St. Irenaeus of Lyons (125–202), defender of Christian doctrine against the Gnostic heresies.

[2] Irenaeus: Against Heresies, in *The Ante-Nicene Fathers,* Vol. 1, Book IV (A. Roberts and J. Donaldson, eds.), Charles Scribner's Sons: New York, 1926, Chapter XLI.2, p. 525. In his remarks concerning "sons of the devil," Irenaeus declares: "And therefore did the Lord term those [who remain in a state of apostasy] 'a generation of vipers' . . . For He said, 'Beware of the leaven of the Pharisees and of the Sudducees.' " (XLI.3)

[3] Thascius Caecilius Cyprianus (210–258), Bishop of Carthage, pioneer of Latin Christian literature ("De Unitate").

[4] Lapide, Pinchas E. *Three Popes and the Jews,* Hawthorne Press: New York, 1965, p. 29. See also: St. Cyprian, Treatises: The Lord's Prayer, in *The Fathers of the Church,* (R. J. Deferrari, ed.), The Fathers of the Church, Inc.: New York, 1958, Vol. 36, pp. 134–135.

[5] St. Gregory (d. 395), Bishop of Nyssa, ecclesiastical writer

[6] Poliakov, Leon. *The History of Anti-Semitism,* Vol. 1, The Vanguard Press, Inc.: New York, 1965, p. 25. See also: St. Gregory of Nyssa, Homilies on the Resurrection, in *Patrologia Graeca,* Vol. 46, p. 685.

[7] Eusebius Hieronymus Sophronius—St. Jerome (342–420)—Doctor of the church, translator of the Hebrew Bible into the Latin Vulgate.

[8] Flannery, Edward H. *The Anguish of the Jews,* The Macmillan

Co.: New York (Collier-Macmillan Co.: London, Ontario), 1965, p. 47. See also: Simon, Marcel. *Versus Israel,* De Boccard: Paris, 1948, pp. 255–271.

9 "Golden Mouthed" (344–407), Doctor of the Eucharist, Bishop of Constantinople, noted for his homilies and his revision of the Greek Liturgy.

10 Flannery, *op. cit.,* p. 48. See also: St. John Chrysostom, Homilies Against the Jews, in *Patrologia Graeca,* Vol. 48, pp. 843–942.

11 Synan, Edward A. *The Popes and the Jews in the Middle Ages,* The Macmillan Co.: New York (Collier-Macmillan Co.: London, Ontario), 1965, pp. 32,174 (note 3). See also: Pope Gelasius I, in *Patrologia Latina,* Vol. 59, pp. 131D–132A.

12 Pope Gregory, in his reference to Jews as a "Synagogue of Satan," reiterates the metaphor of Revelation 2:9 and 3:9.

13 Synan, *op. cit.,* pp. 65, 184 (note 26). See also: Epistolarum, IX, 2 (E. Caspar, ed.), in *Das Gregors VII, Monumenta Germaniae Historica,* Epist. Select., Vol. 2, fasc. 2, p. 571.

14 Synan, *op. cit.,* pp. 89, 194 (note 29). See also: Innocent Ill, in *Patrologia Latina,* Vol. 217, p. 561D.

15 Trachtenberg, Joshua. *The Devil and the Jews,* Yale University Press: New Haven (Oxford University Press: Oxford; Humphrey Milford: London), 1943, Chapter 3. See also: Reider, Joseph. Jews in Medieval Art, in *Essays on Antisemitism* (Koppel S. Pinson, ed.), Conference on Jewish Relations: Brooklyn, 1942. See also: Poliakov, *op. cit.,* p. 135.

16 Poliakov, *op. cit.,* p. 219 (quoted from the pamphlet, *Schem Hamephoras,* Martin Luther). See also: Pelikan, Jaroslav (ed.), *Luther's Works,* Concordia Publishing House: St. Louis, 1958 (54 volumes).

17 Poliakov, *op. cit.,* pp. 128, 319 (note 188: *Le Mistère de la saincte hostie,* nouvellement imprimé à Paris, A. Pontier, Aix, 1817).

18 Shakespeare, William. The Merchant of Venice, in *The Complete Works of William Shakespeare,* The World Publishing Co.: Cleveland and New York, 1942, Act III, Scene I.

19 Bernstein, Herman. The Jewish Cemetery in Prague and the Council of Representatives of the Twelve Tribes of Israel, in *The History of a Lie,* J. S. Ogilvie Publishing Co.: New York, 1921.

[20] *The Protocols,* apparently French in origin, were incorporated into *The Jewish Cemetery in Prague,* a novel first published in Russia in 1872 and authored by a German novelist, Herman Goedsche, who used the English pen name, Sir John Retcliffe. Over the years, *The Protocols* were revised, elaborated, edited and embellished. Between 1900 and 1922 *The Protocols* were translated into the major languages of the world, appearing in the United States in a series of newspaper editorials in *The Dearborn Independent* (1918–1922), and later republished in book form as *Aspects of Jewish Power in the United States, The International Jew.* See Anonymous. *Aspects of Jewish Power in the United States, The International Jew,* Vol. IV, Dearborn Independent Publishing Co.: Dearborn, 1922.

[21] This line serves as the doctrinal basis for the deicide charge against the Jews.

[22] Flannery, *op. cit.,* p. 47. See also: St. Gregory of Nyssa, Homilies on the Resurrection, in *Patrologia Graeca,* Vol. 46, p. 685.

[23] Flannery, *op. cit.,* p. 46. See also: Pseudo-Ephraim, *De Magis,* Vol. 2, p. 411 (quoted in Williams, A. Lukyn. *Adversus Judaeos,* Cambridge University Press: Cambridge, 1935, p. 104).

[24] St. Ignatius: Epistle of Ignatius to the Magnesians; Epistle of Ignatius to the Trallians, in Roberts and Donaldson (eds.), *op. cit.,* Chapter XI, pp. 64,71.

[25] St. John Chrysostom: Homilies 1 and 8, in *Jews and Christians in Antioch in the First Four Centuries of the Common Era* (Wayne A. Meeks and Robert L. Wilken, eds.), Scholars Press for the Society of Biblical Literature: Missoula, Montana, 1978. See also: Flannery, *op. cit.,* p. 48. See also: St. John Chrysostom, Homilies Against the Jews (Homily 1:4), in *Patrologia Graeca,* Vol. 48, pp. 843–942.

[26] St. Augustine: On the Fifth Feria of Easter (Sermon 10), in *Selected Sermons of St. Augustine* (Quincy Howe, Jr., ed. and trans.), Holt, Rinehart & Winston: New York, Chicago, San Francisco, 1966. See also: Flannery, *op. cit.,* p. 50. See also: St. Augustine, The Creed (3:10), in *The Fathers of the Church,* Catholic University Press: Washington, 1962 (Christian Heritage: New York, 1946; Cima: New York, 1947), Vol. 27, p. 301.

[27] Flannery, *op. cit.,* p. 38.

[28] Stead, William T. (ed.). *The Passion Play at Oberammergau 1930,*

Ernest Benn Ltd.: London (Carl A. Seyfried & Co.: Munich), pp. 230,231, 1930.

²⁹ The Jews who were the subject of this seventeenth-century pamphlet were in reality the rag pickers of Paris, the *fripiers*. Actually Christian, the *fripiers* were accused of murder—and of being secretly Jewish. See Poliakov, *op. cit.*, pp. 190–197,322 (note 265).

³⁰ Abbott, Walter M. (ed.). *The Documents of Vatican II* (Joseph Gallagher, trans. ed.), Follett Publishing Co.: Chicago: 1966, p. 666.

³¹ ". . . What happened in His passion cannot be blamed upon all Jews then living without distinction, nor upon the Jews of today."

³² Lapide, *op. cit.*, p. 25.

³³ *Ibid.* See also: St. Augustine, Epistle (137:16), in *Patrologia Latina,* Vol. 33, p. 523.

³⁴ Synan, *op. cit.*, p. 226. See also: Poliakov, *op. cit.*, p. 242. See also: Bull of Innocent III of January 17, 1208, in *Patrologia Latina,* Vol. 215, p. 1291, No. 190.

³⁵ St. Thomas Aquinas. *Summa Theologica* (Herbert McCabe, trans.), McGraw Hill: New York, 1964, III a Q. 68, 10. See also: Flannery, *op. cit.*, p. 95. See also: Poliakov, *op. cit.*, p. 94. See also: Letter to the Duchess of Brabant, in *De Regime Principum,* Marietti: Turin, 1924, p. 117.

³⁶ Marcus, Jacob R. *The Jew in the Medieval World,* Atheneum: New York, 1973, pp. 121–126. See also: Poliakov, *op. cit.*, pp. 56–64. See also: Trachtenberg, *op. cit.*, Chapters 9,10.

³⁷ The Jew also allegedly practiced a variant of ritual murder, "profanation of the Host." The Host is the sacred wafer of the Christian communion, the bread which according to the Doctrine of Transubstantiation (1215 A.D.) became the actual body of Christ. Jews were repeatedly accused of stealing the sacred Host, burying it, boiling it in oil, piercing it with needles, tormenting it in a myriad sadistic and sacrilegious ways, in recapitulation of the Passion. In response, the wafer "suffered" and "died"—in death miraculously transforming itself into the corpse of a Christian child. *See* Trachtenberg, *op. cit.*, Chapter 8.

³⁸ Chaucer, Geoffrey. The Prioress Tale, in *The Canterbury Tales* (W. W. Skeat, ed.), J. Cape and the Medici Society Ltd.: London, 1928.

[39] Poliakov, *op. cit.*, p. 63.

[40] Official denial of Jewish complicity in ritual murder was asserted in the Golden Bull of Frederick (1236 A.D.) and the Papal Bulls of Innocent V (1247), Gregory X (1272), Martin V (1422), Nicholas V (1447) and Paul III (1540).

[41] Strack, Hermann L. *The Jew and Human Sacrifice (An Historical and Sociological Study)*, Cope and Fenwick: London, 1909.

[42] In 1928 the temporary disappearance of a child prompted a charge of ritual murder against the Jewish community of Massena, New York. See Flannery, *op. cit.*, p. 297, and Trachtenberg, op. cit., pp. 124–139.

[43] Bulls of Popes Clement VI (1348 A.D.) and Martin V (1422).

[44] Trachtenberg, *op. cit.*, p. 97.

[45] The Council of Beziers, 1246. See Poliakov, *op. cit.*, p. 149

[46] Poliakov, *op. cit.*, p. 25. See also: St. Gregory of Nyssa, Homilies on the Resurrection, in *Patrologia Graeca*, Vol. 46, p. 685.

[47] Poliakov, *op. cit.*, p. 31. See also: *Amulonis Epistola contra judaeos*, in *Patrologia Latina*, Vol. 116, pp. 141–184.

[48] Pope Pius V, 1569. See Trachtenberg, *op. cit.*, p. 76.

[49] Council of Elvira, 306 A.D.

[50] Council of Antioch, 341.

[51] Council of Laodicea, 343–381.

[52] Theodosian Code, Constantine to 438 A.D.

[53] Justinian Code, sixth century.

[54] Flannery, *op. cit.*, p. 48. See also: St. John Chrysostom, Homilies Against the Jews (Homily 3:1), in *Patrologia Graeca*, Vol. 48, pp. 843–942.

[55] So dangerous was this text that twenty-four cartloads of it were burned in Paris.

[56] Unlike the Talmud, the Caballah was spared the flames, some of its precepts being adapted for popular use.

[57] For such causes even as building cathedrals and financing Crusades.

[58] *Lit.*, "who would be justified by the law."

[59] Asserting a basic antithesis between spirit and flesh—"flesh lusteth against the Spirit, and the Spirit against the flesh"—(Gala-

tians 5:17), Paul coupled flesh with evil: "(in my flesh) . . . dwelleth no good thing" (Romans 7:18); with death: "to set the mind on the flesh is death" (Romans 8:6); and Jewish law: "whosoever of you are justified by the law; ye are fallen from grace" (Galatians 5:4).

⁶⁰ St. Augustine: The City of God, Book XVIII, Chapter 45, in *The Nicene and Post-Nicene Fathers*, Vol. II (Philip Schaff, ed.), The Christian Literature Co.: Buffalo, 1887, pp. 387–388. See also: Flannery, *op. cit.*, p. 51. See also: St. Ambrose, Commentary on Psalm 1, in *Patrologia Latina*, Vol. 15, p. 1032.

⁶¹ St. Justin Martyr: Dialogue with Trypho, in *The Fathers of the Church*, Vol. 6 (Ludwig Schoop, ed.), Catholic University Press: Washington, 1965, pp. 139–366.

⁶² Flannery, *op. cit.*, p. 46. See also: St. Hilary of Poitiers, Commentary on Matthew 13:22, in *Patrologia Latina*, Vol. 9, p. 993. See also: St. Hilary of Poitiers, Commentary on Psalm 51:6, in *Patrologia Latina*, Vol. 9, p. 312.

⁶³ Meeks and Wilkins (eds.), *op. cit.*, Homily 1:4.

⁶⁴ Flannery, *op. cit.*, p. 48. See also: St. John Chrysostom, Homilies Against the Jews (Homily 6:5), in *Patrologia Graeca*, Vol. 48, pp. 843–942.

⁶⁵ Parkes, James. *The Conflict of the Church and the Synagogue*, Meridian: New York, 1961, p. 276 (quoted in Flannery, *op. cit.*, p. 46).

⁶⁶ Marcus, *op. cit.*, p. 108 (Letter of Ambrose to Theodosius the Great).

⁶⁷ Trachtenberg, *op. cit.*, pp. 20–21.

⁶⁸ Poliakov, *op. cit.*, p. 30.

⁶⁹ Synan, *op. cit.*, pp. 88,194 (note 23). See also: Pope Innocent III, in *Patrologia Latina*, Vol. 217, p. 392B–C.

⁷⁰ Poliakov, *op. cit.*, p. 219 (quoted from the pamphlet *Schem Hamephoras*, Martin Luther).

⁷¹ Reider, *op. cit.*

⁷² Trachtenberg, *op. cit.*, pp. 45,53.

⁷³ Poliakov, *op. cit.*, pp. 135–136.

⁷⁴ The Nuremberg Laws of the 1930s likewise prohibited marriage between Jews and "Aryans".

⁷⁵ Trachtenberg, *op. cit.*, pp. 189,250 (note 22).

[76] Anonymous. *Aspects of Jewish Power in the United States, The International Jew, op. cit.* (editorial of December 10, 1921), p. 133. Even fiction did not fail to repeat this same theme: in the twentieth century horror story, *Couching at the Door*, a young man entering the room of a notorious prostitute finds himself treading on carpet with a "cabalistic" design. See Broster, D. K. *Couching at the Door* (Basil Davenport, ed.), Dodd, Mead & Co.: New York, 1953.

[77] Anonymous. *Aspects of Jewish Power in the United States, The International Jew, op. cit.* (editorial of January 7, 1922), p. 225.

[78] An operation to undo this "mark" (signifying assimilation into Hellenic culture) is mentioned in 1 Maccabees 1:15.

[79] Homosexuality and incestuous marriages were widespread in the upper classes of Graeco-Roman society, as were sexual practices in the conduct of games and sports.

[80] This virulent fourth-century B.C. account of the Exodus, authored by the Egyptian priest and historian Manetho, was subsequently embellished and repeated over the centuries. See Radin, Max. *The Jews Among the Greeks and Romans*, The Jewish Publication Society of America: Philadelphia, 1915, p. 99. See also: Josephus, Flavius, Against Apion, in *The Life and Works of Flavius Josephus* (W. Whiston, trans.), Holt, Rinehart and Winston: New York, 1962.

[81] Traditionally it was from Syria that the largest number of slaves in the Graeco-Roman world was derived.

[82] Radin, *op. cit.*, pp. 216,217,233,395 (note 4).

[83] *Ibid.*, pp. 85,86,92.

[84] A term of Greek poetry alluding to monsters (85).

[85] Radin, *op. cit.*, pp. 182, 186.

[86] *Ibid.*, p. 189.

[87] By the Jews of Alexandria.

[88] Radin, *op. cit.*, pp. 221–225.

[89] The allegation of enslavement may be a later addition to Cicero's address.

[90] Nor is this message restricted to Christians. For Jews themselves, as well as others, subject to the Christ story via unresolved inner conflict, may harbor anti-Jewish feelings. Such Jewish anti-

Semitism finds expression in the "guilt" and "shame" of being Jewish; in a psychologically defensive, apologetic, self-deprecating, passive image; in Jews who try to emulate Christian behavior or overly pride themselves on being Jewish or who display a compulsive adherence to Jewish ritualistic practices or deny outright their Jewishness; in the acts and declarations of rabidly anti-Semitic Jewish converts to Christianity who have historically become the leaders of openly anti-Semitic groups and organizations throughout the ages.

Bibliography

Abbott, Walter M., ed. *The Documents of Vatican II*. Translated and edited by Joseph Gallagher. Chicago: Follett Publishing Co, 1966.

The Anchor Bible. "The Gospel According to John (i–xii)." Translated by Raymond Brown. Garden City: Doubleday & Co., 1966.

Aradi, Zsolt. *Shrines to Our Lady Around the World*. New York: Farrar, Straus and Young, 1954.

Benson, E.E. "The Room in the Tower." In *Third Fontana Book of Great Horror Stories*. Edited by Christine Bernard. London and Glasgow: Fontana Books, Collins Clear Type Press, 1968.

Bernstein, Herman. *The History of a Lie*. New York: J.S. Ogilvie Publishing Co., 1921.

Blackwood, Algernon. "The House of the Past." In *Tales of the Uncanny and Supernatural*. Secaucus: Castle Books, Inc., 1974.

Blackwood, Algernon. "The Wendigo." In *Ghostly Tales To Be Told*. Edited by Basil Davenport. New York: Dodd, Mead and Co., 1950.

279

Blackwood, Algernon. "The Willows." In *Famous Ghost Stories.* Edited by Bennett Cerf. New York: Random House, Inc., 1944.

Bradbury, Ray. "The Small Assassin." In *Tales of Terror and Suspense.* Edited by Stewart H. Benedict. New York: Dell Publishing Co., 1968.

Broster, D.K. "Couching at the Door." In *Ghostly Tales To Be Told. Op. cit.*

Bulfinch, Thomas. *The Age of Fable.* New York: Random House, Everyman's Library, 1948.

Bulwer-Lytton, Edward. "The Haunted and the Haunters." In *Famous Ghost Stories. Op. cit.*

Bultmann, Rudolf. *The Gospel of John: A Commentary.* Oxford: Basil Blackwell, 1971.

Burrows, Millar. *The Dead Sea Scrolls.* New York: The Viking Press, 1955.

Burrows, Millar. *More Light on the Dead Sea Scrolls.* New York: The Viking Press, 1958.

Carol, Juniper B., ed. *"Ineffabilis Deus."* In *Mariology,* Vol. 1. Milwaukee: The Bruce Publishing Company, 1955.

Chamberlin, Ray B. and Herman Feldman, eds. *The Dartmouth Bible.* Boston: Houghton Mifflin Co., 1950.

Charles, R.H. *The Apocrypha and Pseudepigrapha of the Old Testament.* Oxford: Clarendon Press, 1913.

Chaucer, Geoffrey. *The Canterbury Tales.* Edited by W.W. Skeat. London: J. Cape and the Medici Society Ltd., 1928.

Chetwynd-Hayes, R. "Housebound." In *Third Fontana Book of Great Horror Stories. Op. cit.*

Clarke, Arthur C. "Castaway." In *Strange Signposts.* Edited by S. Moskowitz and R. Elwood. New York: Holt, Rinehart and Winston, 1966.

Coupling, J.J. "Mr. Kinkaid's Pasts." In *Beyond the Barriers of Space and Time.* Edited by Judith Merril. New York: Random House, 1954.

de la Mare, Walter. "The Creatures." In *Fireside Book of Ghost Stories*. Edited by E.C. Wagenknecht. Indianapolis: Bobbs-Merrill, 1947.

Derleth, August W. and Mark Schorer. "The Return of Andrew Bentley." In *Famous Ghost Stories. Op. cit.*

Doyle, dir. Arthur Conan. "The Adventure of the Speckled Band." In *Tales of Sherlock Holmes*. Illustrated by Harvey Dinnerstein. New York: The Macmillan Publishing Co., 1963.

Dupont-Sommer, André. *The Jewish Sect of Qumran and the Essenes.* New York: The Macmillan Publishing Co., 1956.

Edwards, Amelia. "My Brother's Ghost Story." In *Supernatural Omnibus*. Edited by Montague Summers. London: Victor Gollancz, Ltd., 1962.

Flannery, Edward H. *The Anguish of the Jews*. New York: The Macmillan Co. (London: Collier-Macmillan Co.), 1965.

Frankfort, Henri. *Kingship and the Gods*. Chicago: The University of Chicago Press, 1948.

Frazer, Sir James George. *The Golden Bough: A Study in Magic and Religion*. London: The Macmillan Co. (New York: St. Martin's Press), 1955. 13 volumes.

Gaster, Theodor H. *The Dead Sea Scriptures*. New York: Doubleday & Co., 1956.

Guignebert, Charles. *The Jewish World in the Time of Jesus*. New York: E.P. Dutton & Co., 1939.

Hawthorne, Nathaniel. "Rappacini's Daughter." In *Strange Signposts. Op. cit.*

Herodotus. Translated by William Beloe. London: E.C. and J. Rivington, et al., 1821.

Jastrow, Morris, Jr. "The Gilgamesh Epic." In *The Religion of Babylonia and Assyria*. Boston: Ginn & Company, 1898.

John, Jasper. "The Spirit of Stonehenge." In *Strange Signposts. Op. cit.*

Kapelrud, Avrid S. *Ras Shamra Discoveries and the Old Testament.* Translated by G.W. Anderson. Oxford: Basil Blackwell, 1965.

Kerenyi, C. *Dionysos, Archetypal Image of Indestructible Life,* Vol. 2. Princeton: Princeton University Press, 1976.

Kronhausen, Eberhard and Phyllis. *Pornography and the Law.* New York: Ballantine Books, 1964.

Lee, Vernon. "Oke of Okehurst." In *Supernatural Omnibus. Op. cit.*

LeFanu, J. Sheridan. "An Account of Some Strange Disturbances in Aungier Street." In *Great Ghost Stories.* Edited by H. Van Thal. New York: Hill and Wang Publishers, 1960.

LeFanu, J. Sheridan. "Carmilla." In *Supernatural Omnibus. Op. cit.*

Lovecraft, H.P. "The Whisperer in Darkness." In *Strange Signposts. Op. cit.*

Lovecraft, H.P. and August Derleth. "The Shuttered Room." In *Third Fontana Book of Great Ghost Stories. Op. cit.*

Machen, Arthur. "The Black Seal." In *Tales To Be Told in the Dark.* Edited by Basil Davenport. New York: Dodd, Mead and Co., 1953.

Machen, Arthur. "The White Powder." In *Ghostly Tales To Be Told. Op. cit.*

Marcus, Jacob R. *The Jew in the Medieval World.* New York: Atheneum, 1973.

Marryat, Frederick. "The White Wolf of the Hartz Mountains." in *Supernatural Omnibus. Op. cit.*

Maus, Cynthia Pearl. *The World's Greatest Madonnas.* New York and London: Harper & Brothers Publishers, 1947.

Miegge, Giovanni. *The Virgin Mary, the Roman Catholic Marian Doctrine.* Translated by Waldo Smith. London: Luttleworth Press, 1950.

Onions, Oliver. "The Beckoning Fair One." In *Famous Ghost Stories. Op. cit.*

Otto, Walter F. *Dionysus, Myth and Cult.* Translated by Robert B. Palmer. Bloomington and London: Indiana University Press, 1965.

Palmer, Paul F. *"Misserentissimus Redemptor."* In *Mary in the Docu-*

ments of the Church. Westminister, Maryland: The Newman Press, 1952.

Parkes, James. *The Conflict of the Church and the Synagogue.* New York: Meridian, 1961.

Pinson, Koppel S., ed. *Essays on Antisemitism.* Brooklyn: Conference on Jewish Relations, 1942.

Pliny the Younger. "Letter to Sura, Book VII." In *Fireside Book of Ghost Stories. Op. cit.*

Poe, Edgar Allan. "A Descent into the Maelstrom." In *Tales of Terror and Suspense. Op. cit.*

Poe, Edgar Allan. "The Devil in the Belfry." In *Beyond the Barriers of Space and Time. Op. cit.*

Poe, Edgar Allan. "The Fall of the House of Usher." In *The Fall of the House of Usher and Other Tales of Horror.* Edited by Joseph W. Nash. East Rutherford, New Jersey: Andor Publishing Co., 1976.

Poliakov, Leon. *The History of Anti-Semitism.* New York: The Vanguard Press, Inc., 1965.

Radin, Max. *The Jews Among the Greeks and Romans.* Philadelphia: The Jewish Publication Society of America, 1915.

Rice, Jane. "The Refugee." In *Ghostly Tales To Be Told. Op. cit.*

Sayce, Archibald H. *The Religion of Ancient Egypt.* Edinburgh: T. & T. Clark, 1913.

Schaff, Philip, ed. *The Nicene and Post-Nicene Fathers.* Buffalo: The Christian Literature Co., 1887.

Schnackenburg, Rudolf. *The Gospel According to St. John.* New York: The Seabury Press, 1980.

Schoop, Ludwig, ed. *The Fathers of the Church.* Washington: Catholic University Press, 1965.

Sheed, Francis J., ed. *The Mary Book.* New York: Sheed and Ward, 1950.

Shelley, Mary. *Frankenstein.* London: J.M. Dent and Sons, Ltd. (New York: E.P. Dutton and Co., Inc.), 1960.

Simon, Marcel. *Versus Israel*. Paris: De Boccard, 1948.

St. Thomas Aquinas. *Summa Theologica*. Translated by Herbert McCabe. New York: McGraw Hill, 1964.

Stead, William T., ed. *The Passion Play at Oberammergau 1930*. London: Ernest Benn Ltd. (Munich: Carl A. Seyfried & Co.), 1930.

Stevenson, Robert Louis. The Strange Case of Dr. Jekyll and Mr. Hyde. New York: Washington Square Press, 1968.

Stoker, Bram. *Dracula*. New York: Grosset & Dunlap, 1974.

Stoker, Bram. "The Squaw." In *Tales of Terror and Suspense. Op. cit.*

Strack, Hermann L. *The Jew and Human Sacrifice (An Historical and Sociological Study.* London: Cope and Fenwick, 1909.

Synan, Edward A. *The Popes and the Jews in the Middle Ages*. New York: The Macmillan Co. (London: Collier-Macmillan Co.), 1965.

Trachtenberg, Joshua. *The Devil and the Jews*. New Haven: Yale University Press (Oxford: Oxford Univesity Press; London: Humphrey Milford), 1943.

Twain, Mark. "A Ghost Story." In *Thirteen Ghostly Yarns*. Edited by Elizabeth H. Sechrist. Turbotville, Pennsylvania: Macrae-Smith Co., 1963.

Wakefield, Herbert Russell. "Lucky's Grove." In *Third Fontana Book of Great Horror Stories. Op. cit.*

Wellman, Manly Wade. "Where Angels Fear to Tread." in *Ghostly Tales To Be Told. Op. cit.*

Wells, H.G. "The Chronic Argonauts." In *Strange Signposts. Op. cit.*

Wells, H.G. *The Invisible Man*. New York: Bantam Books, 1970.

White, Edward Lucas. "The House of the Nightmare." In *Ghostly Tales To Be Told. Op. cit.*

Wilson, Edmund. *The Dead Sea Scrolls*. New York: Oxford University Press, 1969.

The Works of Flavius Josephus. Translated by William Whiston. London: George Virtue, 1844.

Index